Sun Tzu:
War and Management

Sun Tzu: War and Management

Application to strategic management and thinking

Wee Chow Hou
Lee Khai Sheang
Bambang Walujo Hidajat

ADDISON-WESLEY PUBLISHING COMPANY

Singapore • Wokingham, England • Reading, Massachusetts • Menlo Park, California
New York • Don Mills, Ontario Amsterdam • Bonn • Sydney
Tokyo • Madrid • San Juan • Milan • Paris

Many of the designations used by manufacturers and sellers to distinguish their products are claimed as trademarks. Where those designations appear in this book, and Addison-Wesley was aware of a trademark claim, the designations have been printed in initial caps or all caps.

Cover designed and illustrated by Text & Cover Design, Singapore
Text designed by Lesley Stewart
Typeset by Quaser Technology Pte Ltd, Singapore
Printed in Singapore.

First printed in 1991. Reprinted 1991, 1992.

Library of Congress Cataloging in Publication Data
Wee, Chow Hou.
    Sun Tzu: war and management: application to strategic management
    and thinking/Wee Chow Hou, Lee Khai Sheang, Bambang Walujo Hidajat.
    p. cm.
    Includes bibliographical references and index.
    ISBN 0-201-50965-2
    1. Industrial management—Japan. 2. Strategic planning—Japan. 3. Sun-tzu, 6th
    cent. B. C. Sun-tzu ping fa. 4. Military art and science—Early works to 1800. I.
    Lee, Khai Sheang. II. Hidajat, Bambang Walujo. III. Title.
    HD70. J3W42 1991
    355' . 03—dc20

                                                                            90–27770
                                                                            CIP

British Library Cataloguing in Publication Data
Wee, Chow Hou
    Sun Tzu – war and management.
    1. Management
    I. Sun Zi. Art of war II. Lee, Khai Sheang III. Hidajat, Bambang Walujo
    658

ISBN 0–201–50965–2

Preface

The idea of an analogy between the world of business and that of the battlefield is not a novel one. The metaphor is accepted, consciously or not, in such familiar phrases as the US-Japan Trade *War* and a militaristic turn of phrase in the boardroom now borders on being a cliché. It was July 1985 that the *New York Times Magazine* carried Theodore White's argument that while America may have won the military war, Japan was busy winning the economic war. Five years later *International Business Week*, April 9, 1990, carried a front page headline, 'Car Wars', also dealing with US-Japan trade rivalries.

Indeed, various studies relating the application of military strategies to business practices have been undertaken and a recent publication by Ries and Trout (1986), *Marketing Warfare*, chose to rely, for instance, on the works of the German general Karl von Clausewitz, which were written in 1832. Few studies, however, have given recognition and acknowledgement to the oldest known military treatise in the world, Sun Tzu's *Art of War*, and yet this manual, written in China centuries before the birth of Christ, can be said to contain the foundations on which all modern military strategies are based.

It is proposed in this book that the achievement of Sun Tzu's *Art of War* transcends the military context and offers the basis for an insight into the nature of modern business practices. In particular, and this is an underlying thesis, a study and understanding of Sun Tzu provides a valuable platform for exploring the exact nature of the analogy between business and war and in doing so it offers a pregnant framework for interpreting one of the most startling economic trends in the late twentieth century: the relative decline of the US economy at the expense of the Japanese economy.

The trend has been well documented and more than one theory has been advanced as to its underlying cause. This book is not proposing another theory but rather suggesting that we examine some of the implications of the war and business analogy so as to better understand the nature of various business practices around the world and, specifically, the nature of the US-Japan trade situation.

The fundamental analogy is a fruitful one but it is too often taken for granted and some of the assumptions remain unexamined. If, for instance, the world of business is essentially a war situation the question can be raised as to the extent to which this is unashamedly endorsed by the opposing "armies". The word unashamedly is used because one may feel obliged to point out that there are ethical parameters that need to be taken into account. Limits to the analogy may be introduced on the grounds that war is an extreme situation, demanding exceptional responses and a suspension of normal life. War, after all, involves killing and being killed and often allows for various forms of behavior, espionage and control of the media for instance, that would not be countenanced or encouraged in peacetime. Even allowing for the notion of a "just war" one may still feel that a war mentality is not necessary or desirable for successful business life; whereas a war mentality is always likely to contribute to a successful war.

This book will attempt to unlock the nature of the analogy between war and business by attempting to examine in a systematic way the extent to which business practices are capable of being described and understood in the language of war and the implications that may arise as a result of this enquiry. The guiding framework that will allow for a systematic study is provided by Sun Tzu's Chinese classic; a work of the ancient past that reaches across two millennia and helps to clarify the debate now raging between the opponents and defenders of revisionism. A strategic management model, called Sun Tzu's *Art of War* model, is proposed in order to illustrate the course of the argument.

Publishers acknowledgement

The publishers wish to thank the following for permission to reproduce material from published sources: Table 6.1: Euromoney Publications Plc, London; Excerpt from *The Winning Performance* by Donald K. Clifford Jr. and Richard E. Cavanagh. © 1985 by Donald K. Clifford Jr. and Richard E. Cavanagh. Used by permission of Batam Books, a division of Batam Double day, Dell Publishing Group, Inc. Excerpt from Peter F. Drucker, *Management: Tasks, Responsibilities, Practices*, ©

Contents

1 *Battlefields and boardrooms*

1.1 From concubines to Mao Zedong

Sun Tzu's *Art of War* is the oldest military classic known in Chinese literature. It is also the most revered and well known military text outside China. While its exact origin and authorship have been debated, scholars of military history are unanimous that the book existed, and was probably written, around 400 to 320 B.C., 100 years after the births of Confucius and Lao Tze, two well known Chinese philosophers. Thus, the book is today over 2,300 years old.

The significance and importance of Sun Tzu's work in influencing military thought has seldom been questioned. For example, even modern day military writing and thinking bears much inspiration from the works of Sun Tzu. (See Appendix A). His works and military strategies were known to have been used extensively during the period of the Warring States (about 453 to 221 B.C.). In fact, in another famous Chinese military classic, *Annals of the Three Kingdoms*, there were many strategies that mirrored those advocated by Sun Tzu.

One illustration of the genius and ability of Sun Tzu concerns his legendary experience in training the imperial concubines. It was told that after reading Sun Tzu's *Art of War*, the emperor Ho-lu of Wu requested Sun Tzu to demonstrate whether his works were applicable to the training of women. Thereupon, Sun Tzu requested that he be given full authority and asked to be provided with 180 beautiful women from the imperial palace, including Emperor Ho-lu's two most favorite concubines. He divided the 180 ladies into two groups, appointed the two imperial concubines to be in charge of each group and proceeded to give detailed instructions on how they should move upon hearing the drum signals that he was about to give. To show his seriousness, he even ordered that the executioner's weapons be demonstrated. When Sun Tzu beat his drum the first time, all the ladies giggled and laughed hilariously, and did not carry out the orders. Sun Tzu went on to explain to the 180 ladies that if the first time around they could not carry out the instructions, it must be because the orders from the superior commander (himself) were unclear and not thoroughly explained. Thus, he went on to repeat and explain the orders on how they should move upon hearing the beat of the drum. Then, he called them to attention and proceeded to hit the drum. The ladies giggled and burst into laughter again.

This time around, Sun Tzu retorted that if orders were clearly explained and repeated by the superior commander, and yet not carried out, the fault no longer was with the former, but with the ground or field commander. In that particular incident, it was the responsibility of the two imperial concubines who were put in charge of the two groups. Sun Tzu gave orders to have them executed! When Emperor Ho-lu heard about it, he tried to intervene and asked that his two favorite concubines be spared. Sun Tzu refused and even replied that when the commander had been appointed as head of the army, he was not required to accept all the sovereign's orders! Consequently, he still ordered the two imperial concubines be executed as an example to the others. He appointed two new substitutes, and repeated the signals on the drum. On hearing the beats from the drum, the ladies turned left, right, to the front, to the rear, knelt and rose, etc., all in accordance with the prescribed instructions and drills. Not a single lady dared to giggle or make the slightest noise!

Today, Sun Tzu's *Art of War* remains a compulsory text in major military schools around the world and its influence on twentieth century military thinking is undisputed. The well known saying of Mao Zedong, "Know your enemy, know yourself; hundred battles, hundred victories," is in fact a partial quote from Sun Tzu's writings:

> "He who has a thorough knowledge of himself and the enemy
> is bound to win in all battles. He who knows himself but not
> the enemy, has only an even chance of winning. He who knows
> not himself and the enemy is bound to perish in all battles."

知彼知己者，百战不殆；不知彼而知己，一胜一负；
不知彼，不知己，每战必殆。

and

> "Know your enemy, know yourself, and your victory will not be threatened. Know the terrain, know the weather, and your victory will be complete."

知彼知己，胜乃不殆；
知天知地，胜乃不穷。

1.2 Japanese military thought and Sun Tzu

The book is also known to have influenced Japanese military thinking. Sun Tzu's *Art of War* was introduced to Japan around 716 A.D. to 735 A.D. In contrast, the first Western translation did not appear until about 1,000 years later. The first such translation was in French and was published in Paris around 1772, while the first English translation did not occur until 1905. Interestingly enough, the English translation was done by a Captain E.F. Calthrop of the British army who was then studying in Japan. Today, there are translations in Russian, German and other languages. However, the most translations are predominantly Japanese, being over 13 in number.

It is interesting to note that even as early as the 16th century in Japan, Sun Tzu's philosophies were already being applied successfully in battlefields. Takeda Shingen, one of the four famous warriors of the time, had his battle banners embroidered with the following phrases:

> "Swift as the wind
> Calmly majestic as the forest
> Plundering like fire
> Steady as the mountains"

These descriptions are almost identical to Sun Tzu's statements when he discussed the principle of the execution of war strategies:

> "In movement, be as swift as the wind;
> In slow marches, be as majestic as the forest;
> In raiding and plundering, be as fierce as fire;
> In defense, be as firm as mountains;
> In camouflage, be as impenetrable as darkness,
> When striking, be as overwhelming as thunderbolts."

故其疾如风，其徐如林，侵掠如火，
不动如山，难知如阴，动如雷震。

Many Japanese military writings also bear influences from Sun Tzu's works. For example, Miyamoto Musashi's (1974), *Book of Five Rings* (Go Rin No Shu), a Japanese military classic written around 1645 A.D., contains many parallels to Sun Tzu's writings, including his five rings of ground, water, fire, wind and void.

In modern warfare, Sun Tzu's works were also known to influence Japanese military strategies and their conduct of war. For example, during the Second World War, the Japanese told the Americans that Pearl Harbour would never be attacked, when in reality it was making preparations and advances for the bombing. The Americans were caught totally off-guard when the attack came, and consequently suffered heavy casualties. While even up to today, many people still find it difficult to believe that the Japanese were capable of *lying* so blatantly, the act in fact was an application of Sun Tzu's principle of deception. In another example from the Second World War, the British army expected the Japanese to attack Singapore from the sea, and had all their guns fixed facing that way. This was because the most logical and efficient method for the Japanese to capture Singapore was to arrive by sea. To the utter surprise of the British the Japanese came from land, via peninsula Malaya. This was the use of *surprise*, another of Sun Tzu's principles of war.

1.3 The militarization of Japanese business practices

It is a known fact that Japanese military thought and strategies have tremendous influence on Japanese management practice. For example, in the heyday of the craze to learn Japanese management during the 1970s and early 1980s, the *Book of Five Rings*, written by a Japanese samurai, Miyamoto Musashi, was hailed as the book that influenced much of Japanese strategic thinking and practice. It was reputedly a "must read" book for Japanese chief executive officers (CEOs). Its English translation was among the best sellers at that time. This book, as mentioned in the previous section, bears many resemblances to Sun Tzu's *Art of War*.

Besides reading Japanese military texts, there are three Chinese classics that are reportedly among the highly recommended reading list of Japanese CEOs. Top of the list – Sun Tzu's *Art of War*! This is followed by *Annals of the Three Kingdoms* (another famous military classic on strategies) and *Journey to the West* (the legendary classic of the monkey king).

Interestingly, there is another famous Chinese classic that the Japanese CEOs should read, but somehow it is not well received. This classic is *The Water Margin*, and is also filled with illustrations of various strategies for winning battles. One possible reason could be that *The Water Margin* is a classic that depicted rebels who were the good guys and were anti-establishment (the equivalent of stories of Robin Hood of Western folk literature). To depict this rebellious, anti-establishment attitude as not only acceptable but a virtue, is definitely not consistent with the Japanese management value system. Those who are familiar with Chinese classics may argue that the monkey king in *Journey to the West* was also a rebel who fought against the establishment. There is, however, a big distinction here. Unlike the rebels in *The Water Margin*, the monkey king in *Journey to the West* was very much under control! His master, a Buddhist monk, would engage in a chanting that caused the monkey king much pain if he disobeyed his orders. In this way, the monkey king was prevented from doing anything that was unacceptable to the master.

The military influence on Japanese business practices extends beyond the reading of books on the subject. More significantly, Japanese companies are known to conduct annual or regular management camps for their employees and managers. These camps are run in the most militaristic manner, and include many rituals such as meditation, team work, survival techniques, etc. The severity of these camps is evidenced by the fact that some participants cannot endure the rigor of punishments. However, those who survive are reportedly able to become better managers and decision-makers.

Perhaps the best evidence that the Japanese have used military strategies in their business practices is the way they have conquered the world markets in many products and industries. The Japanese conquest of world markets is very much like a well orchestrated military campaign. This, in fact, is the whole thesis of Kotler *et al*'s 1985 book, *The New Competition*. Many Japanese strategies in entering and conquering the various markets in the world (as described in Kotler *et al*'s book) are not only militaristic but resemble very much Sun Tzu's war strategies. It may well be that Sun Tzu's *Art of War* is the inspiration for much of Japan's economic success in the world. The Japanese have traditionally been known for their skills in perfecting someone else's efforts. Some examples will underline that their perfecting skills could have been extended to the works of Sun Tzu. First, the Japanese board game, *Go*, is now internationally well-known, thanks to the Japanese who mastered and popularized it. Many Westerners today probably believe that the game is Japanese and was invented by them. The fact of the matter is that the game had its origin in China more than 1,500 years ago. It is actually Chinese checkers!

Second, the ancient oriental art of *bonsai* – the growing of miniature trees in small pots – is commonly associated with the Japanese. Indeed, the word, *bonsai* is Japanese and literally means "planted in a shallow vessel." However, little do we realize that the art was invented and widely practiced by the Chinese in 8th century A.D. Nonetheless, when the Japanese took over the art, they refined it and it is their achievement in the art over 400 to 500 years that allows them to lay claim to ownership and to the growth of interest in bonsai among Europeans, Americans, and the world at large.

Moving to the area of management, we are all very familiar and impressed with the high quality control standards achieved by Japanese production systems and many Western and other Asian countries have aspired to learn from the Japanese. It is, however, quite ironic and embarrassing to realize that the Japanese actually copied and adapted their concepts of quality control from Deming and Juran, two octogenarian Americans. The Japanese even publicly acknowledged their contributions by naming the highest quality control award in Japan after Deming!

In a related area, we are also very impressed by Japanese quality control circles (work improvement teams), job rotation and on-the-job training. However, it is important to point out these concepts actually have their roots in the works of Reginald Revans, a British octogenarian who is alive today. Revans originated the concept of Action Learning as early as the 1930s and it encompasses much of what the Japanese are practising in their factories today! It is also significant to note that the Japanese have acknowledged the contributions of Revans as well.

Japanese ingenuity in adapting and perfecting the work of others also extends to the ways and manners in which they entered the world markets. This could be best characterised by what could be termed as the "5 Is" strategy. This "5 Is" strategy can best be illustrated in their product development strategy and manufacturing processes which can be briefly described as follows:

1. In the initial stage of Japanese entry into world markets, they were known to be great *imitators*. Japanese manufacturers were known to buy fully assembled foreign products, stripping them down, and remanufacturing them using cheaper materials, parts and labor. They simply copied lock, stock and barrel. This was also the period when Japanese products were known to be cheap and of poor quality. Many people can recall the days when "Made in Japan" stamped on a toy was a sign of poor quality and low price.

2. In the second stage of Japanese development in manufacturing, they started to make minor *improvements* to the products that

they had originally copied. These improvements were concentrated mainly in upgrading the quality of the products, while maintaining a low price strategy. During this period, Japanese products began to gain acceptance.

3. In the third stage, the Japanese started *improvising*. At this stage, more improvements were made and it marked the beginning of local ingenuity in making better products with distinctive features and quality. This was the time when Japanese products begun not only to make their mark, being inexpensive, but were also known to be of good quality. It was also a period when they started to introduce more models and brands of the same product into the market.

4. In the fourth stage, the Japanese began *innovating*. This was a period when their products' superiority began to show over many other similar products made by the West. Through innovations, the Japanese were able to compete effectively in the world, especially in the markets of the Western world. This stage, which began in the mid 1970s, saw the Japanese creating a world image for themselves. Examples of Japanese innovations during this period are numerous – in the camera industry, the watch industry, the automobile industry, the home electronics industry, etc.

5. Today, the Japanese have embarked on the final and most threatening phase of their economic conquest – *invention*. This is characterized by their quest to develop supercomputers, artificial intelligence and bio-technology. These ventures, when successful, will give them an insurmountable lead over the rest of the world in several new industries. As it is, their inventions in the field of robotic engineering are, indeed, startling.

Thus, it seems that the Japanese approach to world markets is well-planned and executed. They seem to do the right things at the right time, and know how best to fit their national abilities to the needs and demands of world markets. As mentioned earlier, scholars such as Kotler even compared the Japanese conquest of world markets to that of a well thought out military campaign. Given the traditional influence of Japanese military thinking on Japanese management, such arguments are very plausible. What is more intriguing, however, is that Japanese military thinking and writings also bear resemblance (and influence) to Sun Tzu's *Art of War*. It must be emphasized again that Sun Tzu's *Art of War* was already known in Japan since the 8th century, and the Japanese probably mastered it 1,000 years before the Western world; it enjoyed the most translations and interpretations in Japan than in any other country today; it clearly influenced the writings and thinking of Japanese military strategists; and it was a well-read text among CEOs of Japan before the Western world got to know about the significance of this book. Given these historical perspectives, and the Japanese skills in perfecting other's ideas and works, it is conceivable that Sun Tzu's *Art of War* may have significant influences on the ways the Japanese conducted their businesses that resulted in their successes today.

1.4 Sun Tzu and the opening of China

The influence of Sun Tzu on Chinese thinking extends beyond the military philosophy of Mao Zedong, and his demise, to what is potentially one of the most significant economic events of the latter half of the twentieth century: the opening of China. Notwithstanding the hiatus created by the events of June 1989, the opening of China is a phenomenon that cannot be ignored and the significance of this event is best described in the words of Napoleon:

> "China is like a sleeping giant.
> Let her sleep on, for when she awakes, she will rock the world"

China is awakening today. Her opening to the outside world has led many businessmen and corporations to begin active negotiations with the Chinese, all wanting to gain a piece of the action. The Chinese, on their part, are also anxious to secure foreign investments and expertise. At times, however, negotiations with the Chinese are met with frustration and disappointment. More often than not, this could be the result of a mismatch of expectations rather than a lack of willingness to conclude business deals. Among other problems encountered with the Chinese, one main obstacle is their lack of understanding of modern management concepts and practices. Often, their lack of comprehension could be interpreted as excessive demands. For example, there were cases in which, after the signing of a contract, the Chinese would try to introduce additional terms and conditions. The Chinese authorities have rightly recognised this problem, and have taken active and positive steps to improve the situation. One of the major concerns of the Chinese is the upgrading of management knowledge and techniques and one of the most welcomed business packages is one which throws in a training and development program with the business deal. Indeed, the Chinese have looked to the outside world for much help in the areas of management training and education.

Another area, one that is very significant, that the Chinese have turned to for help is their own Chinese classics. Today, the Chinese have begun actively researching their classics and relating their applications to management. Sun Tzu's *Art of War* has emerged as a favorite, and today there are already publications in China that attempt to relate this Chinese military classic to strategic thinking and practice. The following are two examples of such publications:

1. Li Shi Jun, Yang Xian Ju and Tang Jia Rei (1984), Sun Tzu's *Art of War and Business Management*, Kwangsi People's Press, China (translated).
2. National Economic Commission (1985), *Classical Chinese Thoughts and Modern Management*, Economic Management Research Institute, Yunnan People's Publishing, China (translated).

1.5 War and business

It should be clear by now that there is an intriguing analogy to be drawn between military thinking and the world of business and yet it is only in recent years that various researchers have begun an active interest in applying military concepts to management and marketing.

The business world is not unlike the battlefield. In fact, businesses have collapsed through poor planning, resulting in the loss of capital and employment. This is no different from war, where poor planning can lead to the loss of men, equipment and the battle itself. In the case of corporations in the business world, the impact of losses can at times be felt throughout many other sectors of the economy; just as losses in war can literally tear a nation apart.

Competition in the business world can also be quite vicious and merciless, and clobbering the competitors are common events of the day. For example, the basic assumptions underlying the use and practice of comparative advertising (where one's products or services are deliberately compared with those of the competitor) are to put the competitor in a bad light and to discredit them if possible. In North America, comparative advertising became so vicious and disparaging at one stage that the law-makers had to step in. For example, in Canada, the "unfair and deliberate" comparisons of Pepsi against Coca-cola in a series of comparative advertisements in 1980-81 led the latter to lodge complaints against Pepsi to the Canadian Advertising Standards Council and other sources. This led to the subsequent amendments to the Canadian Code of Advertising Standards. This illustration goes to show that businesses will not hesitate to take advantage of loopholes in the market system in order to gain strategic advantage over competitors.

In sum, ruthlessness in competition in the business world is no less dramatic than in the battlefield. Perhaps this similarity is acknowledged in no small way by the common Chinese saying, "The business world is like a battlefield (商场如战场) ." It is, therefore, no great surprise that war strategies have found a very receptive audience in the boardrooms of businessmen.

1.6 The military and management

In order to explain more systematically the way in which Sun Tzu can enlighten our understanding of the contemporary world of business a strategic planning model is proposed. Before looking at this in detail it may be worth considering, at a somewhat abstract level, the similarities between the challenges facing a chief executive officer in a boardroom and those confronting a military head of state. The challenges facing the military head of state may well include the following:

1. To consolidate his present government within existing territory. He can achieve this by using current policies, improved policies, or even new policies. The ultimate purpose of this strategy is to strengthen his government within a defined territory and to protect it from external aggression.

2. To expand his rule beyond his present territories. He can achieve this either by:
   (a) Conquering neighboring states, in which case the risks are relatively low. Or
   (b) Embarking on more ambitious expeditions to far away lands and territories. Our history books are filled with numerous accounts of such ambitious expeditions by the Chinese, the Dutch, the British, the French and the Spanish.

Whether the ruler adopts strategy 2(a) or 2(b), he would also have to extend the government of such conquered territories using his current policies, improved policies or new policies, depending on the circumstances. The purpose of territorial expansion is to gain more land so as to increase one's power and area of influence; as well as to prevent the emergence of likely aggressors (since they will now be under the control of the conqueror).

In the business world, the problems facing the chief executive officer of a company are no different from that of the ruler of a state. For example, he must constantly look out for opportunities for growth in order to improve the performance of his company. The problems and challenges he faces can be captured by the product/market expansion grid that was developed by Ansoff (1957) and shown in Figure 1.1. Basically the challenges involve the following decisions (note that these challenges are parallel to those faced by the military head of state):

1. Increasing the market share of current products in current markets.
2. Finding new markets whose needs might be met by the current product.
3. Exploring and developing new products for existing markets.
4. Developing new businesses with new products and in new markets.

The decisions faced by the company would be relatively easy if there are unlimited resources and if there is no competition. However, in reality, every company is faced with the constraints of resources and the threat of competition. A company often faces constraints in the following 7 Ms:

- Management (The problem of leadership).
- Manpower (The problem of human resources).
- Machines (The problem of production systems and equipment).
- Money (The problem of capital).
- Materials (The problem of accessing raw materials).
- Methods (The problem of technology).
- Markets (The problem of accessing customers).

Owing to these constraints, the company will have to design effective strategies to survive and fight in the business world. At the same time, competition has become keener than ever.

The stiffness and ferocity of competition have been accentuated by factors such as:

- The general slowdown in the world economy
- The recent recessions in many countries
- The emergence of new competitors

Product Market	Existing Product	New Product
Existing Market	Market Penetration	Product Development
New Market	Market Development	Diversification

Figure 1.1 Strategic Marketing Problems

- The advent of technology which creates non-traditional competitors (for example, the computer chip, with its multi-purpose usage, has enabled many companies to enter businesses that they could never do before.)

The net result of resource constraints and intense competition is that not only must strategies be effective, but also they must be flexible and adaptable. It is precisely over such concerns that, over the years, many scholars, researchers and consulting firms have developed numerous strategic management and decision-making tools to help companies become more effective. Some examples of such strategic tools include:

- The experience curve
- The Boston Consulting Group (BCG) Product Portfolio Matrix
- The Shell Directional Matrix
- The General Electric Matrix
- Michael Porter's Structural Analysis and Generic Strategies
- The Booz Allen Approach

1.7 Outline of the Sun Tzu *Art of War* model

In order to better appreciate the relevance and applications of Sun Tzu's works to strategic management and thinking, his comprehensive thoughts have been organized and "modelized" in a format that is familiar to students of modern strategic management. At the same time, efforts have also been made to ensure that the model has a certain sequential order so that it can aid the decision-making process of managers. Thus, the Sun Tzu *Art of War* model as presented in this book is a "How To" model, that is, its main intention is to serve as a tool to assist managerial or business decision-making with regard to the choice, development and application of strategy in various situations. In doing so, it is very important to point out that:

(1) Interpretations and applications of Sun Tzu's works to modern business strategies are only confined to his writings, that is, no attempt is made to include other factors or variables that were not considered by him. (See Appendix B for other considerations.)

(2) In presenting the model and the various strategies advocated by Sun Tzu, the authors would not be imputing their own value systems in judging the "acceptability" of such approaches. In other words, the authors are only presenting a school of thought – Sun Tzu's style – and not its social desirability.

The Sun Tzu *Art of War* model to be presented in this book consists of five major components as depicted in Figure 1.2. Note that the model is also presented in terms of a sequential order. The first step in any strategic decision-making process (whether in war or in business) is that of Situation Appraisal. This involves assessing the desirabil-'ity of engaging in combat. In other words, in the context of war, it means a thorough assessment of the situation facing the commander before he decides whether or not to wage war. Situation Appraisal will be dealt with in Chapter 2.

Having thoroughly appraised the situation, the next stage involves the Formulation of Goals and Strategies. Here, the choice and development of a strategy has to be compatible with the goal(s) formulated and has to be appropriate to a given situation. The third stage in the strategic decision making process involves the Evaluation of Strategies. At this stage, the strategist has to assess the effectiveness of the strategy to be applied or used. Once the strategy is evaluated as feasible and effective, the next stage is that of Implementation. During this stage, the tactical and operational aspects for effective implementation

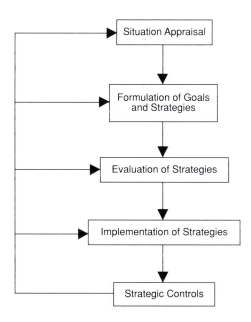

Figure 1.2 Sun Tzu's *Art Of War* Model

would have to be considered. Finally, to ensure success, there must be Controls where feedback mechanisms, such as the methods for acquisition of information, must be in place. This feedback will act as input to refine the earlier stages of the planning process.

2 *Situation appraisal*

2.1 The principle of detailed planning
2.2 Prerequisites of planning
2.3 The eight factors: An overview
2.4 Towards a conceptual model for situation appraisal

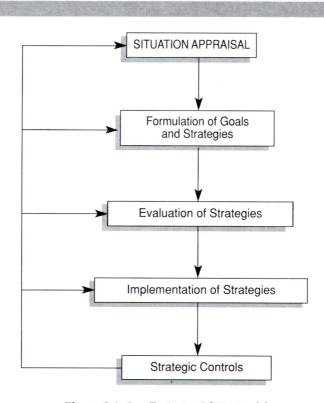

Figure 2.1 Sun Tzu's *Art Of War* Model

The first step in Sun Tzu's *Art of War* model is that of Situation Appraisal (see Figure 2.1). As mentioned in chapter 1, the strategic decision-making process begins with assessing the desirability of engaging in combat. This is the crux of situation appraisal, and it involves an indepth understanding of the principle of detailed planning.

2.1 The principle of detailed planning

According to the opening statement of Sun Tzu's work:

> "War is a matter of vital importance to the State. It concerns the lives and deaths of the people; and affects the survival or demise of the State. It must be thoroughly studied."

> 兵者，国之大事，死生之地，
> 存亡之道，不可不察也。

Thus, it is very important that before a decision to wage war is made, there must be detailed planning. This is echoed in many places in his writings, such as:

> "... With careful and detailed planning, one can win; with careless and less detailed planning, one cannot win. How much more certain is defeat if one does not plan at all! From the way planning is done beforehand, we can predict victory or defeat."

> 多算胜，少算不胜，
> 而况于无算乎！
> 吾以此观之，胜负见矣。

The significance of good planning can be summed up as follows:

> "For this reason, to win a hundred victories in a hundred battles is not the hallmark of skill. The acme of skill is to subdue the enemy without even fighting."

> 是故百战百胜，非善之善者也；
> 不战而屈人之兵，善之善者也。

This can only be accomplished when the general:

> "... attacks the enemy's strategy."

> 上兵伐谋

This is described as the highest form of generalship, and can only be accomplished through detailed planning. Detailed planning involves an assessment of the strengths and weaknesses of yourself *vis à vis* those of your enemies. Such an assessment allows you to gauge the chances of success:

> "He who has a thorough knowledge of himself and the enemy is bound to win in all battles. He who knows himself but not the enemy has only an even chance of winning. He who knows not himself and the enemy is bound to perish in all battles."

知彼知己者，百战不殆；
不知彼而知己，一胜一负；
不知彼，不知己，每战必殆。

In addition, he must also extend his planning to cover the terrain and weather:

> "Know your enemy, know yourself, and your victory will not be threatened. Know the terrain, know the weather, and your victory will be complete."

知彼知己，胜乃不殆；
知天知地，胜乃不穷。

The principle of detailed planning in war applies very much in business. Many textbooks have been devoted to this subject and many researchers and scholars have developed various kinds of planning tools, for example, competitive analysis through the SWOT (strengths, weaknesses, opportunities and threats) approach is conducted by corporate planners before they begin to design their corporate strategies. The essence of SWOT analysis is to determine the company's strengths relative to those of the competitors and to identify possible areas in which the company is likely to be threatened, as well as areas in which the company has distinct advantages. The ultimate purpose is to allow the company to exploit any market opportunities.

Indeed planning has become so important today that more and more larger companies have begun to set up corporate planning departments. The Japanese multinational companies, for example, are known to have large corporate and strategic planning departments that are staffed with highly qualified personnel whose jobs are mainly to scan the environment and detect trends that can impact on the operations of the businesses in the future and to develop intermediate and long term plans to deal with such developments. More often than not, significant gains are made by companies that have focused on those few important decisions that are based on planning rather than on trouble-shooting daily problems. But how does one go about planning? What are the parameters of planning? Sun Tzu provided a very comprehensive way of handling this issue.

2.2 Prerequisites of planning

Owing to the supreme importance and consequences of war, Sun Tzu advocated the need to appraise five fundamental factors (五事) and compare along seven dimensions. The five fundamental factors are:

- Moral Influence (道).
- Climate (天).
- Terrain (地).
- Generalship (将).
- Doctrine (法).

The seven dimensions to be compared are:

- Moral influence of the ruler (主孰有道).
- Ability of the general (将孰有能).
- Advantages of climate and terrain (天地孰得).
- Execution of laws and instructions (法令孰行).
- Numerical strength of troops (兵众孰强).
- Training of officers and men (士卒孰练).
- Administration of rewards and punishments (赏罚孰明).

Since there are areas where the five factors and seven dimensions correspond it is possible for our purposes to reclassify them into eight factors:

1. Moral Influence
2. Generalship (Command)
3. Climate
4. Terrain
5. Doctrine (Law)
6. Strengths
7. Training
8. Discipline (Rewards and Punishments System)

These eight factors form the prerequisites for strategic planning in warfare. In other words, the general must assess these factors thoroughly before starting a war. At the same time, these same factors also hold important implications for strategic thinking and planning in the business world. Each of these will now be discussed, and the implications for the business world will also be highlighted.

2.2.1 *Moral influence* (主孰有道)

When he discusses moral influence, Sun Tzu describes the way in which the people should be in perfect accord with their ruler, and willing to accompany him in life and into death without any fear of danger. Thus, by moral influence, Sun Tzu means the political leadership of the country. If the ruler is wise and capable, he will be able to gain the moral support of his subjects so much so that they will be willing to accompany him through the thick and thin of battles and the ups and downs of the State. The key point here is that these subjects would even be willing to lay down their lives for their State and the ruler. While this may seem unthinkable, in reality, there are such examples. Many of us will recall the many suicidal attempts of Japanese soldiers and fighters during the Second World War. Their willingness to lay down their lives for Japan and their emperor still evokes uncomfortable feelings among veterans of the war today.

In the business world, the moral influence factor is not unlike having a good government that provides leadership to the business sector in the form of proper legal and statutory systems, as well as effective directives and policies. To be successful, such provisions should also be in harmony with the laws of nature, the culture and the sentiments of the people. The moral influence or political factor can best be illustrated by the successes of Japan and other newly developed countries like Taiwan, South Korea, and Singapore. The governments in these countries have played very important roles in the success of their industries and export initiatives. For example, the Japanese Ministry of Trade and Industry (MITI) is known for charting the overall industrial policy for the country. The Japanese government will also not hesitate to support their industries in various ways such as through government guarantees and financing. Similarly, in countries like Taiwan, South Korea and Singapore, the governments have greatly encouraged their companies to have an outward orientation and have packaged various incentives to help them achieve such objectives. The result is that these three countries are very export-driven. Recently, the governments of these countries have also encouraged the development of important projects like the creation of Science Parks similar to that of Silicon

Valley in the United States. The object is to stimulate research and development (R&D) activities, especially in the area of high technology industries.

On the other hand, we have also witnessed corrupt and weak governments that are responsible for the decay in their national economies. Many African, Latin American and Asian countries suffer economically because of poor and incapable governments that are unable to exercise leadership. In fact, the discontent often lead to coups and counter-coups, loss of foreign investments, loss of nationals (who leave the country), worsening economies and lower standards of living.

In today's business world, many countries rely on foreign investment to stimulate economic growth. However, one key determinant of the inflow of foreign investment is the level of political stability, which in turn depends heavily on political leadership. The importance of political stability is best underscored by the fact that much effort has been expended on assessing the political risks of a country. Various methods of doing this have been developed over the years and any textbook on international business or international marketing will contain many such examples. Thus, in the business world, when a company decides to go overseas – whether in the form of direct exporting, licensing, joint ventures or direct investment in manufacturing – the most immediate factor is to consider the political leadership and conditions of that country. History has demonstrated that poor judgement in this area can lead to complete loss of investment (as in the case of nationalization policy). Taking a more current example, one of the constraints facing many companies going to China is still the issue of political leadership. Many China watchers and investors are still uncertain about the future political directions of China when Deng Xiaoping leaves the political scene.

In sum, just as in war an enlightened ruler will create the climate for the rise of a nation, while a weak emperor will pave the way for the demise of the state, in business a capable government will provide political stability and hence attract foreign investments and stimulate economic growth, while a corrupt government will only sow the seeds of economic decay.

2.2.2 Generalship or command (将孰有能)

Sun Tzu clearly made a distinction between the role of the political leader (emperor or ruler) and that of the field commander (general). This was reflected in many places of his writings, for example:

"He whose generals are able and not interfered with by the ruler will win."

将能而君不御者胜

"Hence it is said that enlightened rulers deliberate plans while capable generals execute them."

明主虑之，良将修之

A capable general must possess five important qualities or attributes. These attributes are wisdom (智), sincerity (信), benevolence (仁), courage (勇), and strictness (严). By wisdom (才智), he meant the ability to recognize changing circumstances and to act expediently. Sincerity (诚信) means the ability to have the complete trust of subordinates so that they have no doubt of the certainty of rewards and punishments. Benevolence (仁慈) requires love for mankind, the ability to sympathize with others and to appreciate the hard work and labor of the rank and file. Courage (勇敢) means being brave and decisive and having the ability to gain victory by capitalizing on opportunities without hesitation. Finally, a strict (威严) general is able to instill discipline and command respect as his troops are in awe of him and are afraid of punishments.

While highlighting the positive attributes of a capable general, Sun Tzu also pointed out five common weaknesses which can afflict a general and which can often prove calamitous in the conduct of war. These negative qualities are:

"If reckless, he can be killed;
If cowardly, he can be captured;
If quick-tempered, he can easily be provoked;
If sensitive to honor, he can easily be insulted;
If over compassionate to the people, he can easily be harassed."

必死，可杀也；
必生，可虏也；
忿速，可侮也；
廉洁，可辱也；
爱民，可烦也。

While moral influence in war can be compared to political leadership in business, the generalship factor typifies the element of *corporate leadership* in a business organization (Here, the organization is likened to a division in an army). Viewed in this perspective, it is interesting to note that the above qualities of the capable general mirror the ideal attributes that a chief executive officer (whether he is an entrepreneur or intrapreneur) should have. Any chief executive officer (CEO) who can demonstrate such qualities in the workplace is more than likely to be highly successful because:

(1) He is quick and decisive but not reckless and knows how to capitalize on various business opportunities.

(2) He is able to trust his subordinates in their jobs and let them know that their performances will be rewarded (or penalized) accordingly. In addition, he is not easily provoked when mistakes are made.

(3) He is human relations oriented and understands the problems of his subordinates and appreciates their work. However, he is not overly compassionate to the extent that he is harassed by every little human-related problem.

(4) He has the courage to make bold decisions and hence is willing to take risks when necessary. In other words, he is not afraid of sticking his neck out for the right decisions.

(5) His exemplary, strict lifestyle will instill discipline within the company, an essential ingredient for high productivity. At the same time, he is willing to learn and is not afraid of losing face when people point out his weaknesses.

Just as the success of a war depends very much on the capabilities of the general, in business, the CEO plays an important part in ensuring the success and prosperity of the firm. One good example of an American CEO that demonstrates the above qualities is that of Lee Iacocca of Chrysler Corporation. Through his capable leadership, he was able to steer Chrysler out from bankruptcy to a path of strong business recovery. Note that in exercising his leadership, he was strict and fair to employees and the union, rewarding them once the company recovered, he was able to sympathize with the workers (he took only an annual salary of $1 at one stage), he was willing to make bold decisions (like confronting the unions over substantial wage cuts and inviting union representation on the Management Board) and he was exemplary in behavior.

Besides Iacocca, the history of business is filled with the success stories of companies that have capable CEOs. Many Japanese companies like Honda, Sony and Matsushita have become what they are today largely because of the leadership provided by the pioneers of such companies. Thus, before a company decides on aggressive business moves like entering new markets, it is important that it has the capable leaders to see it through such ventures.

2.2.3 *Climate* (天地執得)

This factor refers to the varying weather, seasons, temperatures, times, and daylight hours. The climatic conditions therefore represent the un-controllable aspect of military campaigns. A capable general capitalizes on the weather by taking into account the opportunities and threats posed by changes in the seasons, the temperature, and other climatic conditions. Using climatic conditions to one's advantage is especially important in conventional warfare. For example, in flying combat planes, wind and cloud conditions must be considered; in the move-ment of sea vessels, wind and wave conditions must be taken into account and in the movement of land forces, the seasons and daily weather conditions become important factors. One of the reasons for the success of the Vietcong in the Vietnam war was their ability to exploit the weather to their advantage.

While in war the general has to contend with the climate and try to use it to his advantage, in business the CEO also faces a set of climatic conditions. Indeed, we often hear of familiar terms like "busi-ness climate" and "economic climate". Any business has to operate within the business and economic climates of the country, the region and the world at large. These would include:

- Business cycles such as recessions, growth, stagnation, inflation.
- The conditions that are favorable/unfavorable for investments, business expansion and operations such as government policies, regulations, incentives, all of which impact on the operations of businesses.
- The cultural and social norms that may either help or retard the practice and operation of businesses. For example, in some cul-tures, businesses are better perceived than in others and they are viewed more as engines of economic growth than exploiters of cheap labor and materials.
- The state of technology and the rate and types of technological changes that might affect the way business is conducted. Often, technology also affects such things as production, or material usage.
- Changes in market structure. New market institutions and systems

may emerge that can upset the status quo for the conduct of business. For example, the formation of labor unions, cartels or common markets will have a significant impact on business operations.

- Other general economic and social factors such as demographic changes, changes in consumer behavior, changes in institutional structures.

To be successful, a firm has to take into account the various changes in the business and economic environment outlined above and adapt its strategies accordingly. It is important to point out that although the company must take into consideration all these environmental factors in its planning processes, they are to a very large extent beyond its control. Unlike corporate leadership which can be voted in and out, as well as recruited and sacked, the company has negligible influence over the environmental factors. It cannot dictate the ups and downs of the business cycles, nor can it influence social and cultural norms overnight. Like climate in warfare where the general has to work within constraints, the CEO also has to work within the constraints posed by the environment. It represents the external factor in planning.

2.2.4 *Terrain* (天地孰得)

By terrain, Sun Tzu meant the area of military operations including factors such as:

- whether the ground for operation is easy or difficult,
- whether the ground is open or constricted,
- the distances of the camping site to and from the battlefield,
- the degree of danger posed by the terrain,
- the scope for operation and maneuvers and,
- the possibilities for attacks and withdrawals.

These variables of the terrain will affect the chances of life and death in battles. It is important to point out here that there is a difference between the terms "terrain" and "grounds" as used by Sun Tzu. The single Chinese character is the same for both words, but they contain different meanings. In terrain (地形), Sun Tzu meant the characteristics of the ground. As such, it is a *fixed* factor once war begins, in that the terrain will constrain the types of strategies that can be employed. In other words, once an army is locked into combat in a specific terrain, it will have to face the consequences that that terrain offers. For example, in the Middle-East conflict, the openness of the terrain dictates that certain types of military strategies be used. At the same time, it also affects the types of weaponry that can be used and the ways that the troops can be employed.

In contrast, by ground (战地), Sun Tzu meant *battlegrounds*. In this case, battlegrounds need not necessarily be a fixed factor. The general can easily decide the type of battleground on which he wishes to engage the enemy. If the ground is to his disadvantage, he may choose not to fight. Thus, battleground is a variable factor and is, to a larger extent, a controllable element. For example, in the Vietnam war, the Vietcong chose not to take on the Americans directly and avoided open confrontations. Instead, they chose to hide in the jungles and only launched sporadic raids and attacks through guerrilla warfare. At the same time, they also embarked on psychological warfare through the spreading of rumors and infiltration techniques. They adopted such an approach largely because of their tremendous disadvantages in combat power and their strengths in jungle warfare. Thus, the Vietcong decided on the type of *battleground* they wanted to fight in. On the other hand, in trying to flush out the Vietcong and going after them into the jungles, the American soldiers were forced to fight in a terrain that was unfamiliar to them. The constricted terrain greatly inhibited the kind of strategies and weapons that they could use and the result was that their combat power was greatly diminished.

In sum, while a general can decide on the type of battleground on which to engage the enemy, he will have to contend with the terrain characteristics of that battleground once battle begins. It therefore goes without saying that different battlegrounds will confer different types of advantages or disadvantages and dictate that certain combat strategies will be more effective than others. The distinction between these two terms of terrain and grounds would be much clearer if the reader comprehends Chapters X and XI of Sun Tzu's writings.

In the same way as the army has to contend with terrain characteristics, the business firm also faces certain physical or infrastructural variables by virtue of its physical location. This is because where the firm is located and positioned in the marketplace will affect how it can compete as it may offer certain advantages or disadvantages. For example, once a firm's location is fixed, it dictates the nature of its competition, its relative market position and its access to:

- the supply of raw materials
- cheap and efficient labor
- capital markets (for financing and loans)
- supplies of machinery and equipment (to run the factories)

- managerial talents and skills
- technology, research and development (R&D) centres
- consumer markets, locally and overseas
- infrastructural services such as telecommunications, transportation facilities, water and power supplies, warehousing facilities.

The above variables will greatly affect the operations of a firm and constrain the competitive stance that it can take. It is, therefore, no surprise that many companies spare no expense in making locational studies (for example, companies like McDonalds and Burger King conduct long and detailed surveys before decisions are made on the suitability of new restaurant sites), especially those that involve substantial investments in fixed and immovable assets. For companies deciding to invest overseas (such as setting up a manufacturing plant), the need for in-depth studies on locational factors becomes even more critical. At times, it is not possible to have all the physical factors in one's favor. For example, it may not be possible to locate near to markets, have access to cheap and efficient labor and access to raw materials, all at the same time (just as it is not possible to choose the ideal battleground). However, the objective is still to ensure that the location chosen can provide the maximum leverage for operation. This is because once the company is locked into a business terrain, it has to face the consequences for a while as it is often difficult to pull out quickly. This is the situation faced by some companies that have hurriedly invested in China in recent years. They found, to their disappointment, that there are many infrastructural constraints in China.

2.2.5 *Doctrine or law* (法令執行)

This factor refers to the organization, control, signals procedures, designation of military ranks, allocation of responsibilities, regulation and management of supply routes and the provision of items used by the army. As war involves the whole state and often the stakes are extremely high, effective doctrines and organization are without doubt crucial. This is because the way the army is structured often affects the behavior of the officers and men and the combat readiness and capability of the forces. Thus, we often hear of sayings like, "the army needs to be re-structured", "the forces are poorly organized". To some extent, organizational and structural factors also affect the morale of the soldiers as well. For example, one of the common reasons cited for the discontent of the Philippines armed forces (which resulted in several coup attempts against the Aquino government) in 1987 was that it required reorganization and structuring so as to combat the communists more effectively.

The importance and significance of the doctrinal factor can be evidenced by the following comments by Sun Tzu:

> "If the army is confused and suspicious, the neighboring states will surely create trouble. This is like the saying: 'A confused army provides victory for the enemy.'"

三军既惑且疑，则诸侯之难至矣，是谓乱军引胜。

> "Do not engage an approaching enemy whose banners are well-ordered; do not attack an enemy whose formations are impressive and strong."

无邀正正之旗，勿击堂堂之陈

> "The management of a large force is similar to that of a small force. It is a matter of organization and structure."

凡治众如治寡，分数是也；

> "To control a large force in combat is similar to that of a small force. It is a matter of formations and signals."

斗众如斗寡，形名是也；

> "Order and disorder depend on organization."

治乱，数也；

Just like the army, a business firm's doctrine is reflected by the way it is structured and organized. This aspect includes effective policies, programs, operating procedures, channels of communication, lines of authority and responsibility. To some extent, these elements would reflect the corporate culture or philosophy.

The organization and structure of a firm is one area that must be considered in strategic planning. What should be the best way to organize the company to face the future? If a company wants to encourage creativity, innovation and entrepreneurial spirit, what is the best way to structure the company? If the company decides to go overseas and intends to grow in that dimension, is it organized to reflect the importance of international operations? Are overseas postings considered a premium for career advancement, or are they considered as serving a necessary corporate sentence or spending a "honeymoon" period abroad? With regard to this aspect of an international (or even global) orientation, it is interesting to note that it is almost impossible for a Japanese manager to make it to a CEO position without substantial overseas experience. In contrast, there are many American CEOs who have never worked for a long period of time in overseas markets. Perhaps this could account to some extent for the greater successes of Japanese companies globally.

2.2.6 Strengths (兵众执强)

By strengths, Sun Tzu refers more to the numerical aspect of the army, that is, the physical strength of the army and he includes the equipping of officers and men. There are definite advantages in numbers in war, especially when both combating forces have about the same state of technology. In ancient times, when weapons were rudimentary, a larger army definitely had the upper hand most of the time. Even in today's conventional warfare, numbers are still important as they dictate the operations of weapons and equipment, and hence the extent of fire power. For example, one of the arguments in favor of better equipment for NATO forces centers around the fact that the Warsaw Pact countries have superiority in numbers. In the Iran-Iraq war of attrition, numerical strengths became important to the extent that Iran even sent teenagers to the war front.

Sun Tzu highlighted the importance of numbers when he said:

"When outnumbering the enemy ten to one, surround him;
When five to enemy's one, attack him;
When double his strength, divide him;
When evenly matched, you may choose to fight;
When slightly weaker than the enemy, be capable of withdrawing;
When greatly inferior to the enemy, avoid engaging him;
For no matter how obstinate a small force is, it will succumb to a larger and superior force."

十则围之，五则攻之，倍则分之，
敌则能战之，少则能逃之，
不若则能避之。
故小敌之坚，大敌之擒也。

In addition, he also said:

> "Therefore, an army that lacks heavy equipment will lose the battle; an army that does not have food will not survive; an army that does not have supplies cannot continue fighting."

是故军无辎重则亡，
无粮食则亡，
无委积则亡。

A company engaging in the business world is no different from an army. It also has its relative strengths or weaknesses in terms of resources such as manpower, management, money, machines, materials, methods of production (including technology) and markets served. These variables form the company's *competitive edges* and there are definite advantages to being big and strong. These advantages include:

- economies of scale
- more operating leverages
- more ways to deploy resources
- the ability to last for longer "combat" period
- the ability to absorb attrition as a result of losing workers.

Before a company takes on its competitors or embarks on aggressive market moves, it must assess its resources carefully. This would become even more important if it intends to take on a larger competitor in an industry where there is little product differentiation. Under such circumstances, the larger competitor always has built-in advantages.

One good example of such a competitive situation is the banking industry. It is generally true that the larger banks often have greater advantages in providing a wider range of services at lower costs. In syndicated loans, the players are often large, international banks. The smaller ones are often left in the cold. Similarly, the larger banks are also able to penetrate more international markets (this is true of Japanese, American and some European banks) owing to their vast financial resources and greater ability to take risks (or absorb losses).

Another example where numbers would confer a distinct advantage is in the labor intensive, low technology industries such as textiles, garments and toys. Hong Kong, as a result of its exodus of manpower through emigration in recent years, has now moved the bulk of these industries to China where labor is both plentiful and cheap.

2.2.7 *Training* (士卒孰练)

While recognizing the advantages of numerical superiority, Sun Tzu also cautioned against relying on sheer numbers alone to win wars:

> "The strength of an army does not depend on large forces. Do not advance relying on sheer numbers."

兵非益多也，惟无武进

What is more important is the training of the men and officers.

> "Therefore, he (the general) is able to select men who are able to exploit situations."

故能择人而任势。

Only through training can strategies be effectively carried out. For example, achieving the correct timing, maintaining momentum in attacks and having the correct military formations in warfare demand that the troops are well trained and obedient. In addition, the practice of deception also requires discipline and training.

Relating the factor of training to the business situation implies that having more employees in the rank and file and having more managers will not necessarily lead to greater advantage over the competitors. What is more important is the quality and not the quantity of the staff. The competitive edge will come with proper human resource development and training. It is very interesting to note that the more successful companies are also those with a heavy commitment to human resource development. Good examples of such companies are IBM and SIA (Singapore International Airline). Perhaps the best example of all could be found in the large multi-national companies of Japan. They believe very strongly in on-the-job training and the young executive starts at the lowest level of the organization and has to work his way up, at each stage receiving new and different training. When he reaches the very top, he is almost thoroughly trained and well-exposed. Thus, he becomes very much a generalist-specialist.

In sum, the level of training will dictate the state of combat readiness of the firm. With well-trained personnel, the firm can engage in more activities with greater confidence. In addition, they are better able to handle difficult situations, and yet produce good results.

2.2.8 Discipline (赏罚执明)

Quantity and quality are definite advantages to any army. However, there is another very important dimension to winning war, and that is discipline. According to Sun Tzu, the army that has a set of stringent rules and administers rewards and punishments in an enlightened way will be in a better fighting spirit. The following quotations sum up his arguments:

> "Too frequent rewards indicate the running out of ideas;
> Too frequent punishments indicate dire distress."

> 数赏者，窘也；
> 数罚者，困也；

> "When the men are punished before their loyalty is secured, they will be disobedient. If disobedient, it is difficult to employ them. If the loyalty of the men is secured, but punishments are not enforced, such a troop cannot be used either."

> 卒未亲附而罚之，则不服，不服则难用也。
> 卒已亲附而罚不行，则不可用也。

> "When discipline is regularly enforced on all rank and file, they will be obedient. When discipline is not regularly enforced on all rank and file, they will not be obedient.
> When orders are consistently executed, it is because of the mutual trust between the commander and his men."

> 令素行以教其民，则民服；
> 令不素行以教其民，则民不服。
> 令素行者，与众相得也。

In the same way, a company needs to have discipline if it is to compete effectively. This discipline may be reflected in various ways, such as:

- A corporate code of conduct and ethics governing issues like corruption, taking of bribes, solicited and unsolicited gifts.
- A company uniform, a corporate song, a corporate logo and flag.
- Regulation of working hours, rest periods, days-off.
- Enforcement of safety standards and productivity goals.
- Rules governing the protection of corporate secrets and sanctions procedures for violation of such rules.
- A reward system of fringe benefits and incentive packages.

The main purpose of having such comprehensive and elaborate measures is to direct human behavior to achieve the organization's goals and objectives. Therefore, a company that has a more effective disciplinary procedure and reward and punishment system will be more geared towards higher performance and will be in a stronger position to compete. This is because the employees are clear about what they will receive and can better identify with the organization. This discipline aspect of an organization reflects to a large extent the *motivational factor*. Just as in training, it is interesting to note that companies that place a premium on the motivational factor are also known to be highly successful. Good examples include many Japanese companies and IBM. They are known not just for their total package of remuneration and fringe benefits for their employees. The Japanese companies, for example, have the tradition of sending their executives for annual executive camps where the training not only incorporates military-style discipline but also includes doses of spiritual and social values such as learning self-sacrifice, humility, hard work, suffering and toleration.

2.3 The eight factors: An overview

Table 2.1 summarizes the eight factors that can be inferred from the works of Sun Tzu to assess the combat readiness of an army before going to war and the corresponding applications to modern strategic planning. Just as a good general appraises the situation before going to war, an organization must carefully weigh these factors in their planning so that they can take on the competitors in any strategic business moves or campaigns.

It is important to emphasize that the assessment of these factors involves comparison with the enemy, evidenced by the interrogative form in which Sun Tzu made his statements:

1. Which ruler possesses more moral influence?
2. Which general is more capable?

Thus, these factors are intended to be assessed in relation to the enemies, the result of which is:

> "I will be able to forecast which side will be victorious and which will be defeated."

吾以此知胜负矣。

Table 2.1 The 8 factors of strategic planning

Sun Tzu	Management Application
1. Moral Influence (主孰有道)	Political Leadership
2. Generalship (将孰有能)	Corporate Leadership
3. Climate (天地孰得)	External Factor
4. Terrain (天地孰得)	Physical or Infrastructural Factor
5. Doctrine or Law (法令孰行)	Corporate Structure & Organization
6. Strengths (兵众孰强)	Competitive Edges
7. Training (士卒孰练)	Human Resource Development
8. Discipline (赏罚孰明)	Motivational Factor

What is intriguing about the eight factors is that they are very comprehensive in scope and coverage. First, there is no doubt that the factors range from the micro to the macro level. In other words, the analysis involves examining individuals (human resource development, corporate leadership, and motivation), the company (corporate structure and organization, and competitive edges), the nation (political leadership) and the environment (external and infrastructural factors).

Second, the factors include the controllable and uncontrollable aspects of planning. Climate and terrain (external and infrastructural factors) are to a large extent uncontrollable. Political leadership is also beyond the influence of the company in most cases. Even in a democratic country, once a government is elected, the people and the business organizations are stuck with the style of political leadership for three to five years. However, among the eight factors, there are some that are controllable. For example, motivation and human resource development can definitely be influenced by the company. To some extent, a competitive edge can also be built up very quickly, for example, by recruitment and soliciting supplies, capital, or equipment. In essence, the uncontrollable factors reflect the external aspects of the firm, which to a large extent are elements that are endowed by the forces of nature and the environment. On the other hand, the controllable factors are the internal variables of the company. They reflect to a large extent the man-made elements that affect the organization.

Third, Sun Tzu also considered the human and non-human components of strategic planning. Political leadership (moral influence), corporate leadership (generalship), human resource development (training) and motivation (discipline) are all human elements, while external factor (climate), infrastructural factor (terrain), structure and organization (doctrine) are all non-human elements. Competitive edges (strengths) would encompass both human and non-human elements.

Fourth, the factors also take into account the static and dynamic forces. For example, terrain (the infrastructural factor) is static to a large extent as it takes a very long time to change. Political leadership can also be quite static (especially in communist countries or countries where there are rarely any elections. Climate (external factor) changes, but not so drastically in the short term. In contrast, strengths (competitive edges) can be very dynamic as they depend not only on what one does, but on what the competitors do as well. Similarly, training (human resource development), and discipline (motivation) tend to be more dynamic than static in nature.

Finally, the tangibles and intangibles are also considered. Competitive edges (strengths) can be more easily evaluated and seen, so are doctrines (corporate structure and organization). However, command and discipline (leadership and motivation) are more abstract and harder to grasp and evaluate.

Given the depth and comprehensiveness of Sun Tzu's prerequisites for planning warfare – that consider the micro to macro factors, the controllable and uncontrollable factors, the human and non-human factors, the static and dynamic forces and the tangible and intangible elements – it is possible to contend that the framework for strategic thinking and planning that we commonly understand today, was perhaps already laid out some 2,400 years ago. In fact, when one talks about strategic planning, it is difficult not to consider the eight factors! They represent important aspects that must be carefully weighed before the formulation of goals and strategies.

At this point, it is important to caution that Sun Tzu was not an advocate of hegemony and war. Rather he thought that war should be avoided at all costs and should only be used as a last resort. Rash decisions which lead to war can result in dire consequences and hence must be avoided. War, according to Sun Tzu should only be waged if the following conditions are satisfied:

(1) that there are some definite advantages to be gained;

(2) that there is a strong assurance of victory;

(3) that there is no other alternative, short of war, to safeguard one's position;

(4) that one's defence is invulnerable.

The above conditions are supported as follows:

> "Do not move unless there are definite advantages to be gained; do not use troops unless you can succeed; do not fight unless you are in danger."

非利不动，
非得不用，
非危不战。

On the necessity of an invulnerable defense, he said:

> "In ancient times, the adepts in warfare first made themselves invincible before waiting for opportunities to defeat the enemy.

昔之善战者，先为不可胜，以待敌之可胜。

> "Those who cannot win must defend; ..."

不可胜者，守也

Indeed, Sun Tzu warned that:

> "A ruler must not start a war out of anger;
> A general must not fight a battle out of resentment.
> Engage only when it is in the interest of the State;
> Cease when it is to its detriment."

主不可以怒而兴师，
将不可以愠而致战；
合于利而动，
不合于利而止。

and the reasons are:

> "For while anger can be restored to happiness and resentment can become pleasantness, a State that has perished cannot be restored and a man who is dead cannot be resurrected."

怒可以复喜，愠可以复悦；
亡国不可以复存，死者不可以复生。

Perhaps the last words should appropriately come from the master himself:

> "Therefore, an enlightened ruler should always be cautious about war, while a good general should always be alert in war. This is the way to secure the State and preserve the army."

故明君慎之，良将警之
此安国全军之道也。

2.4 Towards a conceptual model for situation appraisal

This chapter has been devoted to highlighting and discussing the eight factors that, according to Sun Tzu, must be considered before the waging of war. Their applications to modern strategic management have also been discussed. However, all the discussions and arguments can actually be conceptualized into a model that makes understanding the process of situation appraisal easier. This conceptual model is depicted in Figure 2.2. Note that the eight factors for comparison as proposed by Sun Tzu involve an in-depth analysis with regard to:

- Oneself
- The enemy
- The environment

The analysis of the eight factors along the three dimensions of self, the enemy and the environment is in fact not unlike the modern concept of a SWOT (Strengths, Weaknesses, Opportunities and Threats) analysis in strategic management. In fact, as shown in Figure 2.2, the first five analyses of the ability of the general (the corporate leadership), doctrine or law (corporate structure and organization), numerical strengths of troops (competitive edges), training of officers and men (human resource development) and discipline or administration of rewards and punishments (motivational factor) constitute a comparison of strengths and weaknesses of "oneself" versus the "enemy". On the other hand, the analyses on the moral influence of the ruler (political leadership in the country), the advantages offered by climate (external factor) and terrain (physical or infrastructural factor) require an identification of opportunities and threats that are present in the environment.

A close study of the prevailing situation using SWOT analysis through assessing the eight factors in relation to the self, the enemy

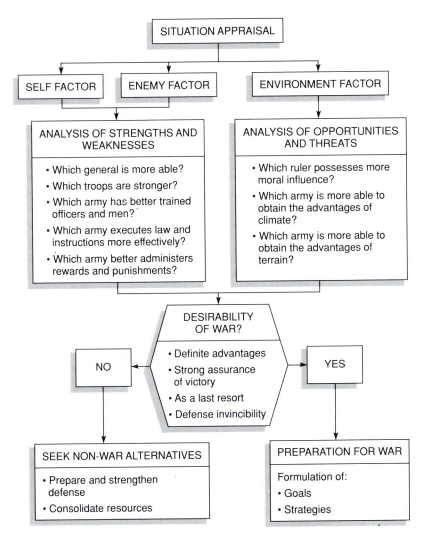

Figure 2.2 Situation Appraisal

and the situation will enable one to determine with greater certainty the chances of success in waging war. Hence, the question of the desirability of war can be answered more confidently (see Figure 2.2 again). If the four conditions for waging war (as discussed earlier) are satisfied, then one proceeds to formulate goals and strategies for a war offensive. However, if the analysis indicates that war is not desirable, then one should seek a "non-war" alternative at the same time not discounting the possibility of a war initiative by the enemy. Sun Tzu said:

"In the conduct of war, one must not rely on the enemy's
failure to come but on one's readiness to engage him;
One must not rely on the enemy's failure to attack but on one's
ability to build an invincible defence."

故用兵之法，无恃其不来，恃吾有以待也；
无恃其不攻，恃吾有所不可攻也。

Thus, though one may not be able to give battle, one should maintain a state of war readiness. In the interim period of peace, one should take the opportunity to be in readiness to counter any enemy offensive by preparing and strengthening one's defenses and be in readiness to seize any opportunities that may arise by consolidating one's resources. The model as depicted in Figure 2.2 can easily be applied to the business world. By now, the readers are probably able to appreciate the relevance and applications of the eight factors in relation to strategic planning. Note that the four conditions governing the desirability of war are very relevant to the situation of a company, say, wanting to declare a marketing war on its competitors. In this case, a marketing war should only be declared if:

(1) There are definite gains to be made such as increased sales, market share, profits, or a higher profile for the company.

(2) There is a strong chance of winning.

(3) It is a measure of last resort, for example, if its market share can never be increased unless it goes on the offensive.

(4) It has built up a ready line of defense, such as financial resources to back up its campaign.

If it is not possible to wage war on the competitors in the market, the company should explore other alternatives. To begin with, the company should strengthen the areas in which it is weak. For example, it can attempt to improve its productivity through better production techniques, increased mechanization, newer technology and higher skills training for employees and managers. It can also seek to increase its marketing competitiveness through better and improved products, more creative and innovative advertising and promotion techniques, more efficient distribution systems and improved customer and clientele relations. In other words, the company should make attempts to consolidate and improve its resources, prepare and strengthen its defenses, and seek non-competitive alternatives.

An example will perhaps illustrate the various points highlighted in the model better. The retail gasoline industry in Singapore (and this is likely to be true in many other countries as well) is known for its aggressive, direct and open marketing campaigns to gain market share. It is perhaps the industry that has had the highest number of marketing and advertising wars over the years. Such aggressive moves to gain market share are not surprising considering that gasoline is a very standardized product that is almost commodity-like in nature. In fact, consumers rarely bother to distinguish one brand of gasoline from another, despite the efforts put in by the oil companies to distinguish their products. At the same time, however, this industry is also driven by economies of scale. This means that the best way to bring down costs (and hence increase profits) is to increase production which necessitates the need for increasing market share.

Besides the above factors, the retail gasoline industry is also oligopolistic in nature. This implies that the first company to introduce a better grade of gasoline and/or use aggressive marketing efforts such as promotional gifts or lucky draws is likely to grab a higher market share if the other competitors do not follow quickly. In Singapore, the retail gasoline market is worth about US$305 million to $330 million a year. At any point in time, if there are no promotional or improved product offers, the sales are very much dictated by the distribution factor (that is, sales of each gas company are dependent on the distribution network). However, when there is a special offer, up to 10% of the total market share (that is, up to US$30 million) can be up for contention. For this reason, companies like Esso (which introduced the Esso Gold), Caltex (which introduced the Caltex CX 3) and Shell (which introduced the SuperShell Formula in 1987) are always looking for opportunities to be on the offensive.

In early 1988, Shell encountered a slight setback in that its Shell Formula gasoline created some valve problems among certain types of vehicles. The other gasoline companies did not hesitate to capitalize on this opportunity and waged very aggressive advertising campaigns to discredit Shell. However, within a month, Shell responded with an improved product and launched an equally impressive marketing campaign to avert its declining image. Shell lost some sales but definitely did not sit back and do nothing. It went on a counter-offensive.

It is important to point out that in launching any offensive move, the gasoline companies are often only able to satisfy two out of the four conditions – that it is a measure of last resort and there are positive gains to be made in the short run. Assurance of victory and defense invincibility are harder to achieve. Thus far, Shell appears to be the most successful because it does have a strong line of defense created by its larger distribution network and by virtue of being the holder of the largest market share (at any point in time, Shell holds about 40% of the total market share in Singapore). The net result is that it has greater operating leverage than the other companies. In fact, when it introduced its improved formula in 1986, it was launched very aggressively and supported by various media over a sustained period of time. The other companies, being smaller and with fewer resources, had a hard time taking on the aggressive moves by Shell.

Taking the illustration further, when a company cannot take on the competitors head-on, it should always look for other means to compete. For example, instead of competing on price, it may want to focus on service and quality. More importantly, it should always try to improve on its existing operations, including improving the product, so as to be more geared up for competition. This should be done in times when competition is not keen or rampant. Taking the retail gasoline industry as an example, when there are no wars going on, the smaller companies should spend more effort in extending and increasing its distribution outlets as a way to strengthen its defense.

The need to be "combat fit" should be the aim of every company. Thus, staff training and development, auditing and improvement of every aspect of the corporate resources should always be part and parcel of the activities of a company. Indeed, all the factors listed in Figure 2.2 should be constantly evaluated and assessed so that the company knows where it stands *vis-à-vis* its competitors and the industry. Such efforts cannot be *ad hoc* attempts, or only receive attention when the company is losing its competitiveness. In fact, two of the main criticisms brought against companies in Singapore during the 1985/86 recession were their unpreparedness in coping with increased competition brought about by excess supply and their failure to monitor the environment. In addition, during the good times, they had never bothered to consolidate their resources so as to be ready for the lean times. However, Singaporean companies are not the exception. Even some Fortune 500 companies have been wiped out of the listing over the years owing to complacency and the inability to remain combat fit.

3 Formulation of goals and choice of battleground

3.1 Formulation of goals
3.2 Formulation of strategies: Choice of battleground

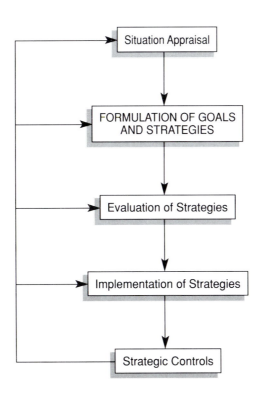

Figure 3.1 Formulation of Goals and Choice of Battleground

Once the situational appraisal is completed and a decision is taken for war, the next step is getting ready for combat. Preparation for war involves formulation along two aspects (see Figure 3.1):

1. Goals
2. Strategies (including choice of battleground)

Each of these two aspects is governed by its own principles. Owing to the substantial coverage of content under the subject of formulation of strategies, it will be discussed in two separate chapters. In this chapter, formulation of goals and choice of battleground will be dealt with. In Chapter 4 we will discuss the other principles governing formulation of strategies.

3.1 Formulation of goals

In war, the ultimate goal or objective must be to win. Nobody enters a war to lose territories! Similarly, nobody enters business to lose money. The final objective must be to make as much money as possible, with the ultimate goal of capturing the entire market share! The paramount purpose in war, according to Sun Tzu, is victory. Thus, those who are skilful in the art of warfare:

> "... subdue the enemy's army without direct battle; capture the enemy's cities without fierce assaults; and destroy the enemy's nation without protracted operations."

屈人之兵而非战也，拔人之城而非攻也，
毁人之国而非久也

In other words:

> "Your aim is to capture all states intact. Thus, your forces are not worn out and your victory can be complete. This is the crux of offensive strategy."

必以全争于天下，故兵不顿，而利可全，此谋攻之法也。

Hence, the aim in war is to win and to win profitably. The parallel in business is to achieve maximum gains with minimum effort. In order to win profitably, goals must:

1. Be prioritized

2. Be achievable

3. Represent some net positive gains

3.1.1 *Prioritizing goals*

It is necessary to prioritize goals because the underlying principle of war is to win profitably. Hence, the general must decide what kind of war objectives are most desirable and beneficial to his state and his forces. For example, the goals for offensive strategy were stated by Sun Tzu in the following priorities:

> "The highest form of generalship is to attack the enemy's strategy;
> The next best policy is to disrupt his alliances;
> The next best is to attack his army;
> The worst policy of all is to besiege walled cities.
> Besiege cities only when there are no other alternatives."

故上兵伐谋，其次伐交，
其次伐兵，其下攻城。
攻城之法为不得已。

Note that the underlying aim of the 4-step offensive strategy is to capture all states intact and with minimum loss of resources and troops. Goals in war are set at the most macro level – to win as many territories as possible, with the ultimate objective of putting all of them under your control. In the same way, it is not unthinkable to say that the ultimate objective of any business is to capture the whole market – to be the pure monopolist!

Prioritizing of goals is very much applicable to business planning, especially given the various constraints that a firm faces (the seven Ms as outlined at the beginning of Chapter 1). It ensures that the company is more focused and separates the important from the trivial. Similarly, the above four priorities in offensive strategy as advocated by Sun Tzu – attacking the enemy's strategy, disrupting his alliances, attacking his army and besieging walled cities – can also be applied to the business world.

Attacking the enemy's strategy

Sun Tzu considered this as the highest form of generalship. Foremost in the mind of every general in war should be to attack the enemy's strategy. This should be the main goal or objective of any military combat. The main intention is to upset the enemy even before the war is started. In the business world, to attack the enemy's strategy is like using pre-emptive measures to upset the competitor's plan. For example, pre-emptive strategies would include:

(1) Introducing a superior product into the market earlier than any other competitor. This would upset any attempts on the competitor's part to erode the company's existing market share. In fact, one of the ways in which technologically superior companies (*vide* IBM) manage to keep their dominant market place is to continuously adopt an aggressive and proactive new product development policy. In this way, they are able to prevent any overtaking moves by competitors.

(2) Entering new segments of the market before any of the competitors. While this does not prevent the competitor from subsequently entering the market segment, it definitely increases the costs of entry. Moreover, being the first to enter the market segment can sometimes bring about distinctive advantages:

> "Generally, those who reach and occupy the battleground early will have time to rest and wait for the enemy. Those who arrive at the battleground late will have to rush into action when they are already tired and exhausted."

凡先处战地而待敌者佚，
后处战地而趋战者劳。

A good example illustrating the advantages of being the first in a market segment is the early entry of McDonald's (as compared to Burger King) into suburban government housing estates in Singapore. Being the first hamburger chain in these estates, McDonald's was in a better position to locate itself in more strategic and higher traffic areas.

(3) Choosing to enter foreign markets long before any other companies. Here, the "early bird catches the worm" phenomenon also applies. The Japanese penetration of various overseas markets typifies this type of proactive strategy. For example, while many other foreign companies are still hesitant to do business with China, Japanese companies are known to be among the earliest entrants into the Chinese market. Today, Japanese workers can be found in many parts of China, working on various types of projects. Traveling through China today, one cannot help but notices that the most visible brands of cars, trucks and other automobiles on Chinese roads are Japanese. While many other countries are still fussing over political differences with Vietnam, Japanese businessmen are quietly sounding out their business contacts with the Vietnamese, and some have already concluded business deals and are doing business with the Vietnamese.

In sum, to attack the competitor's strategy requires a continuous monitoring of the competitive environment as well as the various forces that shape the industry concerned. It requires a proactive and deliberate effort on the part of the company.

Disrupting the enemy's alliances

The next best thing to attacking the enemy's strategy is to disrupt his alliances. During the times of Sun Tzu, there were many warring states, each with its own warlord. Often one of the ways to prevent being attacked by a larger enemy was to align with a neighboring state. Thus, very often alliances were formed for military and political purposes. In fact, marriages among immediate relatives of the war lords were one means of cementing alliances. When it came to military campaigns, one of the challenges faced by the attacking force was to prevent alliances so that the targeted state for annexation would not grow any stronger.

In the business world, disrupting the alliances of the competitors may seem quite unthinkable. But alliances do exist. At the macro level, common markets, economic unions and free trade areas are examples of alliances. Many countries that are producing commodities also belong to some form of association or union in order to increase their international bargaining power. Perhaps the most familiar kind of alliance is that of the OPEC cartel arrangement. It was this alliance that was responsible for the emergence of the Middle-East nations in world politics. Through their two coordinated oil crises, they managed to tilt the economic balance of power (and accompanying it, considerable political leverage as well) in their favor. Fortunately or unfortunately, the alliance is no longer as strong today. While it is difficult to prove that the alliance was disrupted deliberately, it is definitely true that two of the main reasons for the relatively cheaper oil that many non oil-producing countries are getting today has been the collapse of the OPEC cartel arrangement as a result of their inability to work as an alliance and the undermining efforts by non-OPEC producers who are willing to sell below official prices.

Even within a nation, cartel-like arrangements can appear in the form of cooperatives whereby many firms may get together to advance their own interests. There are also various types of associations and unions that are formed to protect their respective trades. Even without any deliberate attempts to form associations, unions or cartels, certain market structures also dictate that some form of cooperation would be beneficial. A good example would be that of a homogeneous oligopolistic market where there are a few suppliers selling similar products that cannot be easily differentiated. Under such a market structure, a firm's sales and profits are very sensitive to price changes. In fact, it pays to be cooperative and not to upset the status quo of the market price. From the above illustrations, it can be seen that whether contrived or not, alliances among companies and among nations for business interests do exist and are real. While in many Western countries there are laws preventing outright collaboration among companies, such practices may not be considered illegal by other countries. For example, one of the mysteries that still puzzles scholars of international marketing is the way Japanese companies penetrated the overseas markets. Unlike American companies, the approach taken by Japanese companies tends to be more controlled. Somehow or other, one of the Japanese companies would be the first to establish a strong foothold in an overseas market before the other companies are phased in. For example, the first car to enter the Southeast Asian market was Datsun, while Toyota was the first to penetrate the North American market. This pattern of "one company first, then the rest follows" is repeated in many instances of how Japanese products enter the overseas markets. Even its computers follow such a pattern.

Following Sun Tzu's advice, the way to win against alliances is to break them up, or prevent them from forming. As discussed earlier, the OPEC cartel did not work possibly because of undermining efforts by other parties. Besides breaking up alliances or preventing them from forming, another way is to form your own alliance as a counter-measure. There are many examples of such efforts in the business world. Joint-venture is a form of alliance aimed at increasing competitiveness, and is a common way to penetrate overseas markets. In fact, joint-ventures are currently the most popular and prevalent mode of doing business in and with China. Even multinational companies have begun to realize the need to form alliances. Good examples include the joint collaboration efforts of the large American motor companies like General Motors and Ford with Japanese automobile companies. In the high-technology area, we have also witnessed the forming of alliances among companies of various nationalities. It seems to be an acceptable method of making one's company stronger (and hence, relatively speaking, making the competitors weaker).

One of the most recent but significant events in the airline industry is the strategic alliance formed by SIA, Delta Airlines of the US and Swissair of Switzerland. SIA formed this alliance as an alternative to acquiring other airlines. The purpose was to ensure that SIA continued its high growth strategy through accessing other markets and routes. It is important to point out that the three members of the alliance are known to be the best run airlines in the world.

Attacking the army of the enemy

In war, going after the army of the enemy can take one of the following forms:

1. Capturing or assassinating key officers or personnel.
2. Upsetting the morale of the enemy's troops.
3. Burning or cutting off supplies to the enemy.
4. Ambushing the enemy forces and/or conducting periodic raids.

In the business world, it is a very common practice to attack the competitor directly by employing similar tactics as in war, such as the following:

(1) Luring and attracting key personnel away from the competitor's firm. One of the reasons why companies are willing to use head-hunting firms and pay large fees for their efforts is because they hunt for suitable candidates with relevant experience and, more than likely, from the competitors.

(2) Spreading rumors about the poor performance of competitor's firms so as to lower the morale of their employees. At times, such malicious attempts may even involve talks on product defects, drawing attention to poor quality service, or publicizing law suits, even going as far as reporting scandals, all intended to belittle the competitor.

(3) Preventing the access of technology or technical knowledge to competitors. At times, this can be achieved through patents, copyrights and trademarks. At other times, this could simply be a refusal to transfer technology or, when it does occur, deliberately passing on out-dated technology. Japanese companies, for example, have often been criticized for their poor record of technology transfer. Besides preventing the flow of technology, another method of harassing the competitors would be to hinder the supply of important parts and materials to the competitors, including the right type of equipment and machinery for the manufacturing process. This option is possible if the competitors are all small and fragmented and hence the largest market share holder can literally squeeze out the marginal firms.

(4) Attracting rank and file employees from competitors by using either higher salaries, fringe benefits, or both. In a tight labor market situation, "raiding" employees from competitors is quite common.

Thus, it can be seen that in the business world, the military tactics as advocated by Sun Tzu are very relevant. In fact there is an option available to the business firm that is similar to military annexation. This option is going after the competitor's firm itself, that is, embarking on a complete takeover move. Such a move in fact would result in capturing the competitor intact. It is a preferred strategy to the next option of "besieging walled cities." For example, in Singapore, the United Overseas Bank's (UOB) acquisition of the Industrial and Commercial Bank (ICB) in late 1987 is an example of increasing market share without open battles. The net result of that acquisition is that the number of UOB branches increased significantly, and the share prices of both banks increased by more than 20%.

Acquisitions are also used by companies for diversification purposes. For example, Yeo Hiap Seng, one of the largest food and beverage companies in Singapore, made moves to acquire 25.5% of Tsang & Ong Stockbrokers in February 1988. Around the same period, another large property developer and contractor, Lum Chang Pte Ltd also made attempts to acquire City Securities. The moves by Yeo Hiap Seng and Lum Chang allowed them to get into the securities and stockbroking business in a very fast way. It spared them the need to set up new organizations of their own to compete openly in the market for business and market share. This is because the two stockbroking houses would already have their own stable clientele and established market shares. Thus, by "buying into the market", both Yeo Hiap Seng and Lum Chang were able to establish themselves in the securities business without the need to start at base zero.

In recent years, acquisitions and mergers have been pursued by many companies in the international market as well. For example, the Quaker Oats Company of the United States bought Stokely-van Camp Inc. in 1984 for US$220 million. It sold off everything except pork and beans and Gatorade sports drink, making the deal's net cost US$95 million. Indeed, this acquisition is a classic case of an acquisition adding crucial value to a smaller company. Quaker's marketing clout put the Gatorade sports drink into the limelight, and the brand now provides annual operating profits of about US$125 million to Quaker Oats – 25% of the parent company's total! In the same way when Rupert Murdoch paid US$2 billion to buy Metromedia TV stations in 1976 it was considered too much. Today, Metromedia has begun to show good results. In another classic takeover move, Triangle Industries bought National in 1985 and American Can in 1986 for a total of US$1 billion. With superb management Triangle Industries achieved economies of scale by merging the two canmakers, subsequently selling them to France's Pechiney for US$3.7 billion in 1989, raking in a handsome profit of US$2.7 billion!

In fact, merger and acquisition mania has caught on particularly in Western Europe, starting in the late 1980s. With the dismantling of the Common Market's trade barriers in 1992, the cheaper US dollar, and the general American permissive attitudes toward takeover, it is expected that the momentum of international takeovers will be increased, with American companies as likely targets. This surge in over-the-border acquisitions, hostile takeovers and joint ventures is part of a massive corporate restructuring effort aimed at achieving global economies of scale in both production and distribution (that is, penetration of various international markets). In addition, it also gives the critical mass needed to pay for the ballooning research and development (R&D) costs.

Besieging walled cities

According to Sun Tzu, this is the worst policy, and should be avoided unless there are no other alternatives. This is because in attacking walled cities, victory is likely to be long delayed and the ardor and morale of the army will be depressed. The troops will be exhausted and the resources of the state may not be sufficient to support a protracted campaign.

In the same way, a company should avoid competing in the open for market share, especially if:

1. the product is not differentiated
2. the market is not growing.

Competitors under such situations are likely to fight "tooth and nail" to protect their market share and the battles can be quite bitter. For example, when the market is not growing, any attempt to alter the market share of the competitor is likely to create repercussions. This is because in such a competitive environment, it is like a zero-sum game, and the gain of one player has to be translated as the loss by another player in the system. The retail gasoline industry typifies such a situation very well. The product is relatively undifferentiated (although the gas companies have always branded their products), there are economies of scale of production and distribution, and the market is relatively slow growing (it depends on the growth of vehicle sales). Under such circumstances, any attempt to grab market share in the open market is likely to be strongly resisted. This explains why this industry has the highest number of retail wars in many other countries.

It is important to point out that when companies fight in the open for gains in market shares, the process is likely to be long drawn and tedious as every action taken by one company is likely to be counteracted by the others. The net result is that gains in market share will come very slowly, and at very high costs. Thus, there is an intuitive logic in avoiding open confrontation. In fact, a faster way to gain market share would be, as mentioned earlier, to embark on an acquisition trail (going after the army of the enemy) to "...subdue the enemy's army without direct battle."

3.1.2 Achievable goals

Not only must war goals be prioritized, they must also be achievable. Goals can only be achievable when the general has made a thorough and careful assessment of the battle situation, and knows the chances of success and defeat. This underscores the importance of situation appraisal. Achievable goals in war also imply understanding the following:

(1) Who to engage (choosing the right enemy for attack). The first obvious step to the formulation of war strategy is to identify the enemy. When more than one enemy exists, then the logical target should be to select an enemy that can easily be defeated before tackling a more formidable foe:

> "In ancient times, those adept in warfare gained victories by conquering those enemies that are easily conquered."

> 古之所谓善战者，胜于易胜者也。

The rationale for doing so is to become stronger with each successive victory in battle:

> "This is called winning a battle and becoming stronger."

> 是谓胜敌而益强。

In the same way, a company should attempt to tackle its weakest competitor. For example, it is easier to go after the market share of the smallest competitor than the largest competitor, and it is definitely easier to acquire a smaller than a larger company.

(2) How to accomplish them within a reasonable period of time. In war, the campaign cannot keep on going:

"There has never been a protracted war that has brought benefits to the state."

夫兵久而国利者，未之有也。

"Therefore, in war it is advantageous to go for swift victory and not prolonged campaigns."

故兵贵胜，不贵久。

This is because any prolonged campaign will dampen the morale of the attacking troops and deplete the resources of the state. In the same way as goal-setting in war, no company would set goals without specifying when they can be accomplished. At the same time, no company can ever enjoy being engaged in a long campaign against competitors. For example, the soft drinks industry is filled with promotional wars. Pepsi often wages war against Coke. Yet it is remarkable to note that there are periods of truce where both companies can consolidate and recover before preparing for the next round of battles. They simply could not go on fighting continuously. Similarly, in the fast food industry, big players like McDonald's and Burger King need intermittent periods of peace before engaging in fierce promotional battles.

3.1.3 Goals must result in net positive gains

In war, goals are set with the intention of gaining territories or some other tangible benefits. As war can have dire consequences, it must be assessed very carefully:

"War is a matter of vital importance to the State. It concerns the lives and deaths of the people, and affects the survival or demise of the State. It must be thoroughly studied."

兵者，国之大事，死生之地，存亡之道，不可不察也。

The bottom line is that the gains from victory must exceed the costs of waging war, such that it contributes to the synergy of one's strengths. The fact of the matter is, at times a country may win the war but may lose out on many other fronts. A very good example would be the Vietnam war. The Vietcong won the war, and they even successfully (to some extent) annexed the neighboring states of Laos and Cambodia, yet they have not come out any better. While they have gained territories, the economy is in a state of chaos. The people have a standard of living much lower than before the war and the nation is ostracized by many other countries. In this case, the gains from victory have been far less than the costs of waging the war. It is thus not surprising that Sun Tzu warned that:

> "Do not move unless there are definite advantages to be gained..."

非利不动

> "Engage only when it is in the interest of the State;
> Cease when it is to its detriment."

合于利而动，不合于利而止。

In the same way, business goals must reflect positive gains. At times, such gains may be expressed in quantitative or qualitative terms. However, no matter how they are expressed, there must be a net gain to the company – whether in the form of higher sales, larger profits or a better image. It would be erroneous to treat anything short of net gains as a public relations exercise. Today, many companies are also beginning to justify their investment in public relations.

To sum up Sun Tzu's principle of winning profitably, it is important that goals must be prioritized, be achievable and represent some net gains to the aggressor.

3.2 Formulation of strategies: Choice of battleground

There are a few principles governing the formulation of strategies. These include:

- The principle of choice of battleground
- The principle of concentration of forces
- The principle of attack
- The principle of *zheng* (direct) and *qi* (indirect) forces

3.2.1 Choice of battleground

As mentioned in Chapter 2 in the discussion of terrain, the choice of a battleground is a variable and controllable factor. While terrain is fixed and not alterable, a general can decide on the type of battleground on which to engage the enemy. However, once a certain type of battleground is decided upon, he will still have to contend with the characteristics conferred by the terrain. Similarly, in business, a company can choose the areas in which it would like to compete. For example, it can decide on the markets (including the countries) that it likes to operate in. It can also decide on the type of products or services that it wants to produce. Once decided, the company will have to face a set of competitive factors that are applicable to that particular market or product.

There are three factors that relate to the principle of choice of battleground:

- Areas that have distinctive advantages
- Areas ignored by the enemy
- Characteristics of the battleground

Areas that have distinct advantages

In war, it is very important to fight in areas where you enjoy a relative superiority over the enemy. There are two ways to explain this:

(a) By being the first to occupy key grounds. According to Sun Tzu:

> "Generally, those who reach and occupy the battleground early will have time to rest and wait for the enemy. Those who arrive at the battleground late will have to rush into action when they are already tired and exhausted."

凡先处战地而待敌者佚，后处战地而趋战者劳。

(b) By choosing a battleground that is more advantageous to oneself than to the enemy:

> "Therefore, those who are skilled in warfare will always bring the enemy to where they want to fight, and are not brought there by the enemy."

故善战者，致人而不致于人。

Being the first to occupy the key ground allows one to obtain the advantages accorded by the terrain. It also permits one to consolidate one's resources before the arrival of the enemy, and hence be better prepared for battle than the enemy. Similarly, as mentioned earlier in this chapter, there are distinct advantages to being an early entrant into a market. Many Japanese successes in the various markets of the world, especially in Asia, can be attributed to their being early entrants in these markets. For example, while the Western world is still hesitant about doing business in China, the Japanese are already operating in China on a large scale. Also, while other countries are debating about doing business with Vietnam, Japan has quietly entered the Vietnamese market. Thus, when these two countries are finally opened up in a big way, the main beneficiary will be the Japanese. This is because by then, they would have built up a substantial market share as well as contacts within these two countries.

A battleground more advantageous to oneself is one in which the terrain fits the nature of one's resources more than those of the enemy. Such a ground amplifies one's strengths while it also shields one's weaknesses. Hence, by bringing the enemy to such ground for battle, one obtains a stronger assurance of victory. To be able to identify advantageous ground, intimate knowledge of the ground is therefore necessary:

> "One must not move troops without being familiar with the conditions of the mountains, forests, dangerous passes, swamps and marshes and so on."

不知山林、险阻、沮泽之形者，不能行军；

The best analogy to date of how the battleground can be changed to one's advantage is still the Japanese. In fact in *The Mind of The Strategist* (1982), Ohmae argues that one of the main factors accounting for the economic success of the Japanese is their ability to change the battle-ground to their advantage:

> "The consciousness of the nation's poverty of natural resources and of its late arrival on the industrial scene has had a significant influence on Japanese corporate strategies. Technology, marketing skills, and capital funds have all been handled very differently from the way they would have been handled in the West." (Ohmae 1982, pp. 233–4)

In business, it is therefore very important to compete in an area where one has distinct advantages. For example, a company should not enter into unfamiliar markets where it has no expertise or experience. Similarly, a company should not compete in products or services where it has no skills. As an illustration, many Singaporean fast food operators tried to copy the Western fast food chain operations without a clear understanding of the competitive factors involved – that they are marketing a complete range of benefits that extend far beyond the food itself, and that they have very sophisticated backup of management and marketing skills. For example, some local operators tried to sell fried chicken (styled on Kentucky Fried Chicken) but in the coffee shops of government housing estates, while others tried to put a group of food stalls in air-conditioned shopping centers without any coordinated management or marketing efforts. The net result is that many of these local imitators were out of business as quickly as they were set up because they failed to grasp the subtleties of fast food operations.

In the same way, when Japanese management was highly successful in the late 1970s and early 1980s, many American companies tried to follow suit without clear understanding of how Japanese management works. For example, American companies tried to use the Japanese "just-in-time" system in production management, but encountered dismal results. The reason for this was that the American production and distribution systems operate on a totally different format that contradicts the successful implementation of the "just-in-time" system. In short, it was an area where American companies simply did not have the advantages when compared to the Japanese.

Many companies have also tried to penetrate the overseas markets without a good understanding of the dynamics involved in overseas operations. At times, there are instances of companies who have even tried to set up overseas operations without the foggiest idea about the risks and dynamics involved. To aggravate this matter, little research is done in understanding the overseas operations. To be successful, one needs to gather information about such markets or take time to build up the expertise. Thus, the common strategy for foreign market entry, as depicted in Figure 3.2 makes a lot of sense.

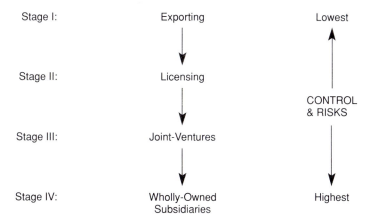

Figure 3.2 Foreign Market Entry Strategy

To begin with, while there is less control, a firm can gather experience of overseas operations through exporting rather than going direct into foreign investments. This is to minimize the risks involved. When indeed, a firm decides to go into overseas operations, joint-ventures may be a better initial choice than wholly-owned subsidiaries. In fact, such a market entry strategy in the business world is reflected in the military analogy when Sun Tzu said:

> "One cannot have advantages of topography without the use of local guides."

不用乡导者，不能得地利。

Having then selected the critical ground to do battle, one needs to devise ways to bring the enemy to such ground. To do this, Sun Tzu suggested:

> "By enticing the enemy with some baits, one can make him come on his own accord. By inflicting damages and placing obstacles, one can prevent the enemy from going to places that he wants to reach."

能使敌人自至者，利之也；
能使敌人不得至者，害之也。

The use of baits to lure the enemy to where you want to fight is therefore a very important way to ensure that you contend in an area where you can have distinctive advantages. At the same time, it is important to inflict damages on the enemy when necessary so as to prevent him from occupying places that are important to you.

The principle of capitalizing on one's strengths is very much applicable to the business world. For example, before the revaluation of the Japanese yen during the mid-eighties, price was used extensively by Japanese car dealers as a competitive edge against continental cars. The Japanese car dealers frequently enticed their competitors into battle by running comparative price advertisements. At the same time, through their relatively low prices, Japanese cars made tremendous inroads into the market shares of other brands of cars. The damages inflicted were tremendous, especially at the lower end of the car market. The European and American car manufacturers simply found that they could not compete against the Japanese car makers. This situation was true in many markets of the world. However, with the increasing value of the yen (especially after 1986), price is no longer a competitive edge for the Japanese car makers. Today, the Japanese brands cost more. The result is that the Japanese manufacturers are today switching strategy. Their advertisements no longer mention prices as a competitive edge or run comparative advertisements that feature car prices. Instead, their advertisements now mention the high engineering quality and superior build of Japanese cars. Some advertisements such as those run by Nissan, interestingly, even talk about the durability of the steel used in the construction of the car, something unheard of some 10 years ago.

It is also interesting to note that the price comparison strategy used by the Japanese manufacturers is today used by some European and Korean car makers. For example, in many countries, the prices of Fiat, Seat and Hyundai cars are now frequently compared with Japanese brands in various advertisements. Thus far, the Japanese have refrained from being lured into battle on the basis of price. They continue to emphasize quality, with an increasing focus on durability as well.

Areas ignored by the enemy

This strategy is different from the previous one. Capitalizing on areas where you have distinctive advantages implies that you exploit your strengths. Choosing areas ignored by the enemy, however, does not necessarily mean that you have strengths in those areas that you have chosen to fight in. You may not have any strengths at all and may even have to build them up. The importance and viability of this principle is illustrated by Sun Tzu, and underscores the idea that there is scope and potential for the smaller and weaker forces in war:

> "To be certain to succeed in what you attack is to attack a place where the enemy does not defend or where its defence is weak. To be certain of holding what you defend is to defend a place the enemy does not attack or where the defense is invulnerable to attacks."

攻而必取者，攻其所不守也；
守而必固者，守其所不攻也。

> "The strength of an army does not depend on large forces."

兵非益多也

In the business world, we can find many examples of avoidance strategy – choosing areas ignored by the enemy – as well as *nicheing* strategy – not relying on large forces (this will be illustrated in greater detail in the next section). The Japanese successes in the various products in the world markets today are perhaps the best manifestation of choosing areas ignored by the enemies. In the words of Ohmae (1982):

> "A key aspect of Japanese corporate strategy, again prompted by the awareness of resource limitations, is the tendency to look for a different battleground on which to compete with the Western giants."
> (Ohmae 1982, p. 240)

> "Choosing the battleground so that they would not have to fight head-on against large Western enterprise has been the key to their success. They have sought out markets, functions, and product ranges where they could initially avoid head-to-head competition. As a result, Japanese production styles, design and engineering approaches and personnel management philosophies are so different today that Western companies find it extremely difficult to fight back or catch up with their Japanese competitors."
> (Ohmae 1982, p. 241)

Thus, despite some early arguments by some scholars that the success of the Japanese in the modern world economy was due to some element of luck in that they were forced to concentrate on the smaller cars because of the characteristics of their people, nation and geography, and that they were aided by the oil crisis (which created the demand for small cars), there is, however, a very disturbing trend. While the Europeans and Americans chose to concentrate on building big and expensive cars, motorcycles, photocopying machines, appliances, television sets and radios, the Japanese deliberately decided to focus on producing smaller but cheaper similar products. The smaller range of products was an area that was totally ignored by the European and American manufacturers. Indeed, they paid no attention to them. In fact, when the Japanese produced smaller automobiles, motorcycles or desk-top photocopiers, they were initially disregarded as toys, and no concerted attempts were made to counteract the Japanese threat. This apathetic and non-urgent attitude was perpetuated in many products and industries. The result is well known today – Europeans and Americans find it so difficult to compete against the Japanese. The reason – the Japanese have inflicted so much damage that it will take a while before they can be threatened. They have built defenses that are quite invulnerable to attacks. Today, Japanese brands dominate many consumer durables such as cameras, motorcycles, watches, televisions, radios, hi-fi stereo components and other household electronic items so that it will take a lot of effort from their competitors before they are in a position to challenge the Japanese.

The irony about the present state of world economic balance of power between the Japanese and the West is that when they chose the areas in which to compete, the Japanese had no strengths in any of those areas! Everything, including technology and materials had to be imported from the Western world. The Japanese had only one thing in their favor – the areas they chose to concentrate on were areas ignored by their enemies, and for reasons best known to their competitors, were continuously ignored until it was too late. In fact, one of the major events that made the Western world make more concerted efforts against the Japanese and view her threats seriously was when Japan decided to build the 5th generation computer. This project would give the Japanese a decisive advantage over her competitors. Today, the Japanese are no longer treated lightly.

One of the most significant recent developments is that business school professors from several leading American universities such as California, Harvard, Columbia, Wharton, Stanford and others have now pooled their resources to try to find out as much as they can by the year 2000 about Japanese manufacturing and commerce. The group, which formed a consortium on competitiveness and co-operation in late 1989 aims to find out ways for American firms to compete more effectively against the Japanese, especially in the areas of exploiting high technology markets and the management of human resources. It is remarkable to note that Professor Peter Jones of the University of California, the leader of the consortium, openly cited an example of how the Japanese are now in a position to play guru. The General Motors plant in Fremont used to be its worst plant. However, since Japanese management techniques were brought in as a result of a joint venture between Toyota and GM, absenteeism, grievances and alcoholism have dropped tremendously and product quality and costs have improved. It is indeed a bold admission that the Japanese have arrived. Yet, as mentioned earlier, they have made it because few competed against them in the first instance.

Characteristics of the battleground

The third factor that relates to the principle of choice of battleground involves a clear understanding of the characteristics of the battleground itself. The characteristics of the battleground can affect, for example, the movement of troops and supplies, the types of weapons to be used and the nature of offensive and defensive strategies. This aspect of war is so important that Sun Tzu devotes more than one chapter of his book to the discussion of it. Chapter XI specifically addresses the nine types of battlegrounds and the kinds of strategies that should be used for each type of ground. However, in at least two other chapters of his work, Sun Tzu also mentions other types of battleground and the relevant strategies to be used. From his discussions of the different types of grounds in Chapters XI, VIII, and X, we propose that there are in fact 13 different types of battlegrounds that can be derived from Sun Tzu's exposition. For ease of presentation, they have been re-ordered by the authors from those of the sequence as presented by Sun Tzu. These 13 battlegrounds, and the chapters in which they were discussed by Sun Tzu are:

(i)   Dispersive Ground 散地 (Chapter XI)
(ii)   Accessible Ground 交地 (Chapters X and XI)
(iii) Frontier Ground 轻地 (Chapter XI)
(iv)   Entrapping Ground 挂地 (Chapter X)
(v)   Constricted Ground 围地 (Chapters VIII, X and XI)
(vi)   Key Ground 争地 (Chapters X and XI)
(vii) Focal Ground 衢地 (Chapters VIII and XI)
(viii) Indifferent Ground 支地 (Chapter X)
(ix)   Treacherous Ground 圮地 (Chapters VIII and XI)
(x)   Desolate Ground 绝地 (Chapter VIII)
(xi)   Distant Ground 远地 (Chapter X)
(xii) Serious Ground 重地 (Chapter XI)
(xiii) Death Ground 死地 (Chapters VIII and XI)

In the following sections, these various grounds will be profiled and their appropriate strategies, as proposed by Sun Tzu, highlighted. They are then related to 13 different business situations where the appropriate strategies will be applied.

(i) Dispersive ground 散地

This is a battle situation in which the army is fighting in its own territory:

诸侯自战其地，为散地。

As such, it is not only dispersive, but is also divisive, disruptive and dissentious. Accordingly, Sun Tzu recommended:

"In dispersive ground, do not fight."

散地则无战

This doctrine of war underlines much conventional warfare, even up to today. For example, one of Israel's military strategies has always been to avoid fighting a war within her own territory. This is evident in the various wars conducted with her Middle-East neighbors for the last 15 years. Her occupation of the West Bank, the Golan Heights and the Gaza Strip typify her resolve not to fight in her own territory. However, if one has to combat in his own territory, Sun Tzu advocated the need for the army to be of one common resolve. In other words, one should inspire all the rank and file with unity of purpose:

> "In dispersive ground, unify the determination of the army."

是故散地，吾将一其志

In the business world, one can face a dispersive situation too. For example, at a national level, the United States is facing such a problem. It is today invaded by exports from Japan and the four Asian tigers – South Korea, Taiwan, Hong Kong and Singapore. Instead of taking more aggressive and offensive strategies such as increasing its export capability (which would be analogous to fighting beyond one's territory), it has chosen passive and defensive strategies by trying to fight on its own soil, for example, by taking measures and enacting bills to protect local manufacturers. The irony is that the various parties in the US who are affected by such threats are not united in purpose and resolve! The net result is that the actions taken are hardly effective. Given the complexity and heterogeneity of American society, the best strategy is to push her combat zone beyond her national frontiers.

The British press is another good example of competition in a dispersive situation. Unlike newspapers in the US which rely more on advertising revenue, British newspapers depend more on circulation revenue. Unfortunately, the number of newspapers in Britain is simply too high and they are basically going after the same readership. For example, as of July 1990, there were twelve national newspapers and eleven Sunday papers battling for the daily and Sunday readership. The result is that competition has become so intense that even profitable papers like the Financial Times have to take various measures to cut costs such as reducing perks to employees and journalists in order to remain competitive. Many other papers are now operating treacherously in an overcrowded market.

At the business unit level, the appropriate lesson to be learned from Sun Tzu's exposition on dispersive ground is that a firm should not compete in the same market with too many of its own products and brands. Unfortunately, such a competitive situation is quite typical of many consumer products like detergents, soaps and soft drinks where there are many brands of the same product competing for the same market. For example, if a company has too many brands of the same product in the same market, there are bound to be conflicts and dishar-mony among the different brand managers as they would be very concerned about their own brand performance (which ultimately will reflect on their own work performance). This is because any improve-ment or gain in the market share by one brand is very likely to be achieved at the expense of the other brands in the same market.

Applying the principle of avoidance of competition in a disper-sive ground, a firm should try to minimize the number of brands in each market segment in which it is competing. If a new brand is to be introduced, it should be carefully targeted and focused on a new and/or different segment so as to avoid cannibalization with the existing brand(s). Similarly, if a retailer wants to open a new store, he should ensure that it does not compete in the same trading area as any of his existing stores. The logic is simple: fighting in your own territory in business can only result in cannibalization in most instances. The only way to prevent this from happening is to fight in the markets of the competitors!

However, if a company had to compete in the same market with several of its own brands, then there is a need to ensure that there is unity of purpose among the various personnel involved. This means that everyone concerned must share the same vision and resolve in tackling the market and an aggregate approach will have to be adopted in order to prevent individual interest from dividing the efforts of the company. In other words, there must be directives and guidance from top management to ensure that the company moves with unity of purpose and has common overall goals and objectives. Under such circumstances, it may also make better sense to reward brand managers on the basis of the overall achievement of *all* brands in that market rather than on the basis of the brand(s) under his management.

(ii) Accessible ground 交地

This type of ground is mentioned by Sun Tzu in Chapter X as com-municative ground (通地) and in his Chapter XI as accessible ground (交地) . While the Chinese characters may appear to be different, the de-scriptions of the ground as given by him suggest that they are of the same type:

> 我可以往，彼可以来，曰 “通”
> 我可以往，彼可以来者，为交地。

In fact, the two key Chinese characters could be linked to become 交通地 , and used to describe a ground that is open, highly communica-tive and equally accessible to the enemy and yourself. There is liberty of movement and the enemy can traverse the ground as easily as your forces. Owing to the characteristics of accessible ground, Sun Tzu advocated the following strategies:

"Do not allow your formations to become separated."

交地则无绝

"Pay strict attention to the defense."

交地，吾将谨其守

"Be the first to occupy the higher and sunny positions that are convenient to your supply routes so as to gain advantage in battle."

"通" 形者，先居高阳，利粮道，以战则利。

The above strategies are aimed primarily at preventing the enemy, who can easily enter your territory, from disrupting the formation of your forces and cutting off your supplies.

In the business world, there are also accessible grounds. In fact, this is typical of situations where the market entry and exit are easy. In many small businesses such as the retail food industry, it is very easy to get into the market as the barriers in terms of capital and technology are both very low. At the same time, because of the highly competitive nature of the industry, market exit is also common. Such a business situation is what economists term "perfect competition". For such an industry, there is little product differentiation and consumers can easily substitute one supplier with another. Under such circumstances, it becomes very important to pay attention to good location and the distribution system (the need to occupy sunny positions to gain advantage in battles).

In a perfect competition market structure, there is also a need to protect market share. This is because the competitor can easily produce the same product at about the same cost, and hence can easily take away your market share. Therefore, defense of market share becomes important. In addition, to survive in such a competitive environment, costs of production must be brought down as low as possible and this can only be achieved when all parties within the company work in unison. Thus, one's formations will not become separated.

Perhaps one of the best illustrations of defense and occupation of "sunny positions" in a highly competitive industry is the Western fast food industry. Probably every other person would claim that they can make a better burger than Burger King and McDonalds. Yet few have succeeded over the years. This is because these chains have managed over the years to build up very strong defenses through improvement in their total system – that includes production, marketing, advertising and promotion, inventory control, planning, and distribution outlets – so much so that the walls have become thick and impenetrable.

(iii) Frontier ground 轻地

When the army has made only a very shallow penetration into the enemy's territory, the ground is considered frontier in nature:

入人之地而不深者，为轻地。

In war, this is similar to capturing a beach-head, which is an area in hostile territory that is occupied with the intention of securing further landings of troops and supplies. This initial gain of a foothold is crucial for any further penetration into enemy territory. Accordingly, Sun Tzu recommended that:

"Do not stop in frontier ground."

轻地则无止

"Keep the forces closely linked."

轻地，吾将使之属

Anyone familiar with military strategy will appreciate the soundness of Sun Tzu's advice. In capturing a beach-head, the forces occupying it will attempt to push it as far inward as possible. At the same time, the beach-head position is not easy to defend and the intention is never to defend it for long anyway. However, as this is the first penetration into enemy territory and the main troops would be landing soon after, it is of utmost importance that the landing forces establish links very quickly before being detected by the enemy. Proper communication links and networks have to be set up quickly so that the forces can accelerate their movement into the enemy's territory.

In business, one can also make but a shallow penetration into the enemy's territory when introducing a new product into an existing market, introducing an existing product into a new market segment of an existing market (for example, a company may currently be marketing a product to the youth market, but has decided to enter the adult market as well), introducing an existing product into a new market, like in the case of entering a foreign market through exports or introducing a new product into a new market.

To apply Sun Tzu's strategy to each of the above situations, the business must not be content with just gaining an initial foothold. In other words, it is important not to stop at a small market share after gaining access into a competitor's market or a new market. At this stage of market penetration, it is also very important to keep your "forces" closely linked or in close contact with one another. Thus, it is important to establish, coordinate and monitor the various activities of the company, such as production, marketing, finance, and R&D. This is because in the initial stage of market entry, there are usually many different types of problems that need to be resolved – such as problems relating to the product or marketing which will require a coordinated effort to resolve them.

There are also valid reasons why a company should not stop at a small market share situation. In most manufacturing, there are economies of scale in mass production (which implies the need to capture a large market share). In fact, this is the premise of the experience curve concept – that with large volume of production, there will be lower costs per unit and the larger firm will always have an edge over the smaller ones. Increasing the share of one's market also enhances the leverage of operation and allows the company to have more scope to embark on more expansion.

In the area of foreign market entry, the Japanese can be hailed as the gurus of this strategy of never stopping at frontier ground. Kotler *et al* (1985) documented many instances in which the Japanese demonstrated this strategy. To quote:

> "Toyota focused its strategy on four key West Coast urban
> market areas: Los Angeles, San Francisco, Portland, and Seattle.
> Once a beachhead had been established, then "geographical
> roll-out" could begin. This made it possible to concentrate the
> sales force, closely supervisor marketing activities, and penetrate
> one area thoroughly before tackling the next. In this way,
> mistakes were quickly detected and corrected."
>
> (Kotler *et al* 1985, p. 49)

A demonstration of the coordinated efforts needed in a frontier ground situation is the fact that Japanese companies also did not rush into foreign markets simultaneously. For example, Toyota was the first to enter the U.S. market before the other Japanese automobile companies followed suit. In the case of motorcycles, it was Honda who went in first, followed by Yamaha, Kawasaki and the others. In South-east Asia, the Japanese penetrated the automobile market with the Datsun. This pattern of coordination in foreign market entry appeared consistently in many industries that the Japanese chose to enter.

(iv) Entrapping ground 挂地

Entrapping ground is one in which it is easy to get in, but difficult to get out:

可以往，难以返，曰 "挂"

It is a type of ground that resembles a "quicksand" situation or one which is filled with boobytraps. Therefore, it is both enticing and intricate in nature. In such a situation, if the enemy is unprepared, he can be easily defeated. However, if he is prepared, and is not defeated at the first attempt, it will spell trouble as the attacking forces can be caught in a situation where they are unable to return:

"挂" 形者，敌无备，出而胜之；
敌若有备，出而不胜，难以返，不利。

In business, there are many situations that can be entrapping in nature. For example, businesses with low technology but high capital investment, like exploration, mining and construction can be entrapping. It is possible to spend millions of dollars in exploration without seeing results. Yet to get out would be very expensive, as all the money poured into the project would be gone to waste. At the same time, the company is actually paving the way for the late comers in the field who can benefit from the mistakes and experience of the early entrants.

In the early seventies, many building contractors and sub-contractors in Singapore were entrapped because they did not include an escalating clause in their contracts. When building costs skyrocketed as a result of increasing prices of labor and materials, quite a few were in great financial difficulties. A somewhat different experience was encountered in the mid-eighties. This time, many building developers over-built, hoping that the economic growth would continue unabated. Unfortunately, the recession of 1985/86 shattered all the dreams of these developers, and quite a few, including the larger ones were entrapped. The result was that properties had to be sold at cost in some instances as it was very expensive to hold on to unsold properties.

Businesses with low capital but high operating costs can be entrapping too. This is especially so where there are strong labor unions that prevent the management from retrenching workers. At times, the unions may even obstruct any modernization or mechanization efforts.

The British newspaper and printing industry is typical of an entrapping situation. It suffered because it was not easy for the management to get out.

At a macro level, certain government welfare-related projects can be entrapping too. European and North American societies are filled with numerous such examples, especially with regard to social welfare programs. For example, in the United States, despite President Reagan's tough attitude towards reduction in government spending, he encountered difficulty in reducing welfare spending, especially for the elderly and unemployed. In Great Britain, it took Prime Minister Margaret Thatcher many years before she was able to cut expenditure on welfare-related projects. Undeniably, it is easy to offer welfare programs, but very difficult to get out without great loss of political support.

(v) Constricted ground 围地

Constricted ground is mentioned by Sun Tzu in Chapters VIII, X and XI. The same Chinese characters (围地) are used in Chapters VIII and XI, while in Chapter X, it is referred to as "隘地". However, a close examination of the ground description and the strategies to be used suggest that Sun Tzu is referring to the same type of ground in his various descriptions.

In essence, a constricted ground is one in which the access route is narrow and the retreat route is tortuous. It is a type of ground that is difficult to get into and at the same time difficult to get out of. Its hemmed-in nature allows a smaller force to strike with ease at a much larger force through various ambushes.

> 所由入者隘，所从归者迂，
> 彼寡可以击吾之众者，为围地。

> 背固前隘者，围地也。

The strategies to be used in such a ground include the following:

"Devise stratagems."

围地则谋

"Be the first force to occupy the strategic points and await the enemy. Do not attack if the constricted positions are occupied by the enemy. Attack only if the enemy's defense at the occupied points are weak."

"隘" 形者，我先居之，必盈之以待敌；
若敌先居之，盈而勿从，不盈而从之。

"Block the points of entrance and exit."

围地，吾将塞其阙

Constricted grounds remind us of business situations where the competitive advantage is very narrow. This can happen in the case of a product under an expiring patent or where the technological advantage over the competitors is not great. The pharmaceutical business, to some extent, is quite constricted in that it is very difficult to get in and do well in a big way unless one invests substantially in R&D. In doing so, it also becomes very difficult to pull out. At the same time, the discovery of any wonder drug does not prevent the competitors or anyone else from coming out with something even better. When this happens, the newer and better drug can knock the previous drugs out of the market completely. The best way to survive in such a market situation is to look for better drugs. Hence, the competitive edge enjoyed by companies marketing existing drugs is in fact very narrow in that it is very vulnerable to any new and substitutable drug. In essence, the competitive edge lies mainly on the properties of the drug more than anything else. Some of today's high-technology businesses are also becoming more and more constricted in nature. This is especially so if they involve heavy capital, R&D and human resource investments. Computer software is an example. Often, the advantages enjoyed by a software program can be eroded instantaneously when a better version comes on to the market.

To survive in a constricted environment, resourcefulness is required in the design of strategies. This is because the competitive advantage enjoyed is often very narrow and at the same time this advantage is very vulnerable to attacks. For the defending force it becomes very important to protect the constricted points. If technology is the competitive advantage, it becomes very important to build on this strength and defend it as much as possible through continuous upgrading and improvement and through strong and highly protective patents and rights. Such a niche must not be lost and should be defended at all cost. At the same time, the company must guard itself against attacks from small forces. In fact, in the pharmaceutical business, while it is true that it is not easy to produce and commercialize a new drug in a big way without adequate financial support from the large companies, the invention of the drug often takes place in unexpected places. For example, the drug could be discovered by a group of scientists working as part of a university research team or in a private laboratory. There-

ENTRY / EXIT	EASY	DIFFICULT
EASY	ACCESSIBLE GROUND	FRONTIER GROUND
DIFFICULT	ENTRAPPING GROUND	CONSTRICTED GROUND

Figure 3.3 Entry-exit Analysis of Battlegrounds

fore, it becomes important to harness such inventions before they fall into the hands of the competitors.

As the attacking force, the company should avoid direct confrontation with the competitors, as any direct assault attempt is bound to encounter very strong resistance owing to the constricted nature of the situation. What is important is to find a niche in the marketplace and be the first to introduce the product (or service). This is because the first entrant has the opportunity to occupy the constricted position and will enjoy distinct advantages. Indeed, this is very true of the pharmaceutical business. The first company to come out with a drug to cure a disease or sickness that was previously not curable (such as cancer or AIDS) will enjoy tremendous advantages. Yet this company could be anyone, including a small team of researchers (the small force) in any laboratory.

A good way to conceptualize the four different types of ground as discussed above is by using an entry-exit matrix as depicted in Figure 3.3. Note that we can classify the four types of grounds in terms of relative entry and exit. For example, an accessible ground would be one in which it is easy to get in as well as easy to get out. An entrapping ground is one in which it is easy to get in but difficult to get out. On the other hand, a frontier ground is one in which it is difficult to get in but easy to get out. Finally, a constricted ground would be one in which it is difficult to get in as well as difficult to get out.

(vi) Key ground 争地

A key ground is one which is equally advantageous to the enemy and yourself.

> 我得则利，彼得亦利者，为争地。

Owing to its importance, it is highly contentious and the forces of both sides are likely to contest bitterly for it. Interestingly, Sun Tzu also describes this sort of ground as precipitous ("险") in Chapter X:

"In precipitous ground, I must be the first to occupy the sunny heights and wait for the arrival of the enemy. If the enemy is the first to occupy such ground, do not follow him, but retreat and try to entice him away."

"险" 形者，我先居之，必居高阳以待敌；
若敌先居之，引而去之，勿从也。

Similar strategies to cope with the enemy who occupies key ground were also offered in his Chapter XI:

"Do not attack any enemy who occupies key ground."

争地则无攻

"In key ground, I must rush up all my rear forces and elements."

争地，吾将趋其后

It must be pointed out that key ground (争地) or precipitous ground (险要地) is different from the previous constricted ground in that the entry or exit routes to a key ground are not necessarily tortuous or difficult, and that it is less vulnerable to attacks by small forces. In addition, unlike a constricted ground, a key ground confers advantages both to the enemy and yourself.

In the business world, there are certain key grounds that many companies would like to occupy owing to the advantages that they may confer. These key grounds may include new markets locally or overseas. For example, with the opening of China, many multinational companies view the Chinese market as a key market owing to the vast business potential. It is therefore not surprising to witness many companies rushing into Chinese markets.

At other times, however, key grounds may represent situations where your competitors may hold certain definite advantages over you. Such advantages may be in the areas of, for example, R&D technology, marketing or production skills. However, such advantages are also attributes that you want to acquire so as to be successful in the market. For example, your competitor may enjoy economies of scale which give him a distinctive advantage over you. To compete effectively, you also need the economies of large scale production. How then can you compete?

Interestingly, if one were to apply Sun Tzu's strategies, this would mean avoiding direct confrontation with the competitor who has a distinct competitive edge over you – "do not attack the enemy on key ground". Rather, it is important to improve your supporting skills – "rush up all your rear forces and elements". Intuitively, the strategies make good sense. If the ground is a key one to your competitor, you can expect that he would be defending it at all costs and would be unwilling to lose it. To take him on directly would require tremendous effort. Thus, you need the "rear forces and elements" to support the battle.

One of the good illustrations of avoiding enemy on key grounds is the way the Japanese have handled the Americans and the Europeans in the world markets. To begin with, Japan knew that she could not compete directly with the Americans and Europeans who were very strong in certain product lines and markets. What the Japanese did was to improve their supporting skills first, in particular in the area of production. As mentioned in Chapter 1 of this book, the earlier Japanese industrial movement was focused on imitation, improvement and improvisation. At the same time, they chose to excel in their domestic markets before pushing for the international markets. They chose products that the American and European producers ignored and markets that the Western manufacturers were not interested in, such as South-East Asia, to try out their international experience. The Japanese only took on the European and American manufacturers when they had beefed up their rear forces.

(vii) Focal ground 衢地

Focal ground is mentioned by Sun Tzu in Chapters VIII and XI where the same Chinese characters are used. When a state is surrounded by three other states, its ground is considered focal:

诸侯之地三属，先至而得天下之众者，为衢地。

In such a ground, the enclosed state forms the key to the other three states in that the one who captures it can have a commanding situation over the other states. Thus, it can be expected that the focal ground is always under threat of siege. This is where it differs from key ground where the enemy will hesitate to capture it without abundant rear support. Also, unlike a key ground (in which there are advantages to both the enemy and yourself), a focal ground's advantage for one party will become the disadvantage of the other party.

Owing to the continual threat of being captured by her neighboring states, the options open to her are limited in that if she tries to attack any of the other three states, her vulnerability becomes even greater. Accordingly, Sun Tzu's strategies for the enclosed state center on the use of diplomacy by:

"Befriending neighboring states."

衢地則合交

"Strengthening ties with the allies."

衢地，吾將固其結

It must be pointed out that there is a distinction between neighboring states and allies. The neighboring states are those that are surrounding the focal ground. In contrast, allies are not necessarily the neighboring states. Instead, they could be other states that are friendly to the focal state and which have strong relationships established. Such relationships (which probably include military support) would act as deterrents to any aggressive moves by the neighboring states of the focal state. This distinction is easily illustrated with a present example in the world today. Israel is a focal state. Yet because of her strong allies (chief of which is the United States), she has consistently managed to ward off the occasional over-aggressive stances of her neighbors. At the same time, because of her strong allies, she had also occasionally embarked on some ambitious maneuvers against her neighbors!

The focal state situation is very similar to the smaller producer in an oligopolistic market structure in business. In an oligopolistic market situation, if you are the smaller producer, it is very important not to agitate the larger competitors. This is because they enjoy better economies of scale and have more leverage in their operations and management. Consequently, they are in a position to squeeze out the smaller guys. Thus, it is important to befriend the larger competitors and avoid annoying them. It is, therefore, not surprising that for the smaller producer in an oligopolistic situation, it is safer to follow the leader than to lead them. This is especially true if it is a homogeneous (undifferentiated) oligopolistic situation. In the case of a heterogeneous (differentiated) oligopolistic situation, the smaller producer may have more options but it still has to tread carefully.

To survive in such a business situation, there is a need also to "strengthen ties with allies". These allies would include the suppliers, customers, bankers, labor unions and government bodies. Improving the relationships with these parties would increase the chances of survival of the "focal state". A good example of how such good relationships were manifested in the case of a business situation was the turnaround story of Chrysler. Among other reasons, Lee Iaccoca managed to turn the company around because of his ability to build strong allies with the government, the financial community, the labor union, the suppliers and other parties. The strong support received from Chrysler's allies prevented it from going bankrupt or being squeezed out by the much larger General Motors and Ford.

(viii) Indifferent ground 支地

Indifferent or indecisive ground is a situation that is disadvantageous to both the enemy and yourself. In particular, there is absolutely no advantage to making the first move. In such a battle situation, Sun Tzu's advice was that one should resist being drawn out by any bait. Instead, it is important to feign a retreat, and when the enemy's defense is down (for example, when his troops are halved), it becomes advantageous to strike:

> 我出而不利，彼出而不利，曰"支"；
> "支"形者，敌虽利我，我无出也；
> 引而去之，令敌半出而击之，利。

The underlying logic for such a strategy is to avoid incurring a high casualty rate in the capturing of the position. This is because the nature of the ground is such that there is no advantage to rushing into it like the key ground, and if it has to be taken, it should be obtained only at a minimal loss of troops. Otherwise, it is better to forgo the position.

In business, there are also some situations that resemble the indifferent status. The following are two examples:

(1) When China first opened up, many companies were hesitant to go in as they were very uncertain about the Chinese policy. There appeared no tremendous advantages to be the first. Instead, many companies sidelined themselves and preferred to gain from the experiences of the early entrants.

(2) In the areas of R&D some companies prefer to let others take the lead and create the learning experience for them. In fact, in the early stages of Japan's industrial development, they allowed American and European firms to take the lead in basic R&D while they concentrated on applied R&D and production technology. The Japanese at that time did not have the necessary skills to do the basic R&D, and there were no advantages to being the first. Rather a more viable strategy was to ride on the inventions of the pioneers.

The above examples show that indifferent situations do exist in business, just as in war. At times, companies may deliberately choose not to compete in certain businesses, products or markets as they do

ENEMY SELF	ADVANTAGES	DISADVANTAGES
ADVANTAGES	KEY GROUND	FOCAL GROUND
DISADVANTAGES	FOCAL GROUND	INDIFFERENT GROUND

Figure 3.4   Relative Advantage Analysis

not see any advantages in doing so. Rather, they let others take the risks before getting into action.

Figure 3.4 summarizes the three types of grounds that have just been discussed. Note that the differences are depicted in terms of relative advantage analysis.

(ix) Treacherous ground 圮地

Treacherous ground is mentioned in Chapters VIII and XI. According to Sun Tzu, when the army is traveling in mountain forests, dangerous passes, marshy swamps, or other difficult terrain, it is in treacherous ground.

行山林、险阻、沮泽，凡难行之道者，为圮地。

This type of ground differs from serious ground (to be discussed later) in that the army faces the difficulty of nature and terrain, rather than the enemy. Treacherous ground also differs from constricted ground where one may deliberately choose to enter as there are advantages to be gained in occupying constricted positions for battle purposes. An army may face constricted ground at any point of the battle. In the case of treacherous ground, it is a situation faced by the army as a result of movement of troops, often in order to get to battle. In other words, it is the terrain encountered as a result of movement through time and space. However, owing to the difficulty of the terrain, the troops can face enemy ambushes. Thus, Sun Tzu advised that in treacherous ground, one should:

"Move swiftly".

圮地则行

"Do not encamp".

圮地无舍

"Press on over the roads".

圯地，吾将进其涂

The treacherous situation in war resembles very much the matured stage of a product life cycle in a business situation. At this stage of the product life cycle, the market is saturated with all kinds of competitive products and, at the same time, the market is not expanding and new users are harder to come by. In fact, the consumers are more than likely to be infatuated with newer and better products. Thus, the marketer is faced with an increasingly difficult environment. It is therefore important not to stay too long in matured markets ("do not encamp"). Rather the marketer should actively look for new and better opportunities so as not to fall into a decaying maturing stage (move swiftly and press on over the roads). This can be accomplished by market modification (for example, looking for new markets, new users or finding varied and new ways to use the product) and/or product modification (for example, adding new features or design and style improvements). In addition, the marketer should also look for new and different products that have growth opportunities so that they can eventually replace the matured products.

(x) Desolate ground 绝地

In war, one of the main reasons for occupying certain types of ground is to use it with the ultimate objective of winning the war. Grounds are therefore occupied not merely to gain territories but also for strategic reasons. However, as the battle progresses, grounds that were originally captured and deemed valuable might lose their appeal as they become less crucial to the subsequent conduct of the war. Sun Tzu clearly recognizes the dynamism of battlegrounds when he describes a desolate ground as one in which there are no more advantages to be gained. In such a situation, one must not linger in that ground. It should be abandoned:

"Do not stay on desolate ground."

绝地无留·

In business as in war we can find desolate ground. These are declining markets, where sales are declining due to technological advances that bring about new and better products, consumer shifts in tastes, increased domestic and foreign competition. Typically, these conditions lead to over capacity and price competition, resulting in erosion of corporate profits.

On a broader level, a company may have in its business portfolio various losing ventures typical of the "dogs" quadrant of the Boston Consulting Group (BCG) Business Portfolio Matrix. They have low market growth and low relative market share and are no longer cost effective. Overall, they tend to be a liability to the company. Accordingly, the company should divest itself of them so as to gather some crumbs rather than hold on to them, ultimately losing the whole loaf. Desolate ground should be abandoned.

Unfortunately, companies at times tend to linger too long in desolate grounds. They are reluctant to get rid of weak products and declining businesses. Some argue that business will improve when the economy improves, that they still contribute to overall company's business, that the situation will be different if the strategy is revised, etc. No matter how seemingly valid the arguments are, the failure to recognize and remove weak products and declining businesses can be very costly, tying up valuable resources that could be more productively utilized elsewhere. Sun Tzu's advice to them is to cut their losses before they damage the company.

In international business it is interesting to note that Japanese companies are adept at foregoing desolate grounds once they realize that they are no longer useful. For example, in the years following World War II, many Japanese companies were competing in the labor-intensive industries such as textiles and low-technology manufacturing and assembly. However, once they realized that the other developing countries were able to operate more cheaply than them, the Japanese deliberately abandoned such industries and moved to higher technology and higher value-added products. They did not linger on desolate grounds.

Today, Japan is tackling a new challenge in that it is facing a chronic labor shortage that might hamper its economic growth. The common cliche that "Japan has run out of Japanese" has encouraged many Japanese companies to deliberately restructure and invest for higher efficiency at home, while consciously building up foreign production sites and linking up with foreign partners through various types of joint production ventures. The result is that Japanese companies will be going from strength to strength once they have restructured to cope with the labor shortage problem at home. The reason is that they are able to recognize desolate grounds, and make deliberate efforts to move on.

(xi) Distant ground 远地

In distant ground, both sides are away from home base and are equally matched in forces. In such a situation, Sun Tzu advocates that it is to the best interest of both sides to avoid direct battles which would confer little advantage to either side:

"远" 形者，势均，难以挑战，战而不利。

An analogous situation in business is competition among various manufacturers or businesses of the same country in various overseas markets (distant ground). They might be, for example, attempting to penetrate or enter the overseas market. Here Sun Tzu would have recommended a strategy of avoidance of direct confrontation as any battles between two armies in distant ground are likely to bring negative effects to both forces.

The Japanese penetration of foreign markets again provides a very good example of this avoidance of direct battle in distant ground. For some strange and unexplained reasons which can best be explained only by the Japanese themselves, they have a very unique but observable pattern in entering foreign markets. Unlike their Western counterparts who would all rush into a foreign market that has potential, the Japanese foreign market entry strategy is very controlled, disciplined, ordered and scheduled. Typically, only one Japanese company would enter the foreign market first, establishing a strong beach-head, to be followed by a systematic "roll-out". When this company is successful, the other Japanese companies will then follow suit. More intriguingly, the Japanese also appear to have allocated their foreign markets so that every Japanese competitor has his own foreign territory clearly demarcated. In this way, no two Japanese competitors would rush into battle in the same distant ground! For example, in automobiles, Japan used Datsun (now known as Nissan) to enter the ASEAN market. In the United States, Toyota was the first entrant. In motorcycles, it was Yamaha that penetrated the ASEAN market first, while Honda was used to enter the American market. After the successful launching and penetration of Honda into the American market, Yamaha and other Japanese brands like Kawasaki followed suit. Similar patterns were observed in the ASEAN market. Indeed, the Japanese foreign market entry strategy of non-direct confrontation was observed in many product categories.

(xii) Serious ground 重地

A serious ground is one in which the army has penetrated deep into enemy territory and has left behind them many of the enemy's fortified cities and towns:

入人之地深，背城邑多者，为重地。

In such a situation, the army should attack the enemy when he is unprepared and move on. However, if the attack were to fail, it would spell grave consequences in terms of returning to the home base. This is because the return route is now filled with enemy fortified towns and cities. Under such circumstances, the ways to ensure the survival of the army are:

"Plunder the resources of the enemy."

重地则掠

"Protect the supply routes to ensure a continuous flow of provisions."

重地，吾将继其食

As mentioned earlier, serious ground should be distinguished from treacherous ground. In the case of serious ground, the army is now deep into enemy territory, while for treacherous ground, the troops are not necessarily in hostile grounds. In treacherous ground, the difficulties and obstacles are likely to come from the forces of nature. In serious ground, the obstacles are man-made (fortified cities and towns). These man-made obstacles in serious ground also distinguish it from constricted ground where the advantages/disadvantages are conferred by the forces of nature. In addition, a constricted ground is difficult to enter. However, penetration into enemy territory up to the serious ground stage could be made relatively easy by the enemy who may want to entice you into their territory in the first instance.

What would be serious grounds in business situations? In general, when companies are involved in direct foreign investments, they can be considered to be in serious grounds. This is because not only have they penetrated deep into hostile territory, but they would have to compete with both local manufacturers and other foreign competitors operating in the same market. Inevitably, the risks are higher as the environment is very different. In addition, once heavy investments are poured into the foreign business venture, it is often no longer that easy to pull out. It is therefore not surprising that most companies are reluctant to invest overseas, and when they do have to do so, they tend to take a very cautious approach.

The Japanese companies, for example, have for many years resisted moving their production plants overseas. It was only when their local costs of production and the Japanese yen went up substantially that they took such a step. Even so, one often finds reports of friction between the Japanese owners and their local counterparts.

To survive in serious ground, Sun Tzu advocated that one should plunder the resources of the enemy and protect supply routes. The logic underlying these strategies is best summed up by the following two quotations:

> "Therefore, the wise general sees to it that his troops feed on the enemy, for one cartload of the enemy's provisions is equal to twenty of his own; and one picul of the enemy's fodder to twenty piculs of his own."

故智将务食于敌，食敌一钟，当吾二十钟；䓤秆一石，当吾二十石。

> "The reason why a country can be impoverished by military operations is because of distant transportation; the carriage of supplies over long distances will render the people destitute."

国之贫于师者远输，远输则百姓贫。

In the same way, a company operating in a foreign market should seriously consider relying as much as possible on local resources. These would include all the factors of production like labor, capital, technology, management, raw materials and other supplies. If these resources could be sourced locally, it is definitely cheaper and faster than transporting them from home. In addition, sourcing locally, especially in the areas of depleting resources would not strain the supplies at home. At the same time, such efforts would also be helping the development of other sectors of the local economy, contributing to the building of goodwill with the local government.

It is interesting to note that Japanese overseas operations have subscribed to most of these practices of sourcing locally with one glaring exception. They have traditionally resisted employing top management personnel locally. Almost all the top level positions in Japanese overseas companies are staffed by Japanese. Over the years, this has created much unhappiness and resentment on the part of the local employees. Today, the Japanese are beginning to change this attitude.

Besides using local resources, another important aspect of doing well in an overseas market is to ensure that distribution channels and sources of supply are carefully established (protecting supply routes). Distribution channels for supplies and final products are more vulnerable in foreign markets. The company must ensure that there is a continuous supply of resources to the overseas plant and more efforts must be made to improve relationships with suppliers to ensure that such supplies are not suddenly terminated. If necessary, alternative sources of supply must be explored. More often than not, the purpose of overseas production is to increase capacity, production and overall market share and business. Unfortunately, this has to be accomplished at the cost of higher risks and greater competition. Thus, it is very important that the company's access routes to the various markets are well established and protected. This would require a continuous monitoring of the changes in the environment, tastes and preferences of the clients and the competitive moves made by the other competitors. In particular, it is important to build relationships with the international channel members, just as it is important to develop ties with your suppliers.

(xiii) Death ground 死地

The final type of battle situation mentioned by Sun Tzu in Chapters VIII and XI is death ground. This is a situation in which the army can only survive if it fights with the courage of desperation, where the only way to survive is to fight:

> 不疾战则亡者，为死地。

Accordingly, Sun Tzu's strategies for the death ground are:

> "Fight."

> 死地则战。

> "Make it evident that there is no chance of survival (except through fighting)."

> 死地，吾将示之以不活。

In death ground, it is very important to have the spirit of "comrades in adversity". According to Sun Tzu, it is the nature of soldiers to resist when surrounded and to fight to the death when there is no other alternative. Therefore, the general must make it very clear that there is no other way out except through fighting for their survival. Only then would the courage of soldiers be multiplied. The moment they are aware of escape routes, their hearts and minds would be on the escape route and their spirit for battle will be greatly diminished.

In business, a company can also face death ground. Perhaps two internationally well known examples would illustrate this point. Chrysler Corporation of the United States was at the verge of bankruptcy between 1978 and 1982. The company lost more than US$3.5 billion which was the biggest financial loss of any company in the history of the United States at that time. Despite the bailout by Congress in December 1979 under the Chrysler Corporation Loan Guarantee Act, the company almost collapsed. It was literally in death ground.

The turnaround came when Lee Iacocca took over the company. Among many other measures, he made it abundantly clear to his employees that the only way to survive was to fight. He was able to convince the otherwise militant United Auto Workers Union to take a pay cut that left the members earning about US$2 less per hour than their counterparts at General Motors and Ford. The total of their relinquished benefits amounted to US$1 billion. His efforts resulted in a drastic change in the behavior and loyalty of the workers towards management, an occurrence that is very unusual in America's heavily unionized industries. In his own words:

> "At Chrysler we have one and only one ambition. To be the best. What else is there?"

In sum, Lee Iacocca's ability to motivate his employees and get the best out of them enabled Chrysler to make a miraculous recovery and in 1984, Chrysler's pre-tax earnings of US$2.4 billion was more than its cumulative earnings in the previous 58 years!

Another spectacular turnaround event in the automobile industry is that of Jaguar cars from Britain. Again, it was a company at the brink of collapse that was turned into a multi-million dollar success story. How did Jaguar Cars Ltd. do it? In essence, the ultimatum to the workers was short, clear and blunt: break-even in six months or fold up. The no-holds-barred message was passed down to every worker. And the bitter prescription worked. In 6 years, the dying British car manufacturers did a complete turnaround – from losses of US$62 million a year, the company began to make profits of US$207 million.

Jaguar's turnaround strategy could be described as a three-step survival process. In the first stage, the survival plan was drawn up. Workers were told explicitly that the company was facing a crisis and that they must break even in six months or would have to fold-up. Operating costs were cut, efficiency and quality were improved. Staff cutbacks of as much as 40% were effected. Changes in work environment such as the introduction of more efficient methods were carried out. Suppliers, dealers and distributors were told to shape up or lose their contracts. It must be pointed out that at this stage, no alternative was given – they had to either shape up or ship out.

At stage two, the company focused on "hearts and minds" campaigns. To survive in adversity, there had to be comradeship in spirit and purpose. During this stage, five-year plans were drawn up with clear goals set. Workers were trained and wages were linked to productivity. Parties, sports events, bonfires, pantomime shows and ceremonies to launch new car models were organized for employees and their families. The purpose was to instill in the workers a sense of pride and belonging to the company. In essence, this stage was designed to create the spirit of comradeship in adversity.

The third stage which began in 1984 focused on privatisation and expansion. By this time, the company began breaking all previous sales and production records. Productivity went up three-fold and the company made plans to increase output by half. It is significant that the developments and "culture" created in the first two stages were continued at this stage as well as when the company went public, the employees were given first priority in buying shares.

The strategies adopted by Chrysler and Jaguar were very similar and they resemble the advice given by Sun Tzu for coping with a death ground situation: make it abundantly clear that the only way to survive is to fight on.

While these 13 different battlegrounds may not cover all business situations (for example, a monopolistic situation is not discussed; however, it is important to note that in war, the ultimate objective is to attain complete control; in business, the ultimate purpose is to attain complete monopoly of the market), they nevertheless cover a very wide spectrum of competitive situations that have relevance to business practices.

4 *Formulation of strategies*

4.1 The principle of concentration of forces
4.2 The principle of attack
4.3 The principle of *zheng* and *qi* (direct and indirect forces)

In Chapter 3, it was mentioned that there are a number of principles governing the formulation of strategies. These principles include:

(i)   The principle of choice of battleground
(ii)   The principle of concentration of forces
(iii) The principle of attack
(iv)   The principle of *zheng* (direct) and *qi* (indirect) forces.

The principle of choice of battleground was discussed extensively, and included three factors that relate to it – areas with distinctive advantages, areas ignored by the enemy and characteristics of the battleground. In this chapter, we shall focus on the remaining three principles governing the formulation of strategies – the principle of concentration of forces, the principle of attack, and the principle of *zheng* (正) and *qi* (奇) forces which essentially implies contingency planning. Figure 4.1 highlights the salient points underlying the formulation of strategies.

4.1 The principle of concentration of forces

The principle of concentration is very similar to Peacock's (1984) principle of economy of force outlined in Appendix A of this book. To

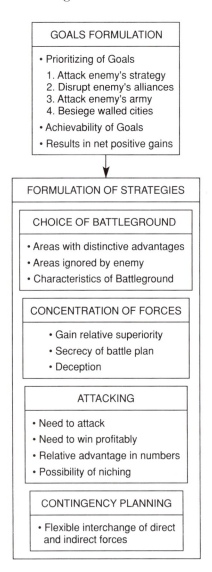

Figure 4.1 Formulation of Goals and Strategies

recap, economy of force simply means the use of minimum strength applied to a point other than the decisive one in order to pave the way for the application of mass force at the point of decision. The idea is to use one's limited available force to strike at the enemy's weakest point where victory can be better assured.

Sun Tzu's principle of concentration of forces recognizes that relative strength, and NOT absolute strength, at the point of contact dictates the outcome of the battle. This principle is evidenced by the following quotations:

> "The enemy must not know where I intend to attack. For if he does not know where I intend to attack, he must defend in many places. The more places he defends, the more scattered are his forces, and the weaker is his force at any one point."

吾所与战之地不可知；不可知，则敌所备者多；
敌所备者多，则吾所与战者，寡矣。

> "If he (the enemy) prepares to the front, his rear will be weak; if he defends the rear, his front will be fragile. If he strengthens his left, he will weaken his right; if he strengthens his right, he will weaken his left. If he tries to prepare for everywhere, he will be weak everywhere."

故备前则后寡，备后则前寡，备左则右寡，
备右则左寡，无所不备，则无所不寡。

The above sayings suggest that at the selected battleground of active combat, the force with the greater number of troops employed will be victorious although he may not have the advantage in terms of his overall army strength. Hence, one who is numerically inferior may still inflict defeat on the enemy by causing the latter to divide while he concentrates his forces at the point of combat. This principle of concentration of forces in order to achieve relative superiority in battle is further supported as follows:

> "The strength of an army does not depend on large forces. Do not advance relying on sheer numbers. Rather, one must concentrate the forces and anticipate correctly the enemy's movements in order to capture him."

兵非益多也，惟无武进，
足以并力、料敌、取人而已。

Relative superiority can be achieved by clever choice of battleground, maintaining strict secrecy of one's battle plan, and using deception.

4.1.1 Choice of battleground to gain relative superiority

This aspect has been discussed extensively in the previous chapter. What is important to re-emphasize here is that one must not treat the battleground as something that is fixed – that is, terrain. Rather, battleground should be treated as a variable factor that can be maneuvered and managed. In the business world, a company may be "fixed" by the terrain when, say, it is in the car manufacturing industry. However, it can vary its battleground by deciding which segment of the car market that it wants to compete in – small, medium or large car segment; economy, luxury or sporty segment, etc. In the previous chapter, it was shown how, by choosing areas ignored by the "enemies", the Japanese were able to:

- take time to build up their strengths and market shares as their competitors were simply not interested in what they were doing.
- enter into product areas and markets where they had no distinctive advantages. In fact, the Japanese had to start from square one in everything they did, and take time to improve upon them. In other words, since there were no serious competitors, it allowed the Japanese time and effort to establish themselves, improve and conquer.
- make mistakes and yet not face serious consequences as there were no threats from competitors.
- use their very limited resources to tackle one area (product or market) at a time, that is, to apply the principle of concentration of forces to achieve relative superiority at the point of combat.

In a typical business situation, a company has to overcome at least three challenges – that of the environment, the competitors and the consumers, assuming that it has a saleable product. By cleverly choosing their battlegrounds – areas ignored by the competitors and areas in which they might have the competitive advantage like production related technology – the Japanese were able to overcome two out of the three constraints. This is because the environment in production technology is more stable and certain than basic R&D (which the Americans and Europeans were doing before the 1970s), and as there were hardly any serious competitors in the areas (products and markets) that the Japanese chose to compete in, they only had to contend with trying to satisfy the customers. This they did very well initially with a low price, penetration strategy before upgrading their product quality. Indeed, the Japanese practiced what was said by Sun Tzu:

"Thus I say that victory can be created. For even if the enemy has a large force, I can prevent him from engaging me."

故曰: 胜可为也。敌虽众, 可使无斗。

The Americans, in contrast, played into Japanese hands. For example, when Japan swept into dominance in consumer electronics in the 1980s, the American government response was that of viewing it from classical trade theory, that is, if Japan was willing to subsidize their exports, American consumers ought to welcome them as gifts. Recent history has shown that this "termite strategy" of the Japanese worked beautifully as the Americans were caught off-guard.

4.1.2 *Maintaining strict secrecy of one's battle plan*

Maintaining secrecy of one's battle plan is critical to the success of any military campaign. This includes not only the battle strategy, but also the deployment of troops, the composition of troops and the use of weapons. In the conduct of war, once the plan is known to the enemy, the element of surprise is lost and the chances of achieving relative superiority come to nought. For the smaller force trying to take on a larger force, secrecy of plan becomes even more critical if it wants to achieve relative superiority at the point of combat. As stated by Sun Tzu:

"If I can uncover the enemy's dispositions while concealing mine, then I can concentrate while he must divide. And if my forces are united while his scattered, I can pit my entire strength against a fraction of his at any selected point of attack. There, I will be numerically superior and the enemy will surely be in trouble."

故形人而我无形, 则我专而敌分; 我专为一, 敌分为十, 是以十攻其一也,
则我众而敌寡; 能以众击寡者, 则吾之所与战者, 约矣。

The attitude of the general, as described by Sun Tzu, should be as follows:

"He only assigns tasks to his soldiers, but does not explain the purpose; he tells them to gain advantages, but does not divulge the dangers."

犯之以事, 勿告以言; 犯之以利, 勿告以害。

As the various aspects of secrecy will be covered in greater detail in Chapter 8, we only wish to make a few comments here. In the business world, a firm must also guard its business and marketing strategies carefully. At no time should such plans be known to the competitors. This is to prevent the competitors from taking preemptive action. This aspect of a company's operations has become so important in today's business operations that books and articles have been written specifically on how to protect company secrets (for example, Unkovic 1985).

The need to maintain secrecy in business has arisen largely because companies have been known to steal secrets from one another. For example, in recent years, there has been a tremendous mushrooming in the piracy business – not only in business stealing, but also in infringement of copyrights and patents. The seriousness of such occurrences has prompted some American firms to sue their Japanese and Taiwanese counterparts for stealing their computer and computer related technology (Singapore *Straits Times*, 24 March 1986).

On the other hand, there are people who advocated "an eye for an eye, a tooth for a tooth" approach in dealing with their business counterparts. For example, a very influential Indonesian business leader who has accused the Japanese of stealing scientific knowledge and technology from the West has even gone so far as to openly advocate that Indonesian firms should steal Japanese technology if necessary because Japanese companies are reluctant to transfer technology or are only willing to pass on obsolete systems (Singapore *Straits Times*, 22 July 1987).

4.1.3 Deception

The various aspects of deception will be dealt with in greater detail in Chapter 7 where we will discuss implementation of strategies. It is important to point out here that we *do not* recommend deception as a way of doing business but we do want to suggest that deception in business is real just as in war. The main purpose of using deception in war is to mislead the enemy from your main intention or line of attack. In other words, by sending out wrong signals to the enemy, the attacking force hopes to achieve the element of surprise as well as relative superiority at the point of combat. Put simply, the purpose is to gain advantage.

Deception has existed in every form since time immemorial. People have tried to pass fake paintings, jewellery, antiques, porcelain as real items. Indeed, the faking industry is big business today. Construction companies have tried to cheat on materials, manufacturers have tried to get by with defective parts and components, service operators have tried to short-change their clients and advertisers are well known for using deceptive advertising and unsubstantiated claims. For these reasons, codes of conduct and practices have to be set up in each business and advertising guidelines established. The fact is that deception exists, and it is important to recognize and tackle it.

4.2 The principle of attack

The third dimension underlying the formulation of strategies is the principle of attack. It is important first of all to point out that Sun Tzu is not an advocate of war. In fact, as mentioned in Chapter 2, Sun Tzu said:

> "War is a matter of vital importance to the State. It concerns the lives and deaths of the people; and affects the survival or demise of the State. It must be thoroughly studied."

兵者，国之大事，死生之地，存亡之道，不可不察也。

4.2.1 The need to attack

To the extent possible, Sun Tzu advocated that war is to be avoided. However, if confrontation and war are inevitable, then the only way to win is through attacking:

> "Invincibility in defense depends on one's own efforts, while the opportunity of victory depends on the enemy. It follows that those skilled in warfare can make themselves invincible, but cannot cause the enemy to be vulnerable."

不可胜在己，可胜在敌。故善战者，
能为不可胜，不能使敌之可胜。

The above comment supports the view that offensive actions are necessary to secure victory in war. However, Sun Tzu was not blinded to the need to use other strategies like consolidation and defensive strategies:

> "In ancient times, those skilful in warfare first made themselves invulnerable before awaiting for opportunities to defeat the enemy."

昔之善战者，先为不可胜，以待敌之可胜。

> "Those who cannot win must defend; those who can win must attack. Defend when one's forces are inadequate; attack when one's forces are abundant."

不可胜者，守也；可胜者，攻也。守则不足，攻则有余。

Thus, depending on the situation, appropriate strategy must be taken. For example, during the interim period of peace, when no active battles are fought, one should make use of the opportunity to strengthen one's resources (that is, consolidation). On the other hand, an offensive strategy like attacking should only be used when the four conditions on the desirability of war – definite advantages to be gained, strong assurance of victory, war as a last resort, and defense invincibility – (as discussed in Chapter 2, see also Figure 2.2) – are fulfilled.

The need to attack in open competitive situations is also very real. We can quote several analogies to support this. In playing a game of soccer, the only way to win is to kick the ball into the opponents' goal mouth. You cannot win by defending your goal area (unless you have already scored), at most it will be a draw. You cannot win a game of basketball unless you place the ball into the opponent's basket and pile up the points – there is no other way. Yes, you can prevent your opponent from scoring through a solid defense system, but to win, you must score! In boxing, you cannot rely on your opponent to box himself into exhaustion to win. You must attack and land that winning punch! Mike Tyson did not win by defending, he attacked his opponents! In fact, over 90% of his wins were through knockouts.

In the United States, one of the nation's most favorite sports is American football. It is quite frustrating at times to hear some American football commentators remarking that a team can win by strong defense. While we do not dispute the need for a strong defense to assure the team of "non-loss" (in fact, as mentioned earlier, Sun Tzu advocated that those skilful in warfare first made themselves invulnerable – through building up a strong defense – before awaiting opportunities to defeat the enemy), we definitely disagree that one can win by defending. To win in American football, and it is no different from many other ball games, you must put the ball in the opponent's goal area. There is no other way.

In business, when you have to compete openly, you cannot win by defending your market share. You cannot rely on your competitors to fail so that you will succeed. If you have to compete openly for market shares, the only way to win is to take the offensive. This is especially true if the market is not growing, for example, in a matured or stable market, or in a recessionary market. In the latter case, it is even more important to go after the competitor's market share as the pie is in fact shrinking (Wee 1985).

Japanese manufacturers exhibited the principle of attack very well in their economic conquest of world markets. In the computer industry, for example, the Japanese have invested heavily over the years to establish their market dominance – they have out-invested the Americans since 1981. The result is very startling. Since 1985, the Japanese share of world chipmaking tools and chip production has outstripped that of the US (concentrated mainly in Silicon Valley). In addition, the key technologies in this industry such as flat-panel displays for laptop computers, color flat-panel displays for most computers and high definition television, CD-rom drives (used with computers to read information published on optical discs), laser printer mechanisms (for desktop publishing), tape automated bonding (for placing more components on a circuit board and for helping miniaturization) and erasable optical disc drives (for storing huge files) are now dominated by the Japanese. Their computer sales in the US are also increasing day by day. In fact, by the 1990s NEC of Japan is likely to mount the stiffest challenge to US supremacy in supercomputers. The Japanese company is introducing its SX-3 system which is likely to outstrip the product its competitors, Gray Research Inc are producing. Judging by the aggressive posture of the Japanese (they have done it in consumer electronics as mentioned earlier), it will not be surprising if they beat the Americans in worldwide computer sales by 1995.

The concept of product life cycle planning in marketing dictates that one must actively seek new products, or extend the existing product in order to survive the market forces. It is rarely possible to rely on an unchanged product to survive. Many of today's leading products and brands have taken the initiative in modifying and improving their features. For example, Colgate toothpaste has added fluoride, minty flavor, tartar control, etc. to its formula, and changed and improved its packaging over the years in order to maintain its market position. Gillette razor blades have done likewise. From a single-blade razor, it moved on to twin-blade, adjustable twin-blade, disposable shavers. Even Wrigley, the famous single product company, has been improving and extending its product in order to extend its product life cycle. The same can be said of soft drinks manufacturers (Coca-cola, Pepsi-cola, 7-Up, etc.), gasoline companies (Shell, Esso, Caltex, Mobil, etc.), car makers (all major automobile manufacturers have some kind of planned obsolescence strategies), hi-fi equipment manufacturers, ... the list goes on. The point is, most successful companies do not simply react to the competitors, consumers and market trends. They attempt to manage such forces and adopt a proactive approach.

The need to be on the offensive so as to gain market share in open competitive situations must be recognized by all companies. It is a pity that the failure to recognize this need has resulted in the collapse of many successful companies. One good example which many readers will be familiar with is that of Coleco, the Connecticut company whose Cabbage Patch Kids were briefly the best-selling toys in history. By July

1988 it had filed for bankruptcy amid collapsing sales of the pug-nosed rag dolls and a rebellion by the company's creditors. Indeed, sales of the dolls, which children adopted complete with birth certificates, tumbled from US$600 million in 1985 to US$125 million in 1987. Besides its failure to recognize that it is in the fad business (and fads change very quickly), Coleco allowed its competitors to chip away at its share through various imitations. Meanwhile, the company failed to look beyond its Cabbage Patch products. It took a reactive and passive stance as opposed to the preemptive and active role so necessary in a business that is highly competitive and volatile. The lesson is simple, to survive and win in an open, competitive market, a company must go on the offensive. It cannot just defend its market position. The only valid reason for building up a strong defense is that it acts as a strong deterrent to any potential attacking force. In other words, when you have strong defenses, your competitors will think thrice before trying to enter your market. For example, Japanese manufacturers are today so established in a wide variety of consumer durables (like watches, television sets, cars, hi-fi and stereo sets) through their varied models and brands that other manufacturers have found it difficult to penetrate the Japanese defenses.

Moving to a more macro level, we can extend the analogy of attack to international trade among nations. Over the last two decades, the successes of countries like Japan and the Newly Industrialized Economies (NIEs) – namely Hong Kong, Singapore, South Korea, and Taiwan – have been largely due to their attacking strategies in international trade. They have opted for an export-oriented strategy as the engine for economic growth rather than relying on domestic factors. The results are well known. Unfortunately, instead of taking the appropriate counter-strategies, many developed countries, in particular the United States and Canada, have embarked on defensive strategies. They have tried to enact more laws and pass more bills to prevent exports from such countries entering their markets. As a result, stricter quotas and tariffs were imposed. At the same time, countries like Britain even tried hopelessly to protect, support and revive already uncompetitive, sunset industries.

While such actions are understandable, they will not be effective unless more positive and proactive action is taken. In fact, the best way to counter the export offensive of the Japanese and the NIEs is to embark on a similar export-oriented strategy. Curtailing imports will prevent further erosion of foreign exchange earnings but will not increase a country's foreign reserves. These countries must fight the Japanese and the NIEs by increasing exports to them and to other countries that Japan and the NIEs are trading or not trading with. In other words, they must choose the battlegrounds in which to fight, and fight with the courage of desperation. Defending will only result in being surrounded even more!

4.2.2 The need to win profitably

It is important to point out that although Sun Tzu advocated that offensive strategy is necessary to win wars, he also emphasized that it should be won with *maximum gains and minimum costs*:

> "For this reason, to win a hundred victories in a hundred battles is not the hallmark of skill. The acme of skill is to subdue the enemy without even fighting."

> 是故百战百胜，非善之善者也；
> 不战而屈人之兵，善之善者也。

In fact, Sun Tzu recognized that there is a high price to be paid when the army has to resort to open combat and delayed battle:

> "When victory is long delayed, the ardor and morale of the army will be depressed. When the siege of a city is prolonged, the army will be exhausted. When the army engages in protracted campaigns, the resources of state will be impoverished."

> 久则钝兵挫锐，攻城则力屈，
> 久暴师则国用不足。

According to Sun Tzu, the greatest ideal is to win a war without even fighting. The rationale for this is in line with the principle of winning profitably and taking "all-under-Heaven" intact. Hence, certain priorities must be established. These priorities – attacking the enemy's strategy, disrupting his alliances, attacking his army and besieging walled cities – have been discussed extensively in the previous chapter under prioritizing of goals. It is sufficient to underline here that the obvious logic to the order of these four courses of action is the avoidance of direct confrontation and minimization of the costs involved in capturing an enemy objective. It is also interesting to note that to do so involves using indirect and more subtle tactics and strategies than brute force. For example, the order of priorities as advocated takes on a continuum from the use of counter-strategy and psychology (attacking the enemy's strategy), through social (disrupting alliances) and personal (attacking the enemy's army) courses of action, before applying physical force as a measure of last resort (attacking walled cities). This is because Sun

Tzu recognised that it is more important to:

> "... subdue the enemy's army without direct battle; capture the
> enemy's cities without fierce assaults; and destroy the enemy's
> nation without protracted operations."

屈人之兵而非战也，拔人之城而非攻也，
毁人之国而非久也

Thus, psychological victory is far superior to physical dominance. Ultimately, the winners must win the hearts and minds of the people
whom they have conquered, so that there can be harmony between the
rulers and the ruled. In fact, the reliance on psychological victory is
also one of the premises for guerrilla warfare and communist propaganda. For example, in the Vietnam war, the Americans lost in spite of
superiority of forces and weapons. There were several reasons for their
failure. First, the Vietcong avoided engaging the American troops in the
open. Instead, they used hit and run tactics and chose their battlegrounds carefully.

More importantly, the Vietcong used psychology to their maximum advantage. They waged various propaganda campaigns depicting
the Americans as exploiters and abusers of their land and people. For
example, while Americans thought that it was great to show Vietnamese women in bikinis and swimsuits in their commercials, the Vietcong
turned such commercials to their advantage by saying that they de-
meaned the traditionally conservative Vietnamese women and their
value systems. Thus, they created anti-American feelings among the
masses.

The Vietcong also used psychology in the international diplo-
matic front. For example, they managed to successfully present the
presence of the Americans in Vietnam as something evil and unwar-
ranted, and insisted that Vietnam should be left to settle its internal
affairs without foreign intervention. At the same time, they did not fail
to highlight to the international press the atrocities and violence created by American soldiers in Vietnam. Alongside the growing dissatisfaction in the US concerning its role in Vietnam and its own losses, this
psychological warfare contributed to the American withdrawal from
Vietnam.

The need to achieve one's objectives with the minimum cost is
also very true in business. As discussed in Chapter 3 under *Prioritizing
goals*, some business options are more costly than others. It would be
better, for the same cost, to pursue an outcome that is more profitable.
In fact, many "measurement" tools have been developed for assessing
the attractiveness of business projects. For example, financial criteria

like the discounted cash flow, net present value, payback, etc. have been developed for such purposes. Similarly, marketing criteria like market share, potential sales growth and profits have also been used.

4.2.3 *Need to adhere to relative advantage in numbers*

Besides emphasizing the need to attack in an open combat situation, Sun Tzu also provided various guidelines on how to attack. Based on one's strengths, relative to the enemy's, one needs to devise the appropriate course of action. Sun Tzu suggested six alternative courses of action, using relative strengths as the criterion. These include:

(1) When to *surround* the enemy.

"When outnumbering the enemy ten to one, surround him."

十则围之，

(2) When to launch a *direct attack.*

"When five to enemy's one, attack him."

五则攻之，

(3) When to *divide* the enemy.

"When double his strength, divide him."

倍则分之，

(4) When to make a *strategic decision* to engage.

"When evenly matched, you may choose to fight."

敌则能战之，

In such cases, there is a need to use strategies, and the more capable general will win.

(5) When to prepare for *retreat.*

"When slightly weaker to the enemy, be capable of withdrawing."

少则能逃之，

(6) When to *avoid* the enemy.

"When greatly inferior to the enemy, avoid engaging him."

不若則能避之。

Hence, one engages the enemy in active combat only when one's strength is at least double that of the enemy. This is to ensure a greater chance of securing victory. However, when one's force is vastly superior in numbers and quality, it is not even necessary to attack the enemy directly. One only needs to surround him, and the imminent threat is enough to force him to submission. In an equally matched situation, the more able strategist will prevail. The winner will be the one who understands more the characteristics of the battleground and hence knows how to apply the appropriate strategy. At the same time, he is able to execute and maneuver his troops better. For example, in the area of maneuver, he is more capable of controlling the morale, and the mental and physical factors, as well as managing the changing circumstances. In addition, he is probably more able in the use of strategies, such as using the principles of deception, surprise, or speed in order to catch his enemy off-guard. In this way, he is capable of securing quick and decisive victories without great loss of troops.

Finally, when one is weaker than the enemy in all departments, one should avoid confronting the enemy. This is because, according to Sun Tzu, no matter how obstinate a small force may be, it will ultimately succumb to a larger and superior force. If confrontation is not avoidable, it is important to know how to attack the enemy's position profitably, and at the same time be prepared to withdraw in the event of defeat.

It is interesting to note that where there are relative advantages in numbers in war, the same advantage applies in business. Size often comes with more advantages than disadvantages. For this reason, it is always quite difficult for the smaller company to take on a larger one in the same industry, especially if the product is fairly homogeneous. For example, it is an axiom that the smallest firm in a homogeneous oligopolistic industry (where the product is not differentiated) has very few options except to follow the industry leader. Even in a heterogeneous oligopoly market structure like the car, tyre and gasoline industries, the options available to the smallest producer are not many. It is almost impossible to take on the leader head-on in competition. More indirect means, including the use of strategies and finding the right products and right markets must be explored.

The advantages of size have never been denied in business and economics literature. In fact, the principle of economies of scale in large production is a very well established axiom. Similarly, the **experience curve** concept (Wee 1985) of strategic pricing is premised on the economies of large scale production. Thus, pursuing a larger market share becomes important as part of the strategy to achieve economies of scale. Many strategic planning tools like the PIMS (Profit Impact of Market Strategies) and the BCG (Boston Consulting Group) Product Portfolio Matrix (of cash cows, stars, dogs and problem child) operate, among others, on the assumption that the larger producer enjoys greater economies of scale in the areas of procuring materials and supplies, production, R&D, marketing and advertising.

The quest for the advantages of size is also one of the reasons why companies want to exploit their markets beyond their national boundaries. For example, there are many leverages associated with operating internationally. These include program transfers (for example, training and human resource development), system transfers (for example, accounting, budgeting and planning systems), people transfers (for example, moving key management and research personnel), economies of scale (for example, in manufacturing, sourcing of raw materials and purchasing), economies of concentration (for example, on R&D), resource utilization (for example, in sourcing of management, manpower, machines, money, materials, methods and markets) and development of a global strategy.

It is interesting to point out here that while the United States has anti-trust laws to protect the smaller companies, Japan does not seem to be very concerned about their companies getting bigger and bigger at the expense of the smaller companies. In fact, American anti-trust laws are today hampering the growth and competitiveness of the computer industry in Silicon Valley. Most of the US computer firms have to fight two governments – Japan's and their own – before any changes can be affected. Meanwhile, with indecisive and ineffective federal US policies, the Japanese firms continue to roll on. There are also fundamental differences in the foreign market entry strategies of American and Japanese companies. For example, in the area of pricing American companies generally opt for a skimming strategy; pricing high to achieve a larger profit margin per unit. In contrast, Japanese companies, by and large, tend to choose a penetration strategy; pricing low so as to capture a larger market share. Implicit in the Japanese foreign market entry strategy is the idea of achieving a large sales volume so as to achieve economies of scale and lower the costs of production. More importantly, such a strategy is also consistent with their objective of allowing companies to grow as large as possible. Obviously, they seem to believe that size will translate into greater muscle and strength.

The events of recent history seem to suggest that the Japanese strategy of going after market share and allowing their companies to

Table 4.1 Ten largest companies in the world (in, 1988)

Name of Company	Rank	Market Value
JAPANESE COMPANIES:		
Nippon Telegraph and Telephone	1	US$296.00 bil.
Sumitomo Bank	2	69.00
Dai-ichi Kangyo Bank	4	63.50
Fuji Bank	5	63.00
Tokyo Electric Power	7	61.50
Nomura Securities	8	56.50
Industrial Bank of Japan	9	56.00
Mitsubishi Bank	10	56.00
US COMPANIES:		
International Business Machines	3	67.50
Exxon	6	62.00

grow as large as possible is paying off. In 1988, Japanese companies accounted for 48% of the total capitalization of the world's thousand largest companies. In contrast, American companies only had 30% of the share. In fact, eight of the top ten largest companies in the world in 1988 were Japanese (see Table 4.1). Note that the remaining two companies – International Business Machines (IBM) and Exxon – were American and ranked at third and sixth. These two companies were occupying top spots for many years before being toppled by the Japanese.

It must be pointed out that the dominance of the Japanese companies in recent years was probably felt most in the banking industry. As shown in Table 4.2, the top 10 banks in the world in 1988 were all Japanese. In fact, when ranked in terms of market capitalization in 1988, the top 21 banks belonged entirely to the Japanese. As shown in Table 4.3, the first non-Japanese bank (Union Bank of Switzerland) was ranked at 22. Amazingly, the American banks which once dominated the world banking industry, were not even placed in the top 25. There were only two American banks – Citicorp (ranked 26th) and J.P. Morgan (ranked 28th) – among the top 30 banks. The other noteworthy point is that the top ten Japanese banks had market values that were many times greater than the non-Japanese banks. For example, the tenth largest Japanese bank (Mitsui Bank) had a capitalization that was more than 3.5 times that of the Union Bank of Switzerland. Looking at

Table 4.2 World's top 10 Japanese banks (in 1988)

Rank	Name of Bank	Market Value
	WORLD'S TOP 10	
1	Sumitomo Bank	US$69.00 bil.
2	Dai-chi Kangyo Bank	63.50
3	Fuji Bank	63.00
4	Industrial Bank of Japan	56.00
5	Mitsubishi Bank	55.50
6	Sanwa Bank	51.50
7	Long-Term Credit Bank of Japan	33.00
8	Tokai Bank	31.50
9	Mitsubishi Trust & Banking	31.00
10	Mitsui Bank	30.50

Table 4.3 World's top 10 non-Japanese banks (in 1988)

Rank	Name of Bank	Country	World Rank	Market Value
	WORLD'S TOP 10 ELSEWHERE			
1	Union Bank of Switzerland	Switz.	22	8.75 bil.
2	Deutsche Bank	W. Germ.	23	8.50
3	Barclays Bank	Britain	24	8.00
4	National Westminster Bank	Britain	25	7.75
5	Citicorp	US	26	7.50
6	Swiss Bank Corporation	Switz.	27	7.00
7	J.P. Morgan	US	28	6.50
8	Banco De Santander	Spain	30	6.00
9	Credit Suisse	Switz.	35	5.50
10	Banco Central	Spain	37	5.00

the figures, the Japanese have built up such great gaps in terms of size that it is unlikely that any other non-Japanese bank will be able to match them in the foreseeable future.

Judging by the results and performances of Japanese companies in recent years, it is plausible to infer that they have no hesitancy in pursuing a relentless policy of unabated growth and dominance. This is very evident from the way in which they go about expanding their overseas markets and clobbering their international competitors. Today, it is a known fact that they dominate the world in many industries. Judging from their strategies, they appear to subscribe to the belief that there are definite advantages to be gained by being large.

4.2.4 Possibility for nicheing

It is important to note that while Sun Tzu explicitly acknowledged the advantages conferred by having a larger force, he also underlined that it must be of superior quality:

> "For no matter how obstinate a small force is, it will succumb to a larger and superior force."

故小敌之坚，大战之擒也。

In other words, while there are advantages to be enjoyed when one has a larger force, such advantages are not absolute unless the force is well trained. Thus, this is consistent with his statement that:

> "The strength of an army does not depend on large forces. Do not advance relying on sheer numbers."

兵非益多也，惟无武进，

What is more important, as discussed in Chapter 2 is the training of officers and men. Thus, Sun Tzu implicitly acknowledged that there are possibilities of victory for the smaller forces. In fact, he suggested that there are several ways in which a smaller force can win in battle. First, the smaller force can create advantages by seizing opportunities:

> "If someone asks: 'What should I do when faced with a large and well-organized enemy troop about to invade my territory?' My reply is, 'First capture something that he treasures most, and he will conform to your desires.'"

敢问：敌众整而将来，待之若何？曰：先夺其所爱，则听矣。

The strategy of seizing and exploiting opportunities by capturing something that is very much treasured by the opponent is the premise underlying political kidnapping and hijacking. The capturing of an airplane loaded with innocent passengers in order to extort political and other demands is one such example. In fact, the world has been so plagued with such events in recent years that countries like the Great Britain and Israel have developed anti-terrorist forces and strategies.

The second way that the smaller force can win is, as discussed in the previous chapter, to choose areas in which you have distinct advantages. This can be achieved by being the first to occupy key grounds or by choosing a battleground that is more advantageous to you than the enemy. Finally, the smaller force can also win by choosing areas ignored by the enemy.

In business, it is also very true that size alone is not sufficient to ensure victory. Just as in the army, there must be an emphasis on quality. For example, as explained in Chapter 2, the strength of an army does not depend on sheer numbers alone. What is of equal importance is the training of officers and men. Similarly, the strength of an organization relies both on the absolute numbers as well as the quality of the labor force and management. Perhaps this understanding of both size and quality as advocated by Sun Tzu has prompted the Japanese to pursue both aspects religiously. Indeed, the Japanese companies do not dominate by size alone, they also dominate by virtue of their high quality products and services.

It is interesting to point out that while economies of scale and various operating leverages are closely associated with size, quality is not. Herein lies the opportunity for the smaller operator. This is because the small firm does not necessarily have to suffer any distinct disadvantages if it can find its appropriate niche and develop its quality. For example, it can choose markets that no one has entered before, or choose products that no other companies are interested in manufacturing. As discussed earlier in this book, this was exactly what the Japanese did when they first entered the international market. Market nicheing is in fact very much part of the marketer's strategies (Kotler 1984, pp. 410–2). In the early 1980s, there were many small breweries in Canada and the United States who managed to carve out very credible market niches for themselves by producing beers that catered to specific tastes and the demands of selected market segments. Indeed, the whole exercise of market segmentation and targeting is designed to benefit the smaller producer who can then try to identify where his product fits into the market place.

Finally, we would also like to state that in business we do not encourage the smaller competitor to go about "seizing something that is treasured by the opponent." However, we would like to warn the reader that such a practice, nonetheless, exists and companies must be aware of it. The business of head-hunting is exactly the practice of seizing someone who is treasured by the competitor. Smaller companies are known to head-hunt key personnel from larger firms in order to benefit from their contacts and experience. Similarly, industrial espionage is very much like "seizing treasures" from your competitors. For example, smaller producers in Taiwan, Thailand and Hong Kong are known for stealing technology from the more advanced countries and using them to manufacture pirated or unlicensed products. In fact, as highlighted in Chapter 1 of this book, the Japanese started off as imitators in the early stages of their industrialization program. They were accused of borrowing and stealing technology from other people, adapting them, before finally putting their own trademarks on the products. Thus, while it is true that the issue of industrial espionage and staff pinching is a moral and ethical one, it is important to recognize that such practices do exist and companies must learn how to cope with them.

4.3 The principle of *zheng* and *qi* (direct and indirect forces)

So far, in the formulation of strategies, we have discussed the principles of choice of battleground, concentration of forces and attack. The fourth and final principle to be considered in the formulation of strategies is that of the employment of the *zheng* and *qi* forces. *Zheng* (正) force can be referred to as the actual, normal, or direct force. Similarly, *qi* (奇) force can mean the surprising, extra-ordinary, indirect, or deceptive force. For lack of better translations, we shall use the terms direct and indirect forces. According to Sun Tzu:

> "That the army is able to sustain the attacks of the enemy without suffering defeats is due to operations of the indirect and direct forces and maneuvers."

三军之众，可使必受敌而无败者，奇正是也；

In this principle, it is recognized that to win battles one needs an extra edge to swing the battle to one's favor. This can be achieved through the employment of the direct and indirect forces, where the former normally paves the way for the application of the latter:

> "In warfare, one generally uses the direct force to engage the enemy, but uses the indirect force to win."

凡战者，以正合，以奇胜。

The indirect force also represents the strategic advantage that one possesses in order to win a battle. In the use of these forces, one must exercise flexibility such that the two forces are interchangeable:

> "In battle there are only the direct and indirect forces, yet their combinations are limitless and beyond comprehension. For these two forces are mutually reproductive; their interactions are endless like those of interlocking rings. Indeed, who can tell where the variations begin and end?"

战势不过奇正，奇正之变，不可胜穷也。
奇正相生，如循环之无端，孰能穷之？

The interchangeable employment of the two forces will make it difficult for the enemy to guess the real intention and at the same time create deception. This is because the enemy may conceive the direct force as the indirect force and the indirect force as the direct force. The element of surprise is always maintained when these two forces are used interchangeably. In other words, these two forces are meant to be equally effective in war – one can be used to replace the other at any time.

It is important to note that employing the two forces interchangeably takes into account the contingent factor, that is, what if the enemy does not respond as anticipated? Now, if after the launch of the direct force the desired response from the enemy is not forthcoming then a different combination must be utilized. This can be done by transforming the indirect force to be the direct force and vice versa. The number and degree of transformations are limitless, and so the resultant combinations of the two forces are also limitless. Hence, the flexible employment of the *zheng* and *qi* forces allows for contingencies.

In any corporate planning decision, it is a norm that contingency planning must be included. At times, a company may even develop more than two courses of action or alternatives. In fact, any effective budgeting and forecasting systems would invariably include the element of contingency planning by using sensitivity analyses, scenarios or other methods. The basic idea is to ensure that other effective actions are available when required.

It must be pointed out that formal planning is based on events that have a high probability of happening. However, at times, there could be other less likely conditions that can create serious difficulties for the company, if they actually happen. Thus, contingency planning is exercised in order to handle such less likely events if they do occur. In the words of Steiner (1979, p. 230):

> "The fundamental purpose of contingency planning is to place managers in a better position to deal with unexpected develop- ments than if they had not made such preparations. By failing to anticipate certain events managers may not act as quickly as they should in a critical situation and the event may create more damage than it otherwise would have. Contingency planning should eliminate fumbling, uncertainty, and time delays in making the needed response to an emergency. Contingency planning also should make such responses more rational."

The example of using alternative but equally effective courses of action can also be applied in the area of foreign market entry strategies. While it is true and perhaps advisable that a company should enter a foreign market by stages – moving from exporting to licensing to joint-venture to wholly-owned subsidiary (see Figure 3.1 of Chapter 3) – so as to minimize risks and maximize control, such an approach should not be rigidly adhered to. Rather, the mode of entry should depend on the various constraints faced by the company, restrictions imposed by the host country, competitive and environmental forces. At times, as in the case of companies wanting to operate in China, joint venture may be the only mode available for entry. Thus, a company must be prepared to use alternative modes of entry if necessary, and at the same time to be able to exploit and use these modes equally effectively.

Going beyond market entry, the strategy to be used by an inter- national company in foreign markets expansion must also be varied so that the competitors will not be able to detect the strategy easily. This is because easy detection may lead to counter strategy or to pre-emptive or defensive actions on the part of the competitors. A good example is the global market expansion paths used by the Japanese. Kotler *et al* (1985, pp. 174–83) identified three distinctive paths used by the Japanese as follows:

Path   I: Japan ⟶ Developing Countries ⟶ Developed Countries
Path II: Japan ⟶ Developed Countries ⟶ Developing Countries
Path III: Developed Countries ⟶ Japan ⟶ Developing Countries

Examples of Path I strategy include products like watches, steel and passenger cars. The type II Japanese expansion path is found in high technological content industries such as computers and semicon- ductors. Finally, Japan has also developed some products where they sell to the developed countries first before the home market (Path III). Examples include videotape recorders (VTRs), color televisions and sewing machines. Thus in pursuing such a varied global expansion strategy, the Japanese have made it difficult for their competitors to predict where and how they are going to strike. In this way, they are able to maintain their market dominance.

5 *Evaluation of strategies*

5.1 Subjective evaluation
5.2 Numerical evaluation
5.3 Business applications

There is no chapter in *The Art of War* specifically devoted to the evaluation of strategy but Sun Tzu alludes to it many times. Sun Tzu mentions that war is a matter of vital importance and hence must be thoroughly studied (evaluated). His recommended five fundamental factors and seven dimensions were discussed in great detail in Chapter 2 of this book. In addition, it is also important to satisfy the four conditions for waging war – definite advantages to be gained, strong assurance of victory, war as a measure of last resort and defence invincibility – before determining the desirability of war and the type of offensive strategy that could be used (see Figure 2.2). If the four conditions cannot be fulfilled, war is definitely undesirable and non-war alternatives must be explored. Thus, Sun Tzu has already considered the issue of evaluation at the earliest stage of the planning process. The following quotations lend more weight to this:

> "He who has a thorough knowledge of himself and the enemy is bound to win in all battles. He who knows himself but not the enemy has only an even chance of winning. He who knows not himself and the enemy is bound to perish in all battles."

知彼知己者，百战不殆；不知彼而知己，一胜一负；
不知彼，不知己，每战必殆。

and

> "Know your enemy, know yourself, and your victory will not be threatened. Know the terrain, know the weather, and your victory will be complete."

知彼知己，胜乃不殆；知天知地，胜乃不穷。

In order to give the formulation of goals the proper priority, there is the need to evaluate the effectiveness of each one of them. For example, Sun Tzu obviously recognized that certain goals are preferred over others when he advocated his four-step offensive strategy – attack enemy strategy, disrupt his alliances, attack his army and besiege walled cities (to be used when there are no other alternatives).

In the formulation of strategy there is an implied need to evaluate the effectiveness of the different strategies in varying situations so as to achieve one's goals. One factor affecting choice of strategy is the characteristics of the ground. In all, as mentioned in Chapter 3, there are 13 different strategies to be used, one for each of the 13 different types of battleground.

It must be pointed out that the purpose of evaluation is to ensure that the strategy to be used is effective, that it can provide the greatest chance of victory and can result in net tangible gain; in essence, a strategy that allows us to win profitably. Throughout Sun Tzu's writings, there is no lack of contributions on the subject of evaluation of strategies. Indeed, it is implied in many of his evaluative statements:

> "Hence, the wise general must consider both favorable and unfavorable factors in his deliberations.
> By taking into account the unfavorable within the favorable factors, he ensures his plan is feasible.
> By taking into account the favorable within the unfavorable factors, he can resolve difficulties."

是故智者之虑，必杂于利害。
杂于利，而务可信也；
杂于害，而患可解也。

For the purposes of discussion, we have grouped Sun Tzu's treatment of this subject along two dimensions – subjective evaluation of strategy effectiveness and numerical evaluation of strategy effectiveness. This classification may not be fair to Sun Tzu's works, but it is an attempt to facilitate understanding and discussion. Figure 5.1 highlights the salient points that will be discussed in this chapter.

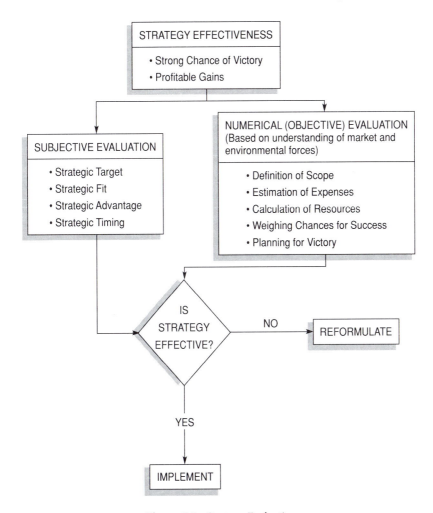

Figure 5.1 Strategy Evaluation

5.1 Subjective evaluation

A general's leadership is very important during times of war. His appraisal of the battle situation is critical to the success or failure of the
military campaign. Sun Tzu explicitly recognized the importance of the
military commander when he said:

> "He who knows when to fight and when not to fight will win;
> He who knows how to deploy large and small forces will win;
> He whose whole army is united in purpose will win;
> He who is well-prepared to seize opportunity will win;

He whose generals are able and not interfered with by the ruler will win."

知可以战与不可以战者胜，识众寡之用者胜，
上下同欲者胜，以虞待不虞者胜，
将能而君不御者胜。

Sun Tzu was able to predict the outcome of the battle using these five factors. Note that four of the five factors relate to the commander himself. Similarly, five of the eight factors discussed in Chapter 2 are also related to the leadership of the commander – generalship, doctrine (law), strengths, training and discipline. Thus, how the commander trains his army in peace time, how he leads his men in war time, how he develops and executes the war strategies are all fundamental to the success of the state in acquiring territories.

In the area of evaluation of strategy, there are specifically four areas in which the commander must do well. These four areas include the selection of strategic targets, the ability to create strategic advantages, the fitting of strategy to situation, and the sense of strategic timing.

5.1.1 Strategic target

The success of any military conquest depends largely on what kind of enemy the attacking force is facing. If war is initiated on the part of the attacking force, it becomes paramount that the right victim be chosen. This is because Sun Tzu warned:

"Do not move unless there are definite advantages to be gained; Do not use troops unless you can succeed; Do not fight unless you are in danger."

非利不动，非得不用，非危不战。

Therefore, it is important that the target chosen must be an easy prey:

"In ancient times, those adepts in warfare gained victories by conquering those enemies that are easily conquered."

古之所谓善战者，胜于易胜者也。

And the general can achieve this because:

"His victories are won without mistakes. The reason why he does not make mistakes is because he ensures every move he makes and conquers an enemy already defeated."

故其战胜不忒，不忒者，其所措必胜，胜已败者也。

While it is important to capture targets that are easily defeated, it is equally important to bear in mind that there must be positive gains after that. In other words, definite advantages must be achieved, and the net result must be:

"To defeat the enemy and become stronger."

是谓胜敌而益强。

Thus, some targets may appear very easy to capture, yet they could be laid with traps and dangers. The result is that the troops may be locked into unexpectedly protracted campaigns and the morale of the soldiers may be dampened. There could also be great loss of men and equipment in such a campaign. On the other hand, there are some targets that, once captured, may bring more liabilities than gains. In fact, there is one recent example of this – the British recapturing of the Falkland Islands from Argentina. While it was a political and military victory for the British, the economic price that they are paying is extremely high. The islands have negligible resources, are located in a very remote area and it costs the British millions of pounds to maintain their presence there. In the words of Sun Tzu:

"There are some routes not to follow, some armies not to assault, some cities not to attack, some grounds not to contest and some commands of the sovereign not to be obeyed."

涂有所不由，军有所不击，城有所不攻，
地有所不争，君命有所不受。

The choice of the right target to engage in war led Sun Tzu to develop various decision criteria for the use of troops. For example, he advocated that it is important to adhere to relative superiority in numbers in attacking. To launch a direct assault requires a superiority ratio of 5:1, while a ratio of 2:1 only allows a strategy of dividing the enemy. It is interesting to note that this ratio of at least 2:1 for aggressive actions is still adhered to by many modern armies in conventional wars. For example, a ratio of 3:1 is normally used when an army tries to assault an enemy's position.

The choice of target also extends to the type of battleground to be contested. You will recall that Sun Tzu advocates choosing areas in which one has distinct advantages or areas ignored by the enemy. Another piece of advice is that to be certain of capturing a place one must attack one that is not defended. These statements show his concern that targets to be chosen must be arrived at after detailed deliberation. This is the focus of his opening chapter where he discusses the importance of detailed planning. He says that, from the way planning is done:

> "I will be able to predict the winner and the loser."

> 吾以此知胜负矣。

Besides picking targets that are ignored or poorly defended, it is also possible to lure the enemy to where you want to do battle, or discourage him from fighting in another area:

> "By enticing the enemy with some baits, one can make him come on his own accord. By inflicting damage and placing obstacles, one can prevent the enemy from going to places that he wants to reach."

> 能使敌人自至者，利之也；能使敌人不得至者，害之也。

The essence of targeting can best be summed by the following two quotations:

> "Therefore, those who are skilled in warfare will always bring the enemy to where they want to fight and are not brought there by the enemy."

> 故善战者，致人而不致于人。

> "If I wish to engage my enemy, I can do so even if the enemy is taking refuge behind tall and deep defenses. This is because I can draw him out by attacking a position that he must rescue."

> 故我欲战，敌虽高垒深沟，不得不与我战者，
> 攻其所必救也；

In business, the choice of strategic targets is also very much part of the evaluation process before the strategy is fully implemented. For example, a company may have "expansion through acquisitions" as one of its major corporate objectives and strategies. Hence, it may go about formulating various types of acquisition strategies. However, as part of this process, it must carefully assess the target that it wants to acquire. Can it be easily acquired? Often an acquisition move may be resisted heavily by the party to be taken over. Will there be synergism after the takeover? This is important as the company should become stronger after the takeover ("To defeat the enemy and become stronger"). Does the company have a large enough numerical superiority to make the takeover move? Note that before 1985 when Japanese companies were less financially strong, they made few moves in acquiring foreign companies. However, the general fall in the stock prices of US companies after the October 1987 crash made them look like bargains. In addition, with the appreciation of the Japanese yen, Japanese companies have become very strong financially. The result is that they went on an acquisition spree. According to Yoshiharu Senoue, Deputy General Manager at Sanwa Bank's Business Development Department, Japanese takeovers of foreign firms totalled 204 in 1986 compared to 100 in 1985. Such foreign takeovers are expected to rise by 40% to 50% in the next few years (reported in *Straits Times*, 25 July 1988).

When a company wants to encroach into someone else's market share, it had better ensure that the target does not notice its actions and embark on retaliatory action. This targetted competitor should preferably be a smaller one. This is to ensure that relative superiority is maintained and advantages can be enjoyed. Just like the aggressor in war, the aggressive firm in business should choose its enemy target carefully. This is because all markets are occupied by one or more companies that enjoy different competitive positions, strengths and weaknesses. By and large, there are leaders, challengers, followers and nichers, each serving a particular segment or segments of the market. The company has to decide which of these types of companies it wants to take on. Should it challenge the leader, compete directly against one of the followers or another firm of its equal size, or attempt to take over one of the nichers? What kind of target it chooses to engage will, of course, depend on the relative advantages it has over its enemy and how it can pit its strengths against the enemy's weaknesses. In essence, the company will have to do a SWOT analysis (as outlined in Figure 2.3) before deciding on the target.

The choice of targets in business – whether it is a decision to enter a foreign market, to acquire a company or to enter a new segment of a market, must be carefully assessed before the strategy can be implemented. This is because the time and effort involved in capturing the target may make very different demands on the company. For example, would the captured target enhance the company's market position, increase the market share of another market, represent a current strategic thrust into a new market or improve the company's product/service quality and quantity? More importantly, what are the implications to the organization in terms of management, manpower, machines, money, materials, methods, markets (as mentioned in Chapter 2)? All these must be carefully considered.

A good example to illustrate the need to capture the right strategic target is that of LTV (of the United States) acquisition of Republic Steel Corporation in 1984. In making the acquisition, LTV had hoped to propel itself to the No. 1 position in steel production, and enjoy economies of scale as a result of a dramatic increase in size. Unfortunately, the market forces at that time did not favor the largest producer. With the tremendous influx of foreign steel imports, modernization and not size was the key to competition. In addition, the management at that time was not exactly inspiring, and made some bad decisions as well. The result was that LTV filed for bankruptcy in 1986, after incurring US$2.6 billion in debt. The lesson to be learned is that what started out as a good target turned out to be a disaster because of poor understanding of market forces and weak management skills.

Another example of poor choice of targets is Britain's Blue Arrow's acquisition of Manpower in 1987. Blue Arrow had an annual revenue of only US$500 million. However, it acquired Manpower, a company over twice its size for US$1.3 billion. The result was disaster. There were management clashes and the intended hopes of a worldwide power in employment services collapsed. Earnings and stock prices plummeted. Since then, Manpower's management has gradually taken over the running of the company!

5.1.2 Strategic fit

Having selected the target to be captured, the next stage of the evaluation process involves assessing the suitability of the strategy with the battle situation. In fact, Sun Tzu's treatment of the type of strategies to be used on different types of battlegrounds (as discussed in detail in Chapter 3) exemplifies exactly the concept of strategic fit. His concern about what works and what will not even led him to comment that:

> "If a general follows my strategy and acts accordingly, he will win. Retain him. If a general refuses to follow my strategy and acts accordingly, he will lose. Dismiss him."

将听吾计，用之必胜，留之；将不听吾计，用之必败，去之。

As a further illustration of his wisdom in matching strategy with battle situations, let us elaborate a bit further about the strategy he advocated for death ground. According to Sun Tzu, the strategy here is to fight, and the general must make it abundantly clear that there is no chance for survival except through fighting. The logic behind such a strategy is that it is in the nature of well-trained soldiers to resist when surrounded and to fight to the death when faced with no other alternative. In such a desperate situation they will also follow the orders of the commander implicitly:

> "When troops are thrown in a situation of no escape, they will not flee in the face of death. Since they are not afraid of death, there will be unity of officers and men in combat. In a desperate situation, they fear nothing; when faced with no route to escape, they will stand firm. When deep into hostile territory, they will be vigilant. When faced with no alternative, they will fight to death."

投之无所往，死且不北，死焉不得，士人尽力。
兵士甚陷则不惧，无所往则固，深入则拘，不得已则斗。

And the result:

> "Thus such troops need no surveillance to make them be alert; support is obtained without being asked for; faith and affections are gained without restrictions; and trust won without orders."

是故其兵不修而戒，不求而得，不约而亲，不令而信。

It is important to note that Sun Tzu did not advocate only one-sided strategies. For example, he warned that:

> "Do not press an enemy in a desperate situation."

穷寇勿迫，

In sum, the wise general is one who is able to:

> "Deliberate and assess the situation, then move."

悬权而动。

> "... evaluate the enemy's plans to determine which strategy will succeed and which will not."

故策之而知得失之计

Based on what we have discussed so far, it is important to note that the ability to achieve strategic fit depends a lot on the capability of the general. In fact, Sun Tzu explicitly acknowledged the importance of the general when he commented:

> "An army may suffer from flight, insubordination, collapse, ruin, disorganization and rout. These six calamities are not attributed to natural causes. They are due to the faults of the general."

> 故兵有"走"者，有"弛"者，有"陷"者，有"崩"者，
> 有"乱"者，有"北"者。凡此六者，非天之灾，将之过也。

He went on to explain what he meant by the six calamities or disasters:

- "Other conditions being equal, when a force pits itself against another that is ten times its size, the result is flight."

  夫势均，以一击十，曰"走"；

- "When the common soldiers are strong and the officers are weak, the result is insubordination."

  卒强吏弱，曰"弛"；

- "When the officers are strong and the common soldiers are weak, the result is collapse."

  吏强卒弱，曰"陷"；

- "When resentful and insubordinate officers rush into battle without orders, and when the general does not understand their capabilities, the result is ruin."

  大吏怒而不服，遇敌怼而自战，将不知其能，曰"崩"；

- "When the general is weak and lacks discipline, when training and instructions are not clear, when the duties of officers and men are not distinct and when the formations are slovenly, the result is utter disorganization."

  将弱不严，教道不明，吏卒无常，陈兵纵横，曰"乱"；

- "When the general cannot correctly judge the enemy's situation and uses a smaller force to strike a larger force, matches weakness against strength and has no elite troops as vanguards, the result is rout."

  将不能料敌，以少合众，以弱击强，兵无选锋，曰"北"。

According to Sun Tzu, these six conditions will definitely bring defeat to the army, and it is the supreme responsibility of the general to examine them carefully. Besides these, the general must know the following:

(1) How to deploy and use his forces. To achieve this, he must have a good understanding of his army's strengths, the quality of his forces (training issue) and the discipline of the soldiers – three of the eight factors that were discussed in Chapter 2. The clever use of forces is very well put by Sun Tzu:

> "He who knows how to deploy large and small forces will win."

Besides the ability to use small and large forces, the general must also be capable of using the "zheng" and "qi" forces:

> "In warfare, one generally uses the direct force to engage the
> enemy, but uses the indirect force to win."

(2) How to exploit the advantages of weather and terrain.

> "Know the terrain, know the weather and your victory will be
> complete."

Just as in war, the strategy to be implemented in business must be assessed for its strategic fit. Here, it is important to point out that although a company may have a set of corporate operating procedures, or ways of doing things, they must not, however, be rigidly adhered to. The importance of strategic fit in the corporate planning process can be illustrated by the fact that scholars and planners like Lorange (1980) and Steiner *et al* (1982) have devoted much effort to addressing this issue. Lorange (1980) for example, in his chapter on *Tailor-Making the Corporate Planning System's Design*, discussed approaches toward tailor-making the strategic planning system so that the capabilities of the system can be developed to meet the particular needs for planning that different companies have.

Over the years, as part of the evaluation process of business strategies, many analytical tools have also been developed. The first set of such tools were qualitative in nature and included such qualities as individual creativity, judgment, hunches, intuition, gut feeling and experience. Brainstorming, project teams and the Delphi technique could also be classified under this category. Note that many of these techniques rely on the leadership factor, like the general in war. In business, the general is the chief executive officer (CEO) or the most senior manager. It is interesting to observe that just as the general plays a critical role in directing the progress of battle, the CEO has a similar function in charting the strategic direction of his company. In exercising his skills, he relies very much on the art of strategic management. It is for this reason that he is head hunted and commands a high salary premium.

The second category of techniques are older, quantitative methods, and they include accounting systems and models in the accounting systems (such as balance sheets, profit and loss statements, cash flows, accounting and financial ratio analyses, break-even analysis, budgets, cost control models, and variance analysis). Forecasting methods such as trend analysis, econometric models, input-output models and multiple regression are also used. In addition, there are other kinds of techniques in this category, including tracking models, decision trees, critical path models like PERT and others.

As a result of computer technology, a new breed of mathematical models have been developed. They have basically adapted the older quantitative methods, but have greater capability and diversity. For example, financial models (Naylor 1970), PIMS (Profit Impact of Market Strategies), experience and cost curves are quite extensively used. It is important to point out that most of the computer-based models are deterministic rather than probabilistic. The major exception is risk analysis, developed by Hertz (1969).

The last group of techniques can be considered hybrid models. This is because they combine the use of various tools in the analysis. For example, many formal strategic planning systems, program budgeting systems, social science investigations and elaborate cost-benefit analyses use many of the different tools highlighted earlier.

It is obvious from the multiplicity of available models that there is no single ideal technique that can be used for evaluating strategies. Each tool has its own strengths and weaknesses and thought must be given as to the appropriateness of each of them. Decisions such as these are probably best made by the person using it – the manager. In a nutshell, the manager or the CEO is still his own best analytical tool. This point can be well illustrated by Carter (1965, p. 36), a biographer of Winston Churchill when he commented on the latter's leadership. According to Carter, Winston Churchill was deeply interested in all kinds of military strategies as propounded by various experts. Churchill would not only listen intensely, but he would probe and question what he heard. He never subscribed to everything the experts said. To him, it was the duty of the experts to give him all views and options. It was his role as a leader to reach the conclusion.

While there is no magic formula to address the problem of evaluation of a strategy for its strategic fit, certain guidelines have, nevertheless, been developed over the years. Among them, Steiner *et al* (1982) considered Tilles' (1963) set of overarching tests as most significant and even added their own comments and illustrative questions. Taking into account all the contributions by Tilles and Steiner *et al*, we suggest the following criteria that the company must address in order to test its strategies:

(1) Consistency with the environment. By this, we mean it must conform to the constraints imposed by the various parties that operate within the environment. For example, does the strategy contradict government policies? Does it go against the logic of the business cycles? Does it contradict social and cultural norms? Does it capitalize on the existing opportunities offered by the marketplace, such as technology, available labor, possible market openings? Does it take into account the threats as well, such as technological obsolescence, changes in government regulations, changes in political leadership, shortages of labor and capital supply? In sum, the strategy must fit into the environmental framework, or in Sun Tzu's terminology, be consistent with the weather.

(2) Weighing the effects of competition. The strategy must take into account such issues as the correct appraisal of competitors. The CEO must decide if he has a good reading of their likely moves and countermoves in response to his strategies. He must know if his strategies make him vulnerable to attack from any particular competitor, if he can achieve a competitive edge and if his strategy is leading him to a head-on collision with the dominant players in the market. Weighing the effects of competition is tantamount to knowing your enemy.

(3) Consistency with corporate practice and culture. This is another critical area to be addressed. The strategy to be implemented must be in line with the way the company is organized and structured. Otherwise, there will be blurring of roles and responsibilities. The strategy must also be consistent with the corporate mission, philosophy, or values. It must not conflict with existing know-how within the company, existing production skills and other strategies currently under implementation. Otherwise, there will be chaos. In a nutshell, this is the "**doctrine and law**" factor that must be considered.

(4) Matching with quantity and quality of corporate resources. The strategy to be implemented must also fit into the available resources – both quantity and quality – of the company. For example, does the company have the money (capital) to ensure successful implementation of the strategy? Does it have the type of production equipment and technology (methods and machines) to meet the requirements set out in the strategy? Does it have the type of personnel, including managers (manpower and management), to see the strategy through to successful completion? In particular, are the rank and file trained? Are they aware of the new challenges and assignments ahead? Are they prepared? In addition, can the company ensure that it has adequate supplies (materials) to sustain the whole operation? All these are important areas to be assessed and they represent the strengths and training aspects of the company.

(5) Acceptable level of risks. Any strategy to be implemented will have a certain degree of risk. The company, especially the CEO, will have to decide what is the acceptable level of risk. Of course, when risks are higher, the returns are expected to be higher too. At the same time, a company that has larger and more diversified resources (like a larger army with varied forces) will be capable of absorbing greater risks. Whatever the risk preference is, the guiding principle must be, "do not move unless there are definite advantages to be gained," so that the net result would be "to defeat the enemy and become stronger."

(6) Matching strategy with market niches and opportunities. An effective strategy must be one that exploits the opportunities offered by the market place. In Sun Tzu's military terms, it must exploit the terrain so as to gain strategic grounds. To achieve this, the company must understand the characteristics of the market structure and situations (battlegrounds) and have a good grasp of the constraints and opportunities (terrain). Then, and only then, can the strategy exploit whatever niche, opening or opportunity is left unfilled. Alternatively, it can also create its own niche once it understands the battlegrounds and the terrain.

(7) Effective and efficient implementation. A strategy must be capable of being implemented effectively and efficiently. The many principles and factors governing the implementation of strategies will be discussed in the next chapter. At this juncture, it is important to point out that the success of implementation depends a lot on coordination and control mechanisms, as well as the capabilities of the employees and managers who are entrusted with the job of executing the strategy. At the CEO's level, his sense of timing and judgement with regard to when the strategy should be implemented is also critical to its success. This is because, "he who knows when to fight and when not to fight will win."

(8) Avoidance of over-used strategies and tactics. Another important aspect of the evaluation process is to ensure that the strategy is not a rehash of some previously used methods. This is to prevent the competitors easily out-guessing you. A winning strategy in the past may turn out to be a loser once the competitors learn how to react to you. Rather, one must heed Sun Tzu's advice:

"Therefore, do not repeat the tactics that won you a victory, but vary them according to the circumstances."

故其战胜不复，而应形于无穷。

It is interesting to note that the above set of guidelines for assessing strategic fit mirror those advocated by Sun Tzu in evaluating military strategies. Thus, there is no doubt that what applies in war can to a large extent be applied to business as well.

5.1.3 Strategic advantage

As part of a successful and effective battle strategy, the general must also be able to create strategic advantages in order to secure victory:

"Thus I say that victory can be created. For even if the enemy has a large force, I can prevent him from engaging me."

故曰：胜可为也。敌虽众，可使无斗。

The reason underlying the above argument is that victory in war does not necessarily depend on large forces. In fact, Sun Tzu advised against advancing on the strength of sheer superiority of numbers. What is equally important is the training of officers and men and the appropriate use of strategy. For example, if the purpose of one's strategy can be concealed while at the same time one knows the disposition of the enemy troops, then the latter will never know how and where one is going to attack. The result is that he will have to defend everywhere, resulting in a scattering of troops which will favor the attacking force. Thus, it is possible to achieve relative superiority at the point of contact, by concentrating one's forces against the enemy's few.

There are many ways in which a larger force can be prevented from engaging a smaller force. The following are some examples of how to avoid direct confrontation with a larger force:

(1) Keeping a low profile. The purpose of keeping a very low profile is not to attract the animosity of the enemy. This can be achieved through a deep sense of humility and pretended vulnerability:

"In the beginning of battle, be as shy as a young maiden to entice the enemy and lower his defences..... "

是故始如处女，敌人开户

(2) The clever choice of battleground. This has been discussed extensively previously. Using this skill with a thorough understanding of the weather, the capable general will be able to exploit the terrain to his maximum advantage.

(3) Seizing something of value to the enemy. In war, it is common to seize something that is of value to the enemy. This may include the kidnapping of key personnel or even the stealing of battle plans. According to Sun Tzu, such a strategy is very useful to the smaller force under seige:

> "If someone asks: 'What should I do when faced with a large and well-organized enemy troop about to invade my territory?', my reply is, 'First capture something that he treasures most, and he will conform to your desires.'"

敢问: 敌众整而将来，待之若何? 曰: 先夺其所爱，则听矣。

It is important to point out that the purpose of seizing something of value to the enemy is to gain strategic advantage, and this advantage should preferably be sustained throughout the battle. At its least effective, it must be capable of allowing sufficient time for the smaller force to devise a better battle plan. It should be highlighted here, however, that while in war, such a practice is acceptable, in business, it can be highly unethical to seize something of value to the competitors. At the same time it is also true that industrial espionage such as the stealing of trade secrets, technology and patents are not unheard off in the business world today, while luring key executives from competing firms through better and more attractive packages is also widely practised. Thus, in the business world, we are equally guilty of seizing something of value to the enemy!

The reverse of this strategy suggests that there is also the urgent need to protect one's valuables. For example, one has to carefully guard corporate secrets such as patents, copyrights and technology, so as to prevent them from being seized by the competitors. Even key personnel and executives must be well treated to prevent them from being lured away.

Strategic advantage can also at times be provided by the enemy in that he opens up opportunities for the attacking force or allows loopholes in his defenses. For example, if he chooses not to defend a particular battleground, or defends a battleground badly, he is opening the ground for easy occupation. Thus:

> "He who is well-prepared to seize opportunities will win."

以虞待不虞者胜

It was mentioned earlier in this book that the Japanese used this approach in penetrating the U.S. market as well as exploiting opportunities that were opened to them. Today, they are still doing this. As mentioned before, while the South African and Vietnamese markets are widely ignored for political reasons, Japanese businessmen appear to have no qualms about their brisk presence in these countries. This is done in spite of the fact that the Japanese government also opposes the apartheid system in South Africa and is opposed to the Vietnamese intervention in Cambodia.

Besides creating and capitalizing on situations for victory, the wise general also ensures that he is in a position of non-defeat. Again, this requires the ability to create advantages for oneself:

> "Therefore, the adept in warfare ensures that he is in a position of non-defeat, while never missing the opportunity to defeat the enemy."

故善战者，立于不败之地，而不失敌之败也。

It is important at this juncture to point out that to ensure non-defeat, one must have a strong defence. One's vulnerability should never be exposed. For example, in the early years of the Japanese industrialization program, Japan never allowed foreign goods free entry to domestic markets. This was because she was very vulnerable to foreign competition at that time. It was only in the last five years that the Japanese market gradually opened up, and even so, at a very cautious pace. The same experiences can be said about the industrial strategies of both Taiwan and South Korea. They protected their local markets vigorously in order to ensure a non-defeat situation. Yet they have never hesitated to strike their economic "enemies" when the opportunities arose.

In sum, there is a need to find strategic advantages in order to ensure victory and achieve a non-defeat situation. This requires the use of both offensive and defensive strategies. Even when a seemingly effective strategy is adopted, there is still the need to explore strategic advantages. In the words of Sun Tzu:

> "If an advantageous strategy is already adopted, there is still a need to create advantageous situations so as to support its accomplishment. By "situations", I mean one must change according to the circumstances so as to obtain advantages."

计利以听，乃为之势，以佐其外。
势者，因利而制权也。

Carrying the analogy over to the business world there is also a need to search for strategic advantages. Indeed, this has taken on greater importance and significance for several reasons – many industries are maturing, competition is becoming stiffer, technology is fast changing, consumers are becoming more demanding, governmental controls are tighter. In fact, Porter's (1980) book on *Competitive Strategy* provides the tools and techniques for managers to conduct industry and competitor analyses with one main purpose – to find competitive edges. Three generic competitive strategies were advocated by him. **Overall cost leadership** should be pursued if the firm competes industrywide and has the advantages of low cost. To be successful in using this strategy, the firm must have efficient and large scale facilities, be prepared to pursue cost reduction through tight cost and overheads control, be willing to avoid marginal customer accounts, be capable of minimizing expenses in R&D, service, sales force, advertising and promotion, and so on. The bottom line is to achieve lower costs relative to the competitors.

The second generic strategy is that of **differentiating** the firm's product or service offering from the competitors so as to create something that is perceived as unique industrywide. Differentiation may take the form of grading, product features, distribution networks, technology or other dimensions.

The final generic strategy advocated by Porter (1980) is that of **focussing** on a particular buyer group, segment of the product line, or geographic market. Unlike the overall leadership and differentiation strategies which are aimed at the whole industry, the focus strategy is built around serving a particular target very well.

In another equally thought-provoking book, *Competitive Advantage*, Porter (1985) describes how firms can actually create and sustain a competitive advantage in their industry. In particular, he advocates the concept of **value chain** as a way of allowing the manager to separate the underlying activities a firm performs in designing, producing, marketing and distributing its product or services. According to Porter, though firms in the same industry may have similar chains (that is, the same collection of activities), the value chains of competitors often differ. For example, Singapore International Airlines and Air Canada both compete in the airline industry but they have different value chains embodying significant differences in crew policies, aircraft operations, choice of destinations, boarding gate operations, ticketing systems and so on. The differences among competitor value chains are a key source of competitive advantage. Thus, through value-chain analysis, the firm will be able to integrate all its activities so as to find competitive advantages.

Porter is not the only person who is concerned with finding competitive edges for a business. Abell (1975) and Leavitt (1965) have suggested that a firm's strategy should react according to the stage in the product life cycle. For example, in the mature stage, market positions have become established and the primary emphasis should be on nose-to-nose competition in the various segments of the market. The firm should therefore seek advantages in the areas of price competition, minor feature competition or promotional competition.

Kotler (1975) advocates that five factors would affect the way a firm can compete effectively through the use of either a **differentiated**, **undifferentiated**, or **concentrated** marketing strategy. If the company has limited resources, it should pursue a concentrated strategy. If there is substantial product homogeneity or market homogeneity, the firm should pursue an undifferentiated marketing strategy. At the early stage of the product life cycle, the firm should pursue an undifferentiated or concentrated strategy, while at a later stage of the life cycle, a differentiated strategy is more appropriate. Finally, if competitors are using segmented approaches to the market, the firm should adopt a differentiated or concentrated marketing strategy. While Kotler's orientation geared more towards marketing, it is interesting that his three strategies – differentiated, undifferentiated and concentrated – are very similar to those advocated by Michael Porter (1980).

Whatever different views may be forwarded by various scholars, one thing is very evident: for a firm to be successful, there is a need to search continually for strategic advantages. In fact, in an analysis of six organisations in the United States – United States Football League (USFL), Braniff International, F.W. Woolworth, De Lorean Motor Company, The Great Atlantic & Pacific Tea Company (A&P), and International Harvester – Clark (1987) showed that one of the main reasons for their failures was the lack of a competitive strategy. In other words, these six firms that failed did not seek out strategic advantages.

In contrast, Japanese companies never hesitate to look for opportunities to create strategic advantages. Their approach is never to focus on just competitive products or prices. Rather, they would focus their attention on a wide spectrum of factors, including their own core strengths. For example, NEC's focus on core competence, rather than the products in the marketplace, led them to invest heavily in chipmaking. The result is that it was able to switch more quickly than many of its competitors into new products like laptop computers and cellular phones. In the same way, Casio focussed on its competence in the areas of miniaturization and LCD-making skills. The result was that in 1974 they led a Japanese onslaught on the Swiss watchmakers (who were too concerned with more complex mechanical watches then) that had a telling effect on the watch industry. With basic digital watches being sold at less than half the price of cheap mechanical watches, the Japanese taught the Swiss watch industry a very painful lesson. It was only with the introduction of the fashionable, electronic Swatch watch in 1983 that the Japanese stampede was checked.

It is important to point out here again that the ability to create competitive advantages is very much premised on many other aspects of strategic planning that we have been talking about since the beginning of this book. In other words, it is not sufficient to just focus on one or two aspects, such as studying competitive products. Rather, one should go beyond that. For example, a firm will be more capable of finding strategic advantages if it has a better understanding and analysis of:

- Its corporate resources and skills (knowing yourself);
- Its competitors and their strengths and weaknesses (knowing the enemy);
- The market characteristics (knowing the terrain);
- The general business conditions (knowing the weather);
- The target market or customer group (the objective);
- Picking the right market or product/service to compete (choosing the right battleground); and
- The state of technology (something of value to yourself and the enemy).

Such understanding will enable the firm to differentiate its offerings more effectively from those of the competitors, as well as differentiate between its own offerings. Thus, it will be able to position its products or services in such a way so as to gain the maximum market share.

5.1.4 Strategic timing

Timing is one of the most important aspects of conducting war. This is because seasons and weather change depending on the time of the year. More specifically, timing will affect the exact moment to launch a military campaign and the type of strategy that can be used. For example, in conventional warfare, timing affects the following:

(1) The movement of troops and supplies. This can be done more easily during the dry season. In contrast, during the rainy season, the movement of troops and supplies can be greatly hampered. This was one of the difficulties faced by the American forces during the Vietnam war. In temperate countries where there is winter, the problem becomes even more serious.

(2) The deployment and equipping of troops. Depending on the weather and terrain, troops must be equipped and deployed very differently.

(3) The use of weapons. Some weapons are rendered ineffective because of changes of weather. In ancient times, the use of fire in attacks depended a lot on favorable wind direction and was effective especially during the hot, dry season. These conditions, however, do not prevail throughout the year. Thus, Sun Tzu said:

> "There are appropriate times and suitable days for launching attacks with fire."

发火有时，起火有日。

While Sun Tzu's comment was on the use of fire, it is interesting to note that in modern warfare, the use of some weapons is also affected by timing. For example, not all aircraft have night sighting capabilities and hence can only be operational during daylight hours. Similarly, many conventional weapons cannot be used at night and in foggy conditions.

(4) The exact moment of engagement. There are times when it is suitable to engage the enemy, while at other times it is better avoided:

> "In the early stages of a battle, the spirits of the forces are high; later, they will gradually flag. At the end stage, their spirits are low and thoughts of returning set in. Therefore, those adept in warfare avoid attacking the enemy when their spirits are high, but attack them when their spirits are sluggish and the soldiers homesick. This is control of the morale factor."

是故朝气锐，昼气惰，暮气归。
故善用兵者，避其锐气，击其惰气，此治气者也。

The ability to have the correct timing in order to secure victory would require that the general is always well-prepared and ready to seize whatever opportunities are opened to him:

> "When the strike of the falcon breaks the body of its prey, it is because of correct timing."

鸷鸟之疾，至于毁折者，节也。

Exact timing implies the ability to strike at the right moment. Thus, if one's attack is too early or too late, it is useless because the capture of any military target often requires precise timing. For example, air raids or artillery bombardment must precede the assaulting infantry; a beach-head must be quickly captured and well defended before the main force can land; and signals and communications must be established before the movement of troops. The sequence must be right, and the timing of contact must be exact.

In business, timing is equally important. In fact, it can affect the competitiveness of a firm. To quote Porter (1980, p. 144):

> "The costs of entry into a group can be affected by the firm's **timing of entry** into it. In some industries it may be more expensive for late entrants into a strategic group to establish their position (e.g., higher cost of establishing an equivalent brand name; higher cost of finding good distribution channels because of foreclosure channels by other firms). Or the situation may be reversed if newer entrants can purchase the latest equipment or use new technology. Differences in timing of entry may also translate into differences in cumulative experience and hence costs. Thus differences in timing of entry may translate into differences in sustainable profitability among members of the same strategic group."

Porter's view on the importance of timing was further reiterated in his 1985 book on *Competitive Advantage*. He argued that a firm may gain distinct advantages by being the first to take a particular action. For example, the first major brand in the market may often enjoy lower costs of establishing and maintaining a brand name (Porter 1985, p. 80). Gerber exploited this advantage in the baby food business in the United States. This is because experience in doing business is largely related to timing, and the earlier one enters a market, the earlier the learning or experience begins.

However, not every early entrant can enjoy advantages. There are times when the late entrants can also enjoy benefits like buying the latest machines and equipment and using the latest technology available. This is true in businesses that rely on computers and automation to give them competitive edge. By entering a market late, a firm can also avoid high market and/or product development costs. In the personal computer market for example, the early entrants had to educate consumers on the use of such products. The adoption process was slow, chiefly because of the initial high cost of the product and its relative unfamiliarity to the consumer. Consequently the early manufacturers had to do two things well in order to be successful: teach the consumers how to use the computer and bring the price down so as to encourage more adopters. Interestingly, both tasks are inter-related in that if the price is low, the consumer may be more willing to adopt the product but if the consumer is not familiar with the product, even a low price may not attract him. Thus, the early manufacturers of personal computers had to do product and market development at the same time – tasks that are neither easy to accomplish nor cheap to achieve!

There are also other advantages of being late. In the exploration business, late-comers can benefit from the mistakes made by the early explorers (for example, by avoiding areas which have been explored before). In the service industries such as airlines, the late-comers may also benefit from having a cheaper and younger workforce. In fact, this is one advantage that was enjoyed by People Express Airlines in the United States, when compared to established airlines like United and Pan Am where the workforces were not only senior but heavily unionized. Similarly, a firm's costs of operation can also be affected by when it recruits its workforce. In a recession, for example, wage rates tend to be lower and the workers are less interested in unionization. This was the case for the Singapore Mass Rapid Transit (SMRT). It recruited the bulk of its workforce during the recession in 1985/1986 when the wage costs were very low. Thus, it was able to enjoy lower operation costs when the MRT started running.

In business, everything ultimately boils down to the bottom-line. Higher profits can be achieved basically through increasing price or lowering cost. However, the timing of implementing either of these two measures is critical. In the words of Porter (1985, p. 80):

> "Timing's role in cost position may depend more on timing with respect to the business cycle or market conditions than on timing in absolute terms. For example, the timing of purchase of an offshore drilling rig in the industry's cycle strongly influences not only the interest cost but the purchase price of the rig. ODECO has purchased rigs during downturns when prices are depressed as an integral part of its cost leadership strategy. Depending on the value activity, then, timing can either raise or lower costs relative to competitors. Timing can lead to either sustainable cost advantage or a short-term cost advantage. A firm that has low cost assets because of fortuitous timing, for example, may find that the eventual need to replace those assets dramatically raises its relative cost position."

Besides the example of ODECO, Singapore International Airlines (SIA) is another company that capitalizes on fortuitous timing to acquire and expand its fleet of aircrafts. In March 1986 when the airline industry was in a recession and orders for the major aircraft manufacturers was at one of its lowest levels, SIA announced a record US$3.3 billion order for 20 new generation B747-400 aircraft! Of course, it had a relatively good bargain on the purchases. Besides making good purchases at the right time, SIA is also one of the very few airlines in the world that manages to sell its older aircrafts at a profit! In a nutshell, the timing of many management decisions, just as in war, can make or break a company.

5.2 Numerical evaluation

The subjective evaluation of the proposed strategy based on the four elements of strategic fit, target, advantage and timing, provides an indication of the strategy effectiveness with respect to the chances of victory. However, Sun Tzu did not stop at that. There is an objective way of assessing one's chances of victory – that of **numerical evaluation**:

> "Now the elements of the science of war are first, measurement of space; second, estimation of expenses; third, calculation of forces; fourth, weighing of possibilities; and fifth, planning for victory."

兵法: 一曰度, 二曰量, 三曰数,
　　　四曰称, 五曰胜;

Sun Tzu went on to elaborate on the relationships of these five aspects. It can be noted from the following quotations that there is a sequential order to the five elements:

> "Based on the characteristics of terrain, measurement of space is derived.
> Based on the measurement of space, estimation of expenses is made.
> Based on estimation of expenses, calculation of forces is made.
> Based on the calculation of forces, the possibilities for success and failure are weighed.
> Based on the weighing of possibilities, planning for victory begins."

地生度, 度生量,
量生数, 数生称,
称生胜。

5.2.1 *Measurement of space*

In war, before an army is dispatched, it is essential to study the enemy's terrain very carefully. Such a study would include the distance that the army has to traverse, the ease or difficulty of the movement, the directness of routes to be taken, the nature and type of terrain involved and any other characteristics relating to the terrain. This is because the space factor would affect how fast troops and weapons can be moved, the types of deployment that can be used, the kinds of military tactics and strategies to be applied. In addition, the terrain characteristics will also affect military supplies, logistics and communications.

The importance of this space factor applies not just to ancient wars. Even today, in modern conventional warfare, any effective battle plan is built from thorough reports from the intelligence officers, of which detailed analysis of the terrain forms a critical and prominent component.

5.2.2 *Estimation of expenses*

Based on a good understanding of terrain characteristics, the scope (that is, the extent of physical terrain involved) of the military campaign can be determined. Inevitably, if the scope is very large, expenses are bound to be high. This is because if an army needs to travel long distances, more men, equipment and supplies are needed. Long distances also imply longer duration for the campaign, adding further to the total expenses involved. The high costs of the spatial and temporal dimensions of war were recognized explicitly by Sun Tzu:

> "The reason why a country can be impoverished by military operations is because of distant transportation; the carriage of supplies over long distances will render the people destitute."

国之贫于师者远输，远输则百姓贫。

> "When the army engages in protracted campaigns, the resources of the state will be impoverished."

久暴师则国用不足。

The cost of the campaign will play an important role in determining whether the military campaign should carry on. Sun Tzu was very conscious of the economic strains that an army can impose on the warring state:

> "Close to where the army is, prices are bound to go up. High prices will drain the wealth of the people. When the wealth is depleted, heavier taxes will have to be urgently levied."

近于师者贵卖，贵卖则百姓财竭，财竭则急于丘役。

> "With energy exhausted and wealth consumed, innumerable homes will be impoverished."

力屈、财殚，中原内虚于家。

According to Sun Tzu, this depletion of wealth and resources could amount to 70% of the total possessions of the people. In addition, government expenditure on repair and maintenance of the equipment needed for war could take up as much as 60% of its total revenue.

The high inflation rate and high expenses that accompany a nation in a state of war are still very valid today. For example, when Israel was heavily involved in the Middle-East war in the 1970s, she experienced double and triple digit inflation rates. In addition, her defense expenditure was very high in relation to her gross national product. The Iran-Iraq war also demonstrated such consequences; the high military involvement and expenses brought about high inflation rates, food shortages and widespread poverty among their people.

The realization of the high costs involved in military campaigns led Sun Tzu to advocate that:

> "Those adept in warfare do not require a second levy of conscripts nor more than the required supplies. The necessary military supplies are brought from home and they live by foraging on the enemy. In this way, the army will always be sufficient with food and supplies."

善用兵者，役不再籍，粮不三载；
取用于国，因粮于敌，故军食可足也。

> "Therefore, the wise general sees to it that his troops feed on the enemy, for one cartload of the enemy's provisions is equal to twenty of his own; and one picul of the enemy's fodder to twenty piculs of his own."

故智将务食于敌，食敌一钟，
当吾二十钟；蒠秆一石，当吾二十石。

Thus, by living off the enemy's resources and supplies, the wise general not only cuts down the expenses of his own army, but at the same time increases the costs to the enemy. In this way, he can probably sustain a longer campaign and also fight in more and wider territories.

5.2.3 Calculation of forces

If a country has plentiful resources, it may be possible to dispatch a larger force with more weapons, better supplies and support systems for war. However, if resources are limited, and if the general insists on fighting, then he must make do with a smaller and hopefully a more select force, fewer supplies and weapons. Also, the general will have have to cope with greater constraints if he wants to travel long distances and fight in distant ground.

The size of the available budget does affect military commitment. For example, the Soviet Union finally recognized in early 1988 that her military involvement in Afghanistan was taking a very high toll on her nation's economy as well as the army. This was because the theater of operations was not only unfamiliar to them, but was very large and wide. The weather was harsh, and the terrain was very difficult – factors working against the Russians. To win decisively, the Russians would probably have had to pour in many more resources and military personnel, a course of action that they could not afford to undertake, especially with an ailing economy at home. They therefore took a most rational decision: gradual pullout from Afghanistan.

5.2.4 Weighing the possibilities for success and failure

With a given strength, supplies and weapons for a military campaign, the general must now weigh his chances of success. To do so, he has to compare the strengths and weaknesses of his army with those of the enemy. Such strengths and weaknesses are also very much affected by the nature and type of terrain that his army is operating in, the climatic conditions, the firing and combat power available, and the quality of training. Again, taking the example of the Soviet intervention in Afghanistan, although the former had strengths in terms of combat power, such advantages were eroded when they had to fight in very harsh terrain and weather. The result was that the Russians were never able to score decisive victories. In fact, the Soviet encounter was very much a repeat of the American involvement in the Vietnam War in the 1960s and 1970s.

The weighing of possibilities for success and failure is very similar to doing a SWOT (strengths, weaknesses, opportunities and threats) analysis as mentioned in Chapter 2. The difference is that at this stage, SWOT analysis is carried out to ascertain the effectiveness of one's strategy, the decision to engage in combat having already been taken.

5.2.5 Planning for victory

From the comparison of relative strengths and weaknesses, one can therefore determine one's chances of victory through the application of appropriate strategies. Here, it is important to point out that effective strategies help to secure victories. However, to begin with, there must be possibilities for winning. If such a possibility does not exist, there is no point in planning for victory.

Planning for victory therefore gets into the details of allocation of tasks and responsibilities and how resources would be committed. It is the stage of deciding *who* should do *what, where, when*, and *how* to go about executing the plan. In essence, it is the implementation stage.

5.2.6 An example of numerical evaluation

A very good recent example illustrating the five related dimensions of numerical evaluation in war is the Falklands Campaign. After the Falkland Islands were invaded rather suddenly by Argentinian forces on 2 April 1982, the British army made a detailed study of the situation before launching their counter-attack to re-capture the islands.

First, the area of operation had to be carefully studied. The Falkland Islands lie 8,000 miles south-west of the United Kingdom and over 3,500 miles from Ascension Island, but only 400 miles from the Argentinian mainland. The islands are characterized by very difficult terrain in inhospitable conditions, and the weather in the islands is unpredictable and harsh. Moreover, the occupied islands in which combat had to take place were not exactly small. For example, the distance from one end of the East Falkland to the other is almost 50 miles (from San Carlos to Port Stanley). In addition, the narrow stretch of waters separating the East and West Islands – Falkland Sound – makes any approaching ship an easy target for air and land fire.

Upon understanding the characteristics of the terrain, and taking into account the distance involved, detailed measurement of space was considered. It was strictly an out-of-area operation, and the massive area of coverage involved dictated that all the three major arms – navy, air and land forces – had to play equally important and well coordinated roles. The task force had to be assembled very quickly. It had to be stocked and provisioned for at least three months at sea. Even for the aircraft involved, air-to-air refuelling had to be considered. Indeed, the British knew from the very outset that it was going to be an expensive campaign. One source estimated that the improvements and modifications made for the various equipment used for the forces alone exceeded 200 million British pounds (The Falklands Campaign 1982). This figure excluded the costs of weaponry, ships, aircrafts and other essential basic items. Thus, the campaign could not be justified on the basis of economic sense. Margaret Thatcher, the British prime minister, justified her military campaign to the British public on the basis of moral necessity – the rescue of British subjects in distress, the protection of British sovereignty and the restoration of freedom and democracy for the Falklanders.

Once the area of operation was understood, the cause justified and the cost estimated, the British had to assemble their task force. This itself was no easy job. Eventually, within a space of seven weeks, a task force of 28,000 men, over 110 ships (including 44 warships, 22 from the Royal Fleet Auxiliary, and 45 merchant ships with volunteer civilian crews), over 95 aircraft, almost 200 helicopters, various weaponry and ammunition, supplies and other provisions were assembled for the campaign. It is important to point out that various Special Forces like the Special Air Service and the Special Boat Squadron of the Royal Marines were also included to handle the hostile demands imposed by the terrain of the Falkland Islands.

It was obvious that the British calculated their forces requirements on the basis of the scope of operations and the distance involved. In addition, they had to be prepared for contingencies. Unlike the Argentinians whose reinforcements were only 400 miles away, the British had to fight the war 8,000 miles away from home. Thus, calculations were critical to the success of the campaign.

It was apparent to the British that, apart from the spatial and temporal disadvantages, they had the upper-hand in terms of superiority of forces and fire power. For example, they had more superior warships; they knew that their 28 Sea Harriers (fighter aircrafts intended largely for air defense but able to be employed in ground attacks and reconnaissance roles) and 14 RAF Harrier GR3s (fighter aircrafts primarily for ground attacks), after being converted to use Side-winder AIM 9L air-to-air missiles, were far superior to the Argentinian conventional fixed wing fighter aircraft; their land weaponry was superior; their surveillance systems were better; their communications networks well established; and their men highly trained. In addition, they also understood the threat posed by the sea-skimming Exocet missile, and counter-measures to deal with it were available to the task force.

At the very outset, therefore, the British knew that their chances for victory were good. Plans were accordingly made to secure victory. Indeed, history has shown that within a period of seven weeks a task force of 28,000 men was assembled, sailed 8,000 miles, and effectively neutralized the Argentinian navy. It fought off persistent and courageous enemy combat aircraft which outnumbered it six-to-one. Furthermore, it successfully put ashore 10,000 men and fought several fierce battles against an entrenched and well supplied enemy who outnumbered them at all times. Despite having fewer men, the British won the war very decisively and forced General Menendez of Argentina to surrender on 14 June 1982, barely two-and-a-half months after the Falkland Islands were invaded. In fact, the actual combat for the recapture took only three-and-a-half weeks. What was more remarkable was that the British also captured 11,400 Argentinian prisoners of war! Such achievements were made possible because the British were able to take into account the elements of the science of war.

5.3 Business applications

Numerical evaluation applies very much in business as well. Terrain characteristics represent the various aspects of the market place in which the firm operates or intends to operate. A good understanding of the market is very important. For example, what kinds of opportunities and threats are there? Does it provide easy access to raw materials, cheap and efficient labor, capital markets, supplies of machines and equipment, managerial skills and talents, technology, research and development, consumer markets, and so on. In addition, does the market have good infrastructural facilities, services and other support systems? Is it highly regulated and influenced by the government? What is the market structure like, and the nature of competition? All these are but some major market characteristics that will affect how the firm can compete. This part of the analysis is basically doing a situation appraisal.

5.3.1 Defining one's business (measurement of space)

Having understood the market characteristics, the firm can now decide its intended area of operation (measurement of space). This is defining at a very basic level what business it wants to be in. According to Abell (1980), defining the business should be the starting point of strategic planning. Over the years, there have been contrasting views about what constitutes the starting point of planning. In the late 1960s and early 1970s, the common view was that the starting point of planning for a business is the definition of objectives. Once objectives are decided upon, the other functional plans like marketing, manufacturing, research and development, and financing will follow.

During that period, marketing share objectives such as the decision to hold, harvest, or build market share featured prominently in many corporate plans. Such emphasis was not surprising at that time, as there was much widely publicized and recognized research that showed the importance of market share as a determinant of profitability (e.g. Schoeffler, Buzzell and Heany 1974; Buzzell, Gale and Sultan 1975).

The contrasting view to focussing on marketing share objectives was put forward by Drucker (1974, p. 611) who advocated that the prime task of top management should be:

> "... the task of thinking through the mission of the business, that is, of asking the question 'what is our business and what should it be?' This leads to the setting of objectives, the development of strategies and plans, and the making of today's decisions for tomorrow's results."

The argument against reliance on market share objectives is understandable. Market share is the result of effective strategy formulation and implementation, not the strategy itself. Rather, business strategy should depend on defining a business in a way that can lead to competitive edges and superiority in the eyes of the consumers. Drucker's view on defining the business first is also shared by Levitt (1960) and Tilles (1969). Tilles (1969) gave the example of how some tin companies in the United States, as a result of re-defining their business from cans to tins, found themselves facing a completely different set of competitors and opportunities. As such, different strategies had to be developed.

Various authors have suggested different ways to define one's business. Ansoff (1965), for example, suggested that changes in business definition can be conceptualized in the two conventional dimensions of the firm's product/market environment. This view is shared by Corey and Star (1971). However, Abell (1980) suggested that a business can be defined along three dimensions – customer groups, customer functions and alternative technologies. While there may be differences as to how a business should be defined, one thing is certain – the way it is defined will affect how strategies will be formulated and how competitive the firm may become (Levitt 1960).

To reiterate, the way a firm chooses to define its business – for example, automated office systems rather than photocopiers, communication-based systems rather than computers, transportation vehicles rather than cars – will automatically dictate how it has to compete. The wider the scope of definition (the bigger the space of operation), the more difficult it is to compete as it has to contend with more competitors. At the same time, more resources will have to be committed. In other words, it will be more costly to compete. For this reason, a detailed and careful situation appraisal must precede business definition as it will show what can or cannot be achieved. The measurement of space need not be confined to the definition of business at the firm's level. Even at the macro level of the state, it can also define the scope of operation. For example, a country can decide whether to produce mainly for the local market, or to compete internationally in various other markets as well. If the latter option is taken, it must also decide which markets it wants to enter, and how many such markets it wants to penetrate. In other words, the scope of operation has to be defined. Japan, for example, chose to concentrate on the domestic market in her initial stages of industrial development. It was when she gained enough experience from the local market that she launched her international offensive. Even then, she chose to concentrate on selected markets and regions before deciding on competing globally. Japan succeeded, among other reasons, because of her ability to define her area of competition.

5.3.2 *Estimation of financial strengths or expenses*

Once the business is defined, an estimation of available financial resources will have to be made. This estimation is important as it will determine how capably the firm can carry out its mission. Now the order here is very important. It is tempting to argue that estimation of financial resources should be made before business definition. While this may appear pragmatic and logical, it is unfortunately inhibitive and myopic. This is because if financial resources are "audited" beforehand, they can easily become constraints. In practice, it is possible to source for additional financial resources after the business is defined. For example, the firm can always borrow more money, raise more capital through issuing new shares, secure more loans through pledging their assets or selling them, invite new corporate partners or investors and so on. Thus, while it is true that there is a limit to the raising of financial resources and that it can affect how the firm can compete, it is also equally possible to overcome some of the financial constraints.

Even at the macro level of a nation, financial resources can be raised through the sale of national assets, imposition of higher taxes (though such measures are never well received by the public), encouragement of greater voluntary savings, institutionalizing compulsory savings, or a combination of such measures. It is interesting to note that countries that experienced economic successes in recent years – such as Japan, Taiwan, South Korea, and Singapore are distinguished by a very high savings rate. Such savings allow them to channel the funds to more investments (such as factories and various manufacturing infrastructures) which not only increase their competitiveness, but also widen their scope for international competition.

The use of national savings for economic development purposes is best illustrated by the case of Singapore. The government of Singapore clearly recognized that to develop economically, it needed the necessary financial resources. However, to rely on the natural forces of voluntary savings would be a slow process. It thus instituted the Central Provident Fund (CPF) Scheme in 1955 with the purpose of providing the workers with retirement funds. However, over the years, as a result of imposing high contribution rates on both employers and employees, the government has been able to raise substantial savings that were used for economic development. This was possible because in the early years of the scheme, there was not much withdrawal of funds for retirement or other purposes by the contributors. Thus, the "great leap forward" was possible as a result of wise decisions on the part of the Singapore government. It had never let financial constraints dictate the fate of the country.

In the same way, when the Singapore government decided that it was timely and necessary to embark on economic restructuring so as to increase Singapore's international competitiveness, it set up the Skills Development Fund (SDF) in October 1979. The SDF was instituted with the basic aim of upgrading the skills of the employee and retraining retrenched or redundant workers. The approach was very simple. First, decide what is to be accomplished. Then, raise the necessary financial resources to help accomplish it. Financial resources were never considered a constraint.

5.3.3 Calculation of resources

Without doubt, a firm with larger financial outlay will be able to accomplish much more than another with lesser financial muscle. The financially stronger firm will be able to hire more and better skilled workers and managers, buy newer and better machines and equipment, import or license the latest technology and production techniques, source for more, cheaper and better materials, and access more and newer markets. Thus, it is able to assemble a better force for combat. In other words, it is able to acquire the critical mass that is so necessary as a prerequisite for success.

Conversely, a firm with limited financial resources will have to decide how best it can compete under those constraints. Fortunately, just like in war where sheer numbers alone do not translate into definite advantages, in business it is also possible for the smaller firm to survive and compete effectively if:

1. It can find the appropriate niche(s);
2. It can concentrate its resources on those few areas where it can excel most;
3. It constantly seeks to differentiate its offerings from those of the competitors;
4. It focuses more on quality than quantity, whether in the area of its workforce, services or products.

Just like the firm, a nation that has more wealth and resources will be in a better position to compete. However, it does not mean that the smaller and poorer nations will not be able to survive. Japan has hardly any natural resources, and the same is the case of Singapore. Both are not large nations. Yet, both have succeeded so far. The reason is that they have never allowed their constraints to handicap them. Given whatever they have – and they basically have only human resources – they have carved out their respective places in the world economy because they knew what they could and must achieve to survive. In the case of Japan, what started out as niches have become so large that in many industries the Japanese are now world leaders.

The growth in wealth of the Japanese over the years has been phenomenal. In fact, in 1987, Japan invested US$14.7 billion in the United States – a subject of concern among some Americans – in anticipation of the benefits to be derived from the US-Canada free-trade agreement (they knew what they wanted). Japanese investments in Canada also more than doubled for that year. The Japanese also embarked on investment in foreign stocks and shares. In 1987, it spent US$20 billion on foreign equities – more than the amount invested in the 30-year period from 1951 to 1980! It is estimated that its foreign equities probably exceeded US$70 billion as of 1988. Thus, with more resources today, especially in the area of finance, the Japanese are able to pursue many other options that few other nations in the world can match.

5.3.4 *Weighing chances for success*

A good CEO, like the general in war, must weigh the chances of victory in business. Can his strategy be successful? Much of the answer comes from a good understanding of his available resources (knowing himself) *vis-a-vis* those of the competitors. In every non-monopolistic situation, the firm does not operate in a vacuum. Competitive forces change all the time. While marginal competitors are weeded out, new competitors emerge. It is a dynamic situation. At the same time, changes in environment, that is changes in government, laws and regulations and changes in technology, may also provide the impetus for new and perhaps even non-traditional competitors. For example, as a result of the advent of the computer chip, the product and market boundaries of watches, calculators, radios, and other smaller electronic items have become blurred and overlapping. Today, many of these products perform similar functions (like time-telling and calculating) and compete in overlapping markets.

A strategy that is successful in one situation may become a failure in another when competitive and environmental forces change. Thus, each time a strategy is formulated, the CEO must re-evaluate his chances for victory and defeat. It is, therefore, not surprising that many firms use various forecasting techniques and sensitivity analysis to assess the impact of changing scenarios on their business performance. The "what if" analysis should be an integral part of the planning process.

Just like the firm, a nation's chances of succeeding must be weighed against its available resources. Can it go on a high-technology path when it has not enough engineers, scientists, computer experts and analysts? Can it ever be a world financial and communication center if it does not enjoy the strategic temporal and spatial advantages in location? Can it be a large manufacturing nation if it does not have access to materials and supplies, and have the necessary trained manpower? These are important questions that need to be answered. Nations like Japan, South Korea, Taiwan and Singapore that have succeeded in getting out of the poverty trap understand the kinds of options that are available and the chances of success.

However, over the years, these nations also understood that the strategies that made them successful in the earlier years may not be relevant today. Japan knew that the labor-intensive industries that propelled their early economic growth must be discarded once labor wages increased and when their competitive advantages were lost to emerging, newly industrializing countries like South Korea and Taiwan. Thus, they have pursued an industrial policy that is similar to the concept of planned obsolescence used in product planning. Industries that were no longer competitive, like textiles, and shipbuilding and repairing were deliberately phased out.

The economic structure of Singapore is also undergoing similar changes. Businesses that are losing competitive advantages to countries like Thailand, Malaysia and Indonesia are being phased out. New and higher level investments such as computer hardware and software are now being courted with earnest. Only in these higher level technological areas can Singapore maintain an edge over other newly industrializing countries. At the same time, Singapore's wages are still relatively lower than the advanced countries, providing the edge for companies to be sited here. If Singapore's industrial policy had remained the same as in the 1960s and 1970s, the chances for success in the future would be greatly threatened. In fact, it would probably fail miserably.

5.3.5 Tactics and functional plans (planning for victory)

It is only when a strategy is carefully defined, thought out and assessed that tactics and functional plans make sense. While strategy formulation is very much an art, tactics and functional plans (which essentially implement the strategy) are a science. For example, a firm may decide that the best strategy to expand its market share is through acquisition of other smaller companies. The tactic decided upon may involve setting up another company to do the acquisitions and that acquisitions be done through exchange of shares rather than cash payment.

Just as in war, planning for victory in business involves making decisions on:

1. Who should be doing the job(s)?
2. What does it involve?
3. When should it be carried out?
4. Why is it important that it be carried out?
5. Where should it be carried out?
6. Which is the best way to do it?
7. How should it be done?

For a nation, planning for victory will involve all the necessary actions that will help it compete effectively in the world market. While the national strategies adopted by different nations for economic development may be similar, the ways they choose to accomplish them may be very different. For example, one country may decide to industrialize by relying more on local entrepreneurs and business, while for another, as in the case of Singapore, it may decide to rely more on foreign companies, especially the multinational companies. In this case, the government will have to produce various incentives and assistance programs to ensure that it can attract the necessary foreign investments. At the same time, government rules and regulations must be conducive to the conduct of business, infrastructure must be in place, government agencies must be cooperative and helpful, the work force must be disciplined and well-trained and the total investment and business climate must be cordial. This is because, unlike local businessmen, foreign investors are much more mobile and would not hesitate to shift their investments to cheaper and more attractive places.

Even for countries pursuing a policy of reliance on foreign investors, different tactics may be adopted to attract the investments. Some may rely on low wages and costs of production, some may rely on access to raw materials, some may rely on better infrastructure, some may rely on availability of markets (demand), some may rely on more flexible rules and regulations on repatriation of earnings and profits, and so on. In essence, while the end result that is wanted may be the same, the means adopted may differ significantly.

6 *Implementation of strategies: The human factor*

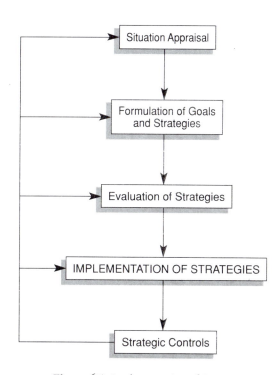

Figure 6.1 Implementation of Strategies

6.1 Introduction

Thus far, we have discussed situation appraisal, formulation of goals and strategies and evaluation of strategies. The next stage is the implementation of strategies which implies going to war or combat (see Figure 6.1). Here, it is important again to emphasize that Sun Tzu would prefer that open combat be avoided and only used as a measure of last resort. If combat is unavoidable, it is important that one must ensure one's invulnerability. In his words:

> "Thus, the victorious army creates opportunities for winning before it engages the enemy. The defeated army engages the enemy first before looking for chances of winning."

是故胜兵先胜而后求战，败兵先战而后求胜。

Invulnerability to defeat can be attained through careful and detailed prior combat preparations and planning and by the strategy implementation stage, whereby all factors which may influence the outcome of the battle have already been taken into account and are incorporated into the strategy to be applied. Implementation consists of two parts: the **human** element, and the **operational** element. The former involves clear understanding of the various roles and responsibilities of the various parties involved in the combat mission. The latter relates to certain principles that are required to ensure successful accomplishment of the mission. In this chapter, the human factor will be discussed, while Chapter 7 will continue discussion on the operational aspects of the implementation of strategies.

Without doubt, one over-riding principle underlying the human aspects of strategy implementation is that of *unity*. To win wars, there must be unity of minds and hearts from the ruler to the subjects of the state. In particular, those who are directly involved in combat must be united in purpose and be one accord in order to achieve victory. For example, it was mentioned in the previous chapter that the British were able to find a moral cause for re-capturing the Falklands Islands. This moral cause helped to unite the people, the military and the government. Hence, the British campaign was made easier as they had only to fight on one front – the enemy – instead of also having to contend with opposition at home. In war, three parties are especially important – the sovereign (ruler), the commanders (generals and senior military officers), and the army (soldiers).

6.2 Sovereign

In Chapter 2 we discussed the importance of the moral influence of the ruler in war. Sun Tzu defined this as:

> "... that which enables the people to be in perfect accord and harmony with the ruler, for which they are willing to accompany him to life and death without the fear of dangers."

令民与上同意也，故可以与之死，可以与之生，而不畏危。

In our business analogy this is equivalent to the political leadership of a nation. Here, we would deal in greater detail with additional aspects of the roles of the ruler; what he should or should not do. To begin with, Sun Tzu said:

> "He whose generals are able and not interfered with by the ruler will win."

将能而君不御者胜。

This clearly means that if the ruler has capable generals to fight the war for him, then he should not interfere with the military operations. It explicitly recognizes that there is a division of roles between the political sovereign and the military commander. In addition it assumes, rightly, that the ruler in most instances will not have sufficient expertise to deal with the military aspects which is a very specialized discipline. Such matters are best left to the general who is the expert in war. Furthermore, the ruler is normally not in the field of battle and will not have the first-hand and up-to-date infor-mation about the latest developments in battle conditions and so is not qualified to decide on the direction of the battle. In addition the embattled army does not have the luxury of time on their side to wait for delayed instructions from the sovereign. This problem was particularly true in ancient times when there were no modern communication facilities. The situation was even more acute if the army was fighting in distant ground. To put it simply, once the war begins the best person to call the shots is the most senior person closest to the field of action – in this case, the military commander or general.

This policy of political non-intervention in the conduct of war was clearly advocated by Sun Tzu when he highlighted that there are three ways in which the sovereign can bring misfortune to his army:

"When ignorant that the army should not advance, to order an advance; when ignorant that the army should not retreat, to insist on a retreat. This is interference with military command."

不知军之不可以进，而谓之进；
不知军之不可以退，而谓之退；是谓縻军。

"When ignorant of the internal affairs of the military, to participate and interfere with its administration. This causes officers and men to be perplexed."

不知三军之事，而同三军之政者，则军士惑矣。

"When ignorant of matters relating to the exercise of military authority, to interfere in the execution of responsibilities and command. This creates doubts in the minds of officers and men."

不知三军之权而同三军之任，则军士疑矣。

The net result of such interferences was also predicted by Sun Tzu:

"If the army is confused and suspicious, the neighboring states will surely create trouble. This is like the saying: A confused army provides victory for the enemy."

三军既惑且疑，则诸侯之难至矣，是谓乱军引胜。

Thus, rather than interfering in the affairs of the military, the sovereign should leave it to the general so as not to create doubt and confusion. The logic is actually quite simple – if the ruler has already appointed the general, he must have enough faith in him to let him carry out his assignment. Otherwise, it defeats the purpose of the appointment. However, it is also important to point out that Sun Tzu did not advocate total abandonment of responsibilities on the part of the sovereign in all circumstances. Note that he highlighted that the generals must be able to justify non-intervention from the ruler. In addition, he prefixed the three possible disasters of intervention with the words, "when ignorant". In other words, if the sovereign was well versed in the art of warfare, he might even lead the army into war. This was so in the case of the warlords in ancient China. However, if the sovereign had no knowledge in warfare, he must adopt a 'hands-off' policy and allow his generals to fight the war for him. In such a situation, the ruler may confine his role to the appointment of capable generals and the initial setting of war objectives and plans:

> "Hence, it is said that enlightened rulers deliberate plans while capable generals execute them."

明主虑之，良将修之。

To make the war a successful one, the appointment of the general(s) must be based on the ability and skills of the candidates. If the appointment is politically motivated, the general is likely to toe the line of the ruler, and is less likely to exercise his professional judgment effectively. Another problem with political appointments is that they may not result in getting the best candidate for the task. Finally, such an appointee may not command the respect of the rank and file, making the job of accomplishing the objectives even more difficult. At its worst, it may lead to chaos and confusion among officers and men, which in turn may lead to defeat of the army in battle.

In summary then, though the sovereign will have to approve the conduct of war after taking into consideration the four conditions to wage war – definite advantages to be gained, strong assurance of victory, war as a measure of last resort, and defense invincibility – and participate in the initial war plans, especially in defining its objectives, the general should be given full authority to decide on how the war should be conducted.

Applying Sun Tzu's concept of non-intervention to business would imply that the government should subscribe to a *laissez-faire* system if it does not have the necessary skills to run business entities. As far as possible, the government should not be involved in business operations that compete directly with the private sector. Rather, it should confine its role to the construction of infrastructures like building roads, railways and other transport systems; the setting up of communication networks like telephones; and the provision of utilities like water and electricity. In addition, it must ensure the existence of favorable conditions for the achievement of economic prosperity and progress. This can be attained through the enactment of equitable laws and regulations to facilitate business operations, the setting of national economic policies and objectives so as to chart the general direction for growth and the attraction of foreign investments.

In essence, the role of government should be to facilitate and assist the growth of business (so as to achieve national economic growth) and not to directly manage them – especially when it has no expertise. This is because business firms are driven by profits, and to

Table 6.1 Economic Performance of World's Top 20 Countries

Rank	Country	Overall economic performance 1988–1990	Projection for real GDP growth, 1988	Average GDP annual 1980–1986
1	Japan	8.36%	4.03%	3.7
2	Korea	8.05%	9.11%	8.2
3	Taiwan	7.66%	7.29%	NA
4	Hong Kong	7.41%	7.13%	6.0
5	Switzerland	7.18%	1.90%	1.5
6	Singapore	7.01%	6.53%	5.3
7	United Kingdom	7.01%	3.08%	2.3
8	Luxembourg	7.00%	1.70%	NA
9	Thailand	6.83%	6.45%	4.8
10	West Germany	6.83%	2.07%	1.5
11	Canada	6.82%	3.04%	2.9
12	Spain	6.56%	4.04%	1.8
13	China	6.54%	7.63%	10.5
14	Finland	6.51%	2.78%	2.7
15	Netherlands	6.41%	1.56%	1.0
16	France	6.28%	1.81%	1.3
17	USA	6.26%	2.71%	3.1
18	Austria	6.21%	1.54%	1.8
19	Sweden	6.15%	1.92%	2.0
20	Malaysia	6.05%	4.20%	4.8

Source: Euromoney Survey, reported in Singapore *Straits Times* on 14th October 1988

achieve them they have to adopt the most effective and efficient measures, which at times would require very quick and drastic changes and actions. In contrast, a government is often constrained by multiple objectives, including welfare-oriented goals, which often retard the decision-making process and result in compromise solutions rather than optimal ones.

While it is not possible to find a truly *laissez-faire* nation, it is significant to note that in countries where the government adopts an assisting and facilitating posture, the country tends to perform better economically. In fact, looking at Table 6.1, it is very apparent that 19 of the top 20 countries that were projected to have the highest economic performance from 1988 to 1990 subscribe basically to the concept of the market-driven economy; that is, they allow market forces to dictate economic growth with minimal direct involvement from the government in the running of business enterprises. Even in the case of China, the only member of the group which subscribes to a centrally planned economy, healthy growth rates have only been achieved after following an open door policy and allowing market forces to play a more dominant role.

While among these 20 countries some governments like Japan, Taiwan and South Korea are more active in assisting and facilitating the conduct of businesses than others, there are also others that prosper with minimal governmental assistance. A good example is the case of Hong Kong whose colonial government provides the least assistance to local businesses and probably adopts the most *laissez-faire* system in its attitude toward business development. Yet, the Hong Kong economy has been thriving and prospering for many years. In fact, even with the prospect of its return to China in 1997, there appears to be no serious dampening effect on its economy. This is because when left alone, there is no lack of entrepreneurship and business vitality among the business people in Hong Kong.

It is also important to point out that the governments of these 20 countries did, at some point in history, get involved in the direct operations of businesses. For example, in the United Kingdom, the government had to come to the rescue of some industries in the 1970s when they ran into financial difficulties. In other instances, such as the case of Chrysler in the United States, the government had to provide substantial federal loans to prevent the collapse of the company. In Canada, the government operated Air Canada in order to serve the geographically disperse population. However, the governments in such countries do not hesitate to sell government-owned companies when the opportunity arises. Among other reasons for doing so, many government-owned companies in these countries are not making money.

In recent years, many governments in the developed countries have begun to realize the need to adopt a non-intervention policy in order to generate greater business efficiency and economic growth. In Britain, the ruling Conservative Party of the Thatcher government at its October 1988 convention mentioned that there were no limits to its policy of returning state-owned firms to the private sector. Besides the already privatized British Petroleum Company, they had plans to privatize steel, water utilities, electricity and even coal. Other countries like Canada and the United States have also moved in the same direction of involving the private sector to take over the running of traditionally key industries. In fact, privatization is fast becoming a buzz word in such countries and has taken so much prominence that some quarters in the United States are also considering privatizing their prisons! This mood of involving the private sector is motivated very much by the fact that these governments have begun to realize that private firms are much more responsive to market forces and would not hesitate to make quick and swift changes that will benefit profit making.

The recognition that the private sector will do an overall better job than the government in operating businesses is also realized by the Singapore government. Despite running many government companies successfully and profitably over the years, the Singapore government recognized the importance and need of adopting a more non-interfering policy. In the earlier years of its industrial development, the government of Singapore set up hundreds of companies that spanned a very wide cross-section of industries to spearhead economic growth. This was because at that time the private sector did not have sufficient capital and expertise to carry out such a massive and comprehensive task. Beginning in the 1980s, having achieved its initial objectives, the government has embarked on a very remarkable effort of systematically privatizing its companies, including Singapore Airlines, Singapore Press Holdings, Resource Development Corporation, RMCA Re-insurance, Singapore Re-insurance and many others – all highly profitable companies. Such efforts are possible because the Singapore government believes fundamentally that it should not be too involved in the running of businesses that can be operated by the private sector. Thus, while other governments privatize their companies because they are inefficient and unprofitable, the Singapore government does it on grounds of basic principle.

In contrast to the market economies of the world, most centrally-planned economies have performed poorly, and today, many of them remain among the poorest nations of the world. As shown in Table 6.1, with the exception of China, none of the others are ranked in the world's top 20 highest growth countries. In addition, as pointed out earlier, China only achieved her high economic growth rates after adopting an open door policy from 1978. In fact, her success has prompted other centrally-planned economies like the Soviet Union, Romania, and Poland to adopt more moderate measures. These countries have begun to "decentralize" more of their decision-making on business operations and other economic issues to organizations closer to the ground. In addition, they have tried to allow some form of market economy to exist.

In fact as a result of the collapse of the Berlin Wall on 9 November 1989, the countries in eastern Europe have experienced a dramatic shift towards Western type free market economies. The winds of change have swept across many of these countries from Poland, Romania,

Hungary to even the USSR where some provinces are now lobbying for a more open market economy. Perhaps the most significant development must be the move towards reunification of East and West Germany. When this is complete the previously communist East Germany will be immersed in one of the most modern and dynamic economies of the western world.

An interesting case of a centrally-planned economy reversing its priorities is that of Vietnam. When South Vietnam was taken over by the North in the mid-1970s, a lot of businessmen were persecuted, jailed and even killed for their pro-capitalist activities. However, barely a decade later, the Hanoi government found that their version of a centrally-planned economy had brought nothing but economic depression and widespread poverty to the nation. This was because they knew little about running businesses and operating the economy. After years of scorning and despising the businessmen and the market economy, they paid a very high price for it – many of their local entrepreneurs left as boat people. Today, the Vietnamese government is beginning to be more market-oriented and is encouraging the people to start businesses. Ironically, in their search for business talents, they turned to the city which they despised most because of its capitalistic past – Saigon.

It remains the case, however, that despite recognizing the merits of a non-interventionist policy, many governments still fall prey to it for political reasons. For example, many industries in Britain and the United States are definitely ailing and no longer competitive internationally (for example, the printing and textile industries). However, their governments have to yield to political pressures and enact laws or adopt various measures to protect such sunset and dying industries at very high costs to their nations. The net result is that there is more confusion and disagreement among various parties involved and the consumer ends up paying for it in terms of higher prices. Perhaps, this is best illustrated in the case of the Japanese farmers. Owing to their strong political lobbying, the Japanese farmers have succeeded over the years in preventing the importation of foreign beef, meat, dairy products, vegetables and fruits. While some inroads have been made in recent years, the result is far from being satisfactory. Meanwhile, Japanese consumers are paying three to five times the world prices for such products. The reason is that the Japanese government has been politically incapable of adopting a non-intervention policy for such products.

Besides non-intervention in business, the government should also avoid appointing political figures into business firms. While this may seem unthinkable in Western societies subscribing to the market economy, it is exactly the case in socialist countries like the Soviet Union,

China, and Vietnam. For example, there were many cases of conflicts in the Chinese business enterprises in the earlier years of her modernization program when the workers had to report to two bosses; the professional manager, and the political appointee of the government who often over-rode the decisions of the former. This led to inefficiency, low morale and low productivity. Fortunately for the Chinese, such problems were minimized when it started its open door policy in the late 1970s. Then the government has given high recognition to the professional factory managers.

Unfortunately, with the Tiananmen Square incident of 4 June 1989, China again took a big leap backward when it began to tighten up on democracy and the free market economy. The old problems resurfaced. Today, China is undergoing a very difficult phase of its economic development. While many East European countries are opening up to the western world and foreign investors, China is struggling to rationalize the tough actions taken against supporters of the free market economy. Yet, we suspect that China knows it cannot go back to its previous policies. It is very likely that it will have to wait for the gradual phasing out of the old guard before bolder, more free market policies are adopted again.

In many centrally-planned economies, political appointees to business positions often plagued the system. There is actually nothing wrong in doing so if they are competent and qualified. Unfortunately, this is often not the case. While this problem is less prominent in Western countries, 'political handouts' also exist in other forms. For example, in the United States, the Reagan administration was accused of giving more than 300 permanent jobs in the civil service to non-career political appointees as farewell gifts (*Straits Times*, October 10, 1988). Again, no wrong is being done by offering permanent jobs in the civil service to political appointees who are able and talented. However, it would be discriminatory if the government were to hold political appointees to a different standard from that of other applicants. In addition, it becomes questionable whether political appointees who accepted permanent jobs in the civil service would be able to adopt the ethics of neutral competence. At the same time, career officials who worked their way up the ladder may see these political appointees as having an unfair advantage, and hence see their careers closed off. This would then cause morale and turnover problems.

6.3 Command

Although the command element was dealt with in Chapter 2, it is useful to reiterate some of the salient points about military leadership. According to Sun Tzu:

"The generalship of the commander refers to the general's qualities of wisdom, sincerity, benevolence, courage and strictness."

将者，智、信、仁、勇、严也。

Besides the five positive qualities of the general, Sun Tzu also highlighted five negative attributes of the general. These five negative traits – recklessness, cowardice, quick temper, sensitivity to honour, over-compassion – can be exploited by the enemy. This, in fact, was explicitly recognized by Sun Tzu:

"If reckless, he can be killed;"

必死，可杀也；

"If cowardly, he can be captured;"

必生，可虏也；

"If quick-tempered, he can be easily provoked;"

忿速，可侮也；

"If sensitive to honor, he can be easily insulted;"

廉洁，可辱也；

"If over compassionate to the people, he can be easily harassed."

爱民，可烦也。

"The destruction of an army and the death of the general are caused by these five shortcomings. They must be carefully understood."

覆军杀将，必以五危，不可不察也。

When we take into account both the positive and negative attributes, a capable general must possess five important traits – caution in action, courage in battle, composure under stress, pragmatism in decision-making and actions and sincerity in the treatment of his subordinates. These traits are also equally applicable to the chief executive officer (CEO) in the business context.

6.3.1 Cautiousness

The general must be cautious in actions. However, being cautious does not mean being indecisive or slow to act. It also does not imply conservatism in decision-making and avoidance of aggressive actions. Rather, it implies the ability to weigh all possibilities and their likely consequences. This is because the fate of the army, and at times the whole state, may depend on how the general makes his decisions. Thus, cautiousness means being detailed and thorough in planning and execution. To achieve this, there are certain definite qualifications that the general must have. Among others, three aspects are especially important:

(1) Ability to plan, especially in the area of strategising. He must know whom he is fighting, why he is fighting, which troops and weapons to use in the fighting, what to capitalize on in fighting, when to fight or not to fight, where he should be fighting or not fighting and how he should go about fighting. His ability to plan effectively will enable him to exploit the situation on the ground to his best advantage:

> "Therefore, the adept in warfare seeks victory from the situation, and does not rely on the efforts of individuals. Thus, he is able to select suitable men to exploit the situation."

> 故善战者，求之于势，不责于人，故能择人而任势。

(2) Ability to execute plans effectively. Some generals are able to plan but are poor in execution. One key characteristic that separates planning from execution is that the latter requires interaction and command of officers and men. In addition, to be able to execute well, the general must also be able to exercise good judgment in the recruitment and selection of officers and men to carry out the plans. In addition, he must provide the necessary guidance to his officers and men.

(3) Ability to manage his army. This requires the general to be able to exercise control over his officers and men through instituting a fair and equitable reward and punishment system. In addition, he must be able to motivate his officers and men so as to achieve high morale, and gain their dedication and commitment.

In the same way, the chief executive officer (CEO) of a company has the responsibility of making key decisions that can make or break the company. For example, if he makes the wrong decision to over-expand, to commit the wrong research and development (R&D) project, to enter the wrong markets, he might be jeopardizing the interests of his company, the jobs of his employees and the welfare of the shareholders. At the same time, he cannot be so conservative as to avoid taking important decisions as this would then retard the growth of the company. However, with careful analysis and planning, he can definitely increase the chances of success and reduce the odds of failure.

6.3.2 Courage

Besides caution, the general must be courageous in battle. Courage means the ability to make bold decisions and be willing to take risks when necessary. At times, this may require him to play the exemplary role and not be afraid of sticking his neck out for the right decision. In addition, when faced with defeat, he must also be courageous enough to admit failure and to accept full responsibility.

In business, the CEO must be courageous too. He is expected to exhibit the entrepreneurial spirit of risk-taking while at the same time, be capable of facing the consequences. Here, it is important to point out that the hallmark of a great leader in business includes not only the ability to accept credit for success and achievement, but also to accept responsibility for failure and defeat. Unfortunately, the common temptation among many CEOs in the Western world is to find a scapegoat when things do not turn out well. This is in sharp contrast to the Japanese ethos whereby the CEO accepts full and complete responsibility for the mistakes committed by his company. A good example was the recent air-crash of Japan Airlines (JAL). At the funeral service, JAL's CEO personally bowed and apologized to every family of the deceased and then resigned as a mark of accepting responsibility for the crash. JAL also compensated the bereaved families very quickly. The JAL case was not an exception but is a common practice among Japanese companies and demonstrates the courage to accept responsibility for failures.

6.3.3 Composure

The capable general is also a person who is composed and not easily provoked into anger and action. In other words, despite his high stature and power, he must not be quick-tempered or succumb to pride and egotism. In fact, he must be able to maintain a sense of humility to the extent of being able to withstand insults and provocations. In this way, he will not be tempted to take rash and reckless decisions. Thus, being composed is very much a complementary trait to being detailed in planning and cautious in actions. In the words of Sun Tzu:

> "… a general must not fight a battle out of resentment."

将不可以愠而致战

> "For while anger can be restored to happiness, and resentment can become pleasantness; a state that has perished cannot be restored, and a man who is dead cannot be resurrected."

怒可以复喜，愠可以复悦；
亡国不可以复存，死者不可以复生。

In the business world, the CEO must exhibit similar traits. He must not be easily provoked by the actions of his competitors. One such tempting area of competition in the business world is the game of corporate acquisitions. Often, a CEO may fall prey to his own weakness. As a result of competitors embarking on an acquisition strategy, he might be tempted to follow suit without having a clear understanding whether such actions would be beneficial to the company as a whole. At times, acquisitions have been made mainly for egotistical reasons rather than for sound policy reasons. In other instances, prices of firms to be acquired were raised to an artificially high level by competitive firms. The main reason was the stubborn refusal to be out-bid by rival firms. Thus, cool-headedness is very much needed on the part of corporate leadership if they want the firm to prosper even more.

At an international level, it is interesting to note the contrasting behavior between Japan and other western countries. For example, when the Tiananmen Square episode erupted, many western countries were very fast in condemning the actions of the Chinese army and government. President Bush even halted a US$600 million arms deal and suspended contact between the two nations military forces on June 5th (one day after the incident). France and Switzerland followed suit and so did many other European countries. They all hurriedly announced some degree of curtailment of ties, including economic and trade measures (such as discouraging tourism in the area). Interestingly throughout these developments, one nation significantly chose to remain silent and that nation was Japan. It remained composed and refused to openly condemn China, nor did it feel it necessary to bring any sanctions against China. Today it continues to enjoy easy access to the Chinese market while many western countries are trying to repair their scarred relations with China.

6.3.4 *Pragmatism*

The general in combat must be pragmatic in his decisions and actions. To be practical and realistic would require initiative on the part of the general. In fact, Sun Tzu said:

> "If the situation is one of victory, the general must fight even though the ruler may have issued orders not to engage. If the situation is one of defeat, the general must not fight even though the ruler may have issued orders to do so."

主曰: 无战, 必战可也; 战道不胜, 主曰: 必战, 无战可也。

It is important to point out that the above saying does not imply disloyalty or betrayal on the part of the general. Neither does it portray betrayal.

Rather, in war, the general is the most senior commander who is closest to the battlefield and knows best how to react to the enemy's actions. If he deems that he can win, he must be allowed to pursue the next logical move. Similarly, if he deems the situation as one of defeat, he must not hesitate to withdraw so that he can live to fight another day. It is the most pragmatic principle to adopt and in fact requires considerable initiative on the part of the general.

On the issue of loyalty, it is interesting to note that the Chinese character for the word, "忠" consists basically of two other words – center (中) and heart (心). Thus, loyalty (忠) literally means centering of one's heart. When one's heart is centered, one's conscience is clear in that he is not biased in any direction. Hence, when a general takes any decision in war, his conscience must be clear. He must always have the interest of the state and the people at heart whether he decides to advance or retreat his forces. This aspect was further illustrated by Sun Tzu:

> "Therefore, the general who advances without seeking personal fame and glory, who retreats without fear of being punished, but whose main concern is for the welfare of the people and the interests of the sovereign, is the precious gem of the state."

故进不求名, 退不避罪, 唯人是保,
而利合于主, 国之宝也。

Thus, every move he makes is with a clear conscience and he does not make his move in expectation of rewards nor fear of punishment. To reiterate the point on loyalty, it is interesting to note that according to the Chinese saying, there is no such term as *loyalty to the ruler* (精忠报君). Rather, the common saying is that of *loyalty to the nation* (精忠报国). Thus, one's loyalty is always pledged to the nation and not to a particular ruler, emperor or political figure. Now when the general's loyalty is to the nation, he will have the interests of all parties at heart – his army, the people, and the sovereign – and not be indebted or biased to any particular group or individual.

However, when a general is not clear on what loyalty implies, it could lead to dire consequences. A good example is General Yue Fei (岳飞) of the Sung Dynasty (960 A.D. to 1280 A.D.). When Yue Fei was a young man, his mother tattooed the four Chinese characters *loyalty to the nation* (精忠报国) on his back. Yue Fei later became a very famous and outstanding Sung general and was responsible for repelling the invaders at the Chinese border. However, owing to the evil plots of the Sung prime minister who was bribed by the enemy, and a weak and indecisive emperor, 13 imperial edicts were issued to recall General Yue Fei from the war zone at the critical point of the battle. At that time, every one of General Yue Fei's officers, including himself, knew that victory was at hand if they had persisted and disobeyed the emperor's orders. Unfortunately, General Yue Fei was blindly loyal to the emperor, and misunderstood the concept of loyalty. He made the fatal error of returning to the capital and was subsequently executed. In his critical moment of decision, General Yue Fei forgot that the four characters engraved on his back read *loyalty to the nation*, and not loyalty to the *emperor*. If he had stayed on to fight, he would have won the war, and more than likely gained an imperial pardon and possibly even a promotion. Unfortunately, by making the wrong decision, he not only lost his life, but jeopardized the welfare of his people and interests of the state. The Sung Dynasty was subsequently conquered by the enemies who established the Yuan Dynasty from 1280 A.D. to 1368 A.D.

In business, the CEO must be equally pragmatic in his decision-making and exercise initiative whenever possible. While he may have already laid out his plans, he must not be constrained by them. Rather, at every opportune moment, he must capitalize on them. If it is necessary to make changes, he must do so without hesitation and this is one of the most important aspects of management for the CEO in today's highly competitive environment. Such changes are not confined to one area at a time. In fact, many changes could be occurring simultaneously in various areas – competition, consumer's tastes and demands, technology and innovation, suppliers' pressures, government rules and regulations, environmental shifts. Thus, to manage effectively the CEO must be flexible and pragmatic in his approach. While adopting a proactive stance, he must also have tremendous reactive capabilities so that he can out-wit his competitors.

On the issue of loyalty, it is important to note that loyalty is to the organization, and not to any particular CEO, or any other individual. Here, it is interesting to note that when one asks a Japanese his profession, the typical response would be: 'I work for Mitsubishi,' 'I work for Toyota,' 'I work for Sony,' – in most instances, he indicates the organization. This is where his loyalty lies – the organization, and not the individual. In contrast, a Western professional would probably indicate his vocation – that he is an engineer, technician or accountant. Rarely is the organization highlighted in an unprobed response. Thus, his answer seems to indicate that his loyalty is to himself!

The contrasting Japanese and Western responses reflect very much what can and cannot be done in the business organizations of both types of societies. In Japan, the corporate identity and orientation has made it possible to develop teamwork, harmonious corporate culture and goals and the like. In Western countries like the United States, the individualistic approach has made it very difficult to harmonize corporate goals and objectives with those of the employees. In addition, when the individual is loyal to himself and does not identify with the company, he will not feel attached to the latter. So, when a better job from another company comes along, he will not hesitate to take it.

On the other hand, when an individual is able to identify with the company, he will develop a sense of emotional attachment that will hold him to that company. In fact, this strong link and identity with the company will even create a sense of guilt should the employee contemplate leaving for another company. It is, therefore, not surprising to note that the employee turnover rates among the large Japanese companies is very low. This is because of their successful inculcation of a very strong corporate identity. In doing so, they have shifted the decision-making process of the employee from the mind to the heart, which is what loyalty is all about.

6.3.5 *Sincerity*

The fifth and final trait required of the general is that he must be sincere in his feelings for his men. In fact Sun Tzu commented on the capable general:

> "When the general regards his men as infants, they will be willing to follow him through thick and thin. When he treats them like his beloved sons, they will be willing to support him unto death."

视卒如婴儿，故可与之赴深溪；
视卒如爱子，故可与之俱死。

At all times, he must have their interests at heart:

> "Pay attention to nourishing the troops, and do not tire them unnecessarily."

谨养而勿劳

However, he must also guard himself against over-compassion as this might be interpreted as weakness by his officers and men and lead to indiscipline and insubordination. Moreover, he could also be vulnerable to exploitation by the enemy. More importantly, he must maintain objectivity and impartiality in judgment at all times and be capable of administering rewards and punishments equitably. In essence, while caring for his men, he must not lose sight of the combat mission.

It is also very interesting to note that Sun Tzu made a subtle distinction between caring for the army versus the ordinary people. The general must be responsive to the feelings of his officers and men, but:

> "If over-compassionate to the people, he can be easily harassed."

爱民, 可烦也。

Apparently, Sun Tzu recognized that a general who is too concerned about the man-in-the-street is likely to encounter difficulties. This is because when a war breaks out, it is inevitable that the people will suffer in various ways – food shortages, diseases, injuries caused by war, loss of lives of family members. Such events are abundant and the general cannot afford to attend to all of them. His main mission should be to win the war and bring an end to the sufferings of his people as soon as possible. If he is distracted by human sufferings and becomes indecisive in taking military actions, the war may be prolonged and the sufferings will continue even longer.

Just like the general in war, the CEO in business must be sincere in his treatment of his employees. As an organization is basically staffed and managed by people, there is no doubt that the CEO must value such human assets and adopt a human orientation in management – the ability to understand the problems of the subordinates and appreciate their work. In fact, one of the ingredients for successful companies highlighted by Peters and Waterman (1982) in their book on *In Search of Excellence* is that of adopting a human orientation approach. However, having a human orientation must not be equated with adopting a welfare-oriented approach in management – giving in to every request and demand by the employees. What is important is that the motivation and incentive system in the company must be fairly administered. At the same time, there must also be disciplinary and censoring procedures for those who do not perform to expectations. Thus, where necessary, employees may have to be removed or retrenched. The CEO must not be bogged down by feelings of the heart to the extent of jeopardizing rationality of the mind.

To be sincere, the CEO must also be able to maintain an exemplary lifestyle. For example, if he wants his employees to work hard, he must be able to take the lead. If he wants employees to make sacrifices such as taking a pay cut, he should be the first to reduce his salary. In this way, he will be able to inspire his subordinates because he has demonstrated sincerity – matching words with actions. It is interesting to point out that many American CEOs failed to abide by such rules. *International Business Week* (May 7 1990) reported that many American CEOs were paid very handsomely, despite relatively poor performance by their companies. For example, despite poor (in fact, negative) shareholder returns, the CEOs of companies such as Chemical Banking, Manufacturers Hanover and Bankers Trust NY continued to receive seven figure salaries. In fact the CEO of Unisys was reported to receive a total pay package in excess of US$12 million when the shareholders were getting −34% return on their equity.

It is also interesting to point out that in business, the CEO has to contend with the people too. Here the term would refer specifically to the constituents – the consumers – that his company is serving. In the Western world, as a result of consumer affluence and increasing sophistication, increasing competitiveness among firms and increasing consumer groups' pressures, many firms are tempted to adopt 'the consumer is king' philosophy. Indeed, every possible attempt is made to satisfy the consumer. However, if one adopts Sun Tzu's view in business it would require a closer examination of whether the consumer should be supreme all the time. Now it is important to point out that this is not tantamount to discarding the need to be consumer-oriented nor the need to practice the marketing concept. Note that Sun Tzu used the words, 'If over-compassionate to the people, he can be easily harassed.' He did not rule out the need to be compassionate. Rather, one should not be overly compassionate to the extent of jeopardizing the combat mission. In the same way, a firm cannot possibly respond to every demand of the consumer. For example, it is not possible to make a defect-free product, neither is it possible to redress every consumer complaint. To do so would require high costs to the company. Instead, the company must decide what is an acceptable (and high) product quality that it can achieve to satisfy the majority of consumers and an acceptable level of consumer dissatisfaction that it is willing to tolerate (bearing in mind it is not possible to satisfy every consumer).

Besides the problems associated with being overly responsive to the consumers (to the extent of being harassed), it is also debatable whether most consumers know exactly what they want. Here it is interesting to note two contrasting styles of marketing to the consumers. In the retail automobile industry, the typical American approach (some of them have deviated recently) is to sell the consumer only the basic model and any additional items such as radio and cassette player, sports rims and tyres, mud-guards, floor mats, power steering, power windows, air-conditioning would be charged separately. At times, these extra items could total up to more than 20% of the price of the car. The underlying philosophy of such an approach is that 'the consumer is right' and he should be given the choice. There are several problems with such an approach. First, it assumes that the consumer knows what he wants, which may not be true. Second, it assumes that the consumer is rational in his decision-making, which again is debatable. Third, it increases the costs of selling as every car sold has to be packaged differently with varying options. Fourth, it increases the effort and time of selling a car, as the salesperson is tasked with selling many other options as well. Finally, it may create consumer dissatisfaction as the final price of the car may be increased substantially.

In contrast, the Japanese manufacturer's approach is to sell the car as a total package which includes all conceivable options at one price. The only choices available to the consumer could possibly be the model (for example, two-door sports, four-door saloon, five-door hatchback) and the colour of the car. While this approach seems to rob the consumer of his decision-making right (he is not the king) and the price of the car may be relatively higher, there are several points in its favor. First, the consumer is spared having to make many decisions in areas that he may not be familiar with. Second, the total package of options and benefits may probably enhance the total perceived value of the car in the eyes of the consumer. Third, the consumer knows exactly what he will get for the price of the car as there are no additional hidden costs. Finally, it is easier for the salesperson to sell the car in terms of time and effort and this probably results in lower selling costs for the company. This seemingly unacceptable approach of deciding for the consumer what he should be buying, however, has yielded tremendous dividends for the Japanese car manufacturers. Their worldwide success is common knowledge today. They obviously must have known what the consumers want (the Japanese manufacturers are 'compassionate') but they also do not bend to every whim and fancy of the consumer (that is, the Japanese manufacturers are not overly 'compassionate'). They are definitely consumer-oriented and they definitely practice the marketing concept but we think Japanese manufacturers do not necessarily subscribe to the concept that the consumer is king. In summary, there is no doubt that in war Sun Tzu placed the onus entirely on the general. In his opinion, the general must bear full responsibility for the actions of his officers and men and for all consequences. For the general to deny responsibility for the actions of his army and to put the blame on circumstantial factors is but a lame excuse not befitting a general. In his words:

> "An army may suffer from flight, insubordination, collapse, ruin, disorganization and rout. These six calamities are not attributed to natural causes. They are due to the faults of the general."

> 故兵有 "走" 者，有 "弛" 者，有 "陷" 者，有 "崩" 者，有 "乱"
> 者，有 "北" 者。凡此六者，非天之灾，将之过也。

In the same way, when employees leave a company in massive numbers; when there are disputes within a company and morale is low; when a company is losing money, losing competitiveness, poorly structured and organized to meet competition; when employees are wrongly assigned; and when a company is constantly threatened by competitors (losing market shares, under acquisition threat), the ultimate responsibility lies with the CEO. It is his fault.

The ability to bear the ultimate responsibility and the skills to make key and important decisions are among the reasons why CEOs command high salaries. In fact, high calibre CEOs command very high premiums. Often such decisions involve very personal judgments that are very much institutionalized within that individual – what we call the art of decision-making and which is very difficult to acquire outside that individual. In contrast, the science of decision making such as demand and financial forecasting tools and various computer statistical packages can be bought and acquired in the open market in a relatively easy way. However, to recognize the need for such acquisitions again requires the art of management, and to use the information intelligently again requires the art of analysis and interpretation. These arts are all institutionalized within the individual, and for the CEO, it is the factor that discriminates him from the rest and which allows him to command a high salary premium. It is only logical then that he bears the burden of responsibility.

6.4 The army

The third important party in the human factor that affects implementation of strategies is the army which includes all officers and men. As mentioned in Chapter 3, there are two important dimensions to an army

– quantity (strengths) and quality (training). It is obvious that when other factors are about equal, the army that has more soldiers will have the distinct advantage. On the other hand, it does not imply that the smaller army will always lose a battle. This is because with superior training, it can overcome the weakness in numbers. At the same time, with the appropriate strategies, it can achieve relative superiority at the point of engagement.

In addition, there are two other related aspects to the management of the army – doctrine (structure and organization) and discipline (motivation) which were also discussed in Chapter 3. When war begins, these two aspects become even more important. Together, they form the control mechanism of the general. Besides control, the general in the combat situation must also pay special attention to communication and state of combat readiness. As control has been discussed previously under doctrine and discipline, only certain salient points pertinent to the combat situation will be highlighted here. More attention will be devoted to the issues of communication and combat readiness as they have not been discussed previously.

6.4.1 *Control*

Control at the implementation stage refers more to operational control than strategic control. In other words, it is concerned with the day-to-day management of the troops in combat. There is no doubt that in war, the general must have a tight rein over his officers and men. Of course, this could be achieved more expediently if in peace-time they are well-trained and disciplined. At the same time, if the army is well organized and structured, it would facilitate the general in directing and commanding his forces and their deployment. On the other hand:

> "When the general is weak and lacks discipline, when training and instructions are not clear, when the duties of officers and men are not distinct, and when the formations are slovenly, the result is utter disorganization.
>
> 将弱不严，教道不明，吏卒无常，陈兵纵横，曰 "乱"

It is therefore no wonder that Sun Tzu recognized this as one of six disasters for the army. Thus, control in the form of discipline and organization is very important to the effective performance of the soldiers:

"If a general pampers his troops but is unable to use them; if he loves them excessively but cannot exercise his commands; if his troops are disorderly but he cannot discipline them; then they are like a bunch of spoilt brats, and are useless."

厚而不能使，爱而不能令，乱而不能治，譬若骄子，不可用也。

Hence, while it is necessary to feel for his men and be compassionate, over pampering will lead to loss of control. When control is lost, it is very difficult to get organized again. At times, it may not even be possible to regain the initiative. This is because when a war begins and as battles develop, the situation becomes very fluid and dynamic. Thus, he must have a sufficient degree of freedom to do what is necessary – for example, in granting field promotions in recognition of good effort, and carrying out executions of soldiers and officers – so as to instil the right discipline as well as unity of purpose in order to accomplish the combat mission.

In the same way, when a business plan is put into action, the person-in-charge must have full control over various resources that are required to ensure its successful implementation. Unfortunately, in many business situations there is a temptation to merely delegate responsibility without commensurate authority. The result is that the manager concerned faces great difficulty in seeing the plan through. While this problem is less significant in the case of the CEO, he is nonetheless answerable to the Board of Directors and the shareholders (if any). Thus, he still must be given sufficient leeway in making decisions.

The control issue becomes more problematic in the case of a CEO or senior manager who manages the subsidiary of a large company. If he has to revert to the parent company for every major decision, his effectiveness is bound to be drastically reduced and the subsidiary is likely to be less responsive to the changing needs and demands of the market. In situations where he is operating in a foreign market, the problem becomes even more serious. Without full authority to operate in that foreign country and having to consult the head-office for directions and decisions, the process is bound to be long, cumbersome and tedious. In addition, his own authority might even be undermined by his own subordinates as they may perceive him as ineffective and powerless. Top management must, therefore, have a clear understanding that the person closest to the place of action is probably the best qualified to make most decisions. Without doubt, certain critical and major decisions may still have to be decided by the head-office but the point is that the most senior manager on the ground must be given authority to run the operation.

6.4.2 Communication

When war begins, one of most critical aspects in ensuring that the general is kept informed on the progress of the battle, the conditions of his army and that of the enemy, is the establishment of effective communication systems. Unlike modern warfare where the general can rely on sophisticated telecommunications, radar and even satellite technology, the general in ancient times did not have such facilities. Instead, he had to rely on a very rudimentary form of signs and signals to achieve this purpose. Thus:

> "*The Book of Military Management* says: As the voice cannot be heard in battle, gongs and drums are used. As the eyes cannot detect human directions and movement from afar, banners and flags are used."

> 《军政》曰：　"言不相闻，故为金鼓；视不相见，故为旌旗。"

From the above quotation, several basic principles about communication systems could be derived. First, the communication system to be used must take into account the situational factor. In other words, it must be relevant to the problem at hand and be appropriate as well. In hand-to-hand combat involving large numbers of troops in ancient times, it would be very difficult to shout orders (as the noise level would be very high) and to use hand signals (as the line-of-sight would be blocked). Thus, gongs and drums, and banners and flags were much more practical and useful in that they could be better heard and seen. Second, an effective communication system must also be identifiable in that it is unique to one particular force. Thus, it would not create confusion. It is therefore not surprising that in ancient times, there were distinctive soundings of the drums and gongs, and varying colours of banners and flags used.

Third, an effective communication system must use more than one means to convey the messages. This would reduce the risks of failure if one of the means failed. Besides these three principles, a fourth principle about an effective communication system is that it must achieve unity among all the target audiences in that system. This is supported by the following statement:

> "Now gongs and drums, banners and flags are used to focus the attention of the troops in battle. When the troops act as an united whole, neither the brave will advance alone nor the coward will retreat alone. This is the art of directing a large troop."

> 夫金鼓旌旗者，所以一人之耳目也；
> 人既专一，则勇者不得独进，怯者不得独退，此用众之法也。

Besides uniting the forces, it has the effects of multiplying their courage, and stimulating them to move in the desired direction – that is, an effective communication system should direct. To achieve this, the system has to be well understood by the troops, and it has to be well co-ordinated. This is because when the communication system consists of several means of relaying messages (like gongs, drums, banners, flags, torches, etc.), there may be confusion unless such means are carefully explained to the troops and their respective commanders. At the same time, the use of several means of communication would also require co-ordination in order to achieve the desired effects. At certain times, perhaps one method is better than the others. At other times, perhaps several methods should be used together so as to achieve greater effects. Thus, close coordination is necessary.

Finally, an effective communication system has also to be flexible and adaptable:

> "Therefore, in night fighting, use many torches and drums; in day
> fighting, use many banners and flags. These different signals are meant
> to direct the attention of sight and hearing."

故夜战多火鼓，昼战多旌旗，所以变人之耳目也。

By being flexible and adaptable, the communication system seeks to exploit the situation at hand. It is thus proactive, and is not necessarily dictated by the situation.

It is very interesting to note that while Sun Tzu had already invented a fairly sophisticated system of communication through various signals, such a development was only a 19th century phenomenon in the Western world. It occurred during the battle of Trafalgar in 1805 – an event that indirectly led to the eventual downfall of Napoleon. The battle was won because Admiral Horatio Nelson of the British army created a secret weapon – a system of sea communication through signal flags. This technique of communicating over long distances by coded flags was then used by the British Royal Navy and it revolutionized how naval warfare would be fought in subsequent generations.

The use of signal flags enabled the British ships to be constantly in touch with the fleet commander, while at the same time covering a vast ocean area. Once the enemy was spotted, communication was quickly established with the commanding ship as well as with other British battle ships. In this way, the battle plan was capable of being altered so as to achieve relative superiority over the enemy.

In contrast, owing to the lack of a system of communication at sea, other navies had to rigidly adhere to their previously agreed upon battle plans. It was simply not possible to alter the plans once the ships set sail. Thus, these navies were time and again confounded by the British navy. In essence, the system of 'talking flags' enabled the British navy to enjoy undisputed rule of the seas for many years. It gave them the tactical superiority that no other navy at that time was able to achieve.

It is important to point out that effective communication as experienced some 200 years ago and even as far back as the time of Sun Tzu, is equally a decisive factor even in modern warfare today. For example, the Milstar satellite system, developed by the Lockheed Corporation, is designed to keep the command of all kinds of forces around the globe in constant touch, from the War Cabinet right down to the platoon commanders. Without a proper system of communication, orders could never be executed, battles would be fought under the foggiest conditions and the end result could be fiasco.

Just like an army in war, an organization must develop an effective communication system if it wants to function properly. This is true regardless of whether the organization is relating to its own employees, to its customers, or any third party outside the organization. In fact, problems often occur in an organization as a result of poor communication. In this aspect, the chief executive officer (CEO) has a key role to play. In their book, Clifford and Cavanagh (1985) highlighted three major skills that are needed for the winning CEO. These are a heightened emphasis on team building, a high level of personal discipline and great skill in communication. In particular, they commented:

> "The CEO in the winning company must be sure that formal controls and information are sufficient to identify major problems and opportunities, but not so sophisticated and complex as to become ends in themselves or require excessive time to generate or to use. He needs to ensure sound feedback to his team and be certain that two-way communication is taking place down within the organization. It's a tough, demanding, time-consuming job to hit the right balance of two-way communication. Perhaps most important, the winning CEO needs to be certain that the signals he sends are unequivocal, consistent, and clear – he can no longer afford the trial balloons or casual wild ideas of his earlier years." (Clifford and Cavanagh 1985, p. 145)

It is worth noting that all the various aspects of an effective communication system mentioned earlier – appropriateness, identity, use of multiple means, and adaptability – can be found in the above quotation.

It is also interesting to note that Japanese companies are also very adept at communication. One good example is that of Honda of America Manufacturing, Inc (HAM). As it operates in a hostile environment that is not familiar with the Japanese way of management, HAM had to communicate change very carefully. This it did beautifully, by allowing its associates and employees to know constantly that change is an everyday, natural occurrence and that everyone participates in it. Today, HAM has revolutionized the way to manage companies in America, and produced the best selling car of 1989.

6.4.3 Morale

When war begins, one of the most important factors that the general must take into consideration is the morale of his troops and those of the enemy. It is a known fact that when a war is fought over a long period of time, the morale of the troops will be affected. In fact, Sun Tzu recognized this when he said:

> "When victory is long delayed, the ardor and morale of the army will be depressed."

久则钝兵挫锐

In Chapter VII, Maneuvers, Sun Tzu also highlighted three factors that affect the combat readiness of troops – morale (spirit or mind), emotion (heart) and physical needs (body) – and they are reflected by the following quotations:

> "In the early stages of a battle, the spirits of the forces are high; later, they will gradually flag; at the end stage, their spirits are low and thoughts of returning set in. Therefore, those adept in warfare avoid attacking the enemy when their spirits are high, but attack them when their spirits are sluggish and the soldiers homesick. This is control of the morale factor."

是故朝气锐，昼气惰，暮气归。
故善用兵者，避其锐气，击其惰归，此治气者也。

> "Use discipline and orderliness to match the enemy's disorderliness; use calmness to handle a clamorous one. This is control of the emotional factor."

以治待乱，以静待哗，此治心者也。

"Use nearness to the battlefield to match the enemy's distance; rest to match enemy's exhaustion; and well-fed troops to match enemy's hungry ones. This is control of the physical factor."

以近待远，以佚待劳，以饱待饥，此治力者也。

It is very interesting to note that these three factors are quite encompassing. To win wars, the morale of one's army must be high and well-motivated. Thus, it is important to cater to their physical needs, that is, matters that relate to their stomachs and bodies. Troops must be well-fed, well-rested, and well-taken care of. Otherwise, it is difficult for them to fight.

Besides taking care of the stomachs and bodies (bread and butter issues) of the soldiers, the general must also be able to assess matters that relate to their minds and psychology. While soldiers may be well-fed, they are no fools in that they would march to war blindly. Even when they are forced to do so, their loyalty will be suspect and they are likely to flee in the face of increased adversary situations. Thus, there is a need to present a rationale or logic for going to war. This is where it is so important to find a moral cause in war that every soldier can identify with.

In addition a capable general must be able to size up the moods of his troops *vis-a-vis* those of the enemy's. When the spirit of his troops is high, it is easier to deploy them in combat. In addition, their courage is also bound to be multiplied.

Besides the physical and morale factors, the general must also control the emotional factor (the heart) in war. It is not sufficient to advance his troops depending on high emotion. Rather he must learn to counteract and control the feelings on the battleground and use them to his advantage. The objective is to frustrate the enemy.

It is important to point out, however, that these three factors – body (physical), mind (morale), and heart (emotion) – should be considered together. In fact, they are very much related. When a general takes great care of his troops in terms of their physical well-being, he is likely to secure their loyalty (an issue relating very much to the heart), and they are likely to obey his commands (an issue relating to the mind). All three factors affect the overall combat readiness of the troops, they must be taken into account at all times. In addition, their effects must also be weighed against those of the enemy's. In other words, the concept of relative superiority is also very much applicable in the case of morale.

The Falklands War is a good example of the inter-related influences of the three factors on morale. The Argentinian generals were initially able to excite the emotions and feelings (hearts) of their fellow citizens with great rhetoric and seemingly heroic attempts at conquering the islands. They could present logical and rational reasons why the Malvinas (Falkland being the British name) islands should belong to Argentina. However, the Argentinian generals made several critical errors.

First, while able to appeal to the Argentinians, they failed to appeal to the Falkland islanders who still regarded themselves as British subjects and refused to support the Argentinian cause. Second, the use of military force failed to gain them the support of the international community and hence dealt a serious blow to their morale. Third, they under-estimated the morale and combat-readiness of the British troops. In fact, they violated one of the principles of maneuvers advocated by Sun Tzu:

> "Do not engage an approaching enemy whose banners are well-ordered; do not attack an enemy whose formations are impressive and strong. This is control of the factor of changing circumstances."

无邀正正之旗，勿击堂堂之陈，此治变者也。

Finally, the Argentinian generals missed out on one of the important influencing factors on combat readiness – they failed to take into account the physical well-being of the troops and the Argentinian public. The body (physical) or the bread and butter issue was ignored. The war was fought at a time when Argentina was in great economic difficulties and the costs of the campaign inflicted heavier burdens on the country. In addition, the army was poorly paid, the conditions of service were far from desirable and the troops were not well trained or equipped. Such undesirable physical conditions did not take long to surface when the war progressed. They took a heavy toll on the morale of the Argentinian soldiers.

In contrast, all three factors that influenced the state of combat readiness were in the British favor. They were able to find a moral cause and justified it to the minds of the British soldiers and public. The British soldiers were very loyal to the crown and their cause. In addition, the campaign was well supported by the public. In fact, various commercial firms even offered food and supplies and the troops were very well equipped. It was no surprise that relative to the Argentinians, the British soldiers' morale was high and they were able to exhibit greater combat competence.

The business organization must also address the three factors that influence the performance of employees. Better working conditions in terms of pay, incentives, medical benefits, the physical environment, leave loans and childcare are likely to attract better employees. Poor working conditions will lead to low morale and job-hopping.

But these alone are not sufficient. The job must also appeal to the intellectual side of the employees. It should offer interesting, challenging opportunities, fit the skills and training of the employees, provide scope for improvement and allow the employee to feel that he is doing something for the benefit of his fellow human beings and his nation. The employee should feel that his efforts are appreciated. In effect, he should feel that he can identify with the organizational cause of his employers.

The third factor, that of the heart, applies to business also. Japanese corporations in particular, excel in the area of corporate loyalty. It is an established practice for lifetime employment to be offered in exchange for corporate loyalty and dedication. Job hopping is discouraged to the point where the large corporations rarely take on workers at the mid-level from another organization. It would be considered an act of corporate betrayal for the employee to change jobs. Japanese workers owe a loyalty to their companies which makes them more willing to accept personal sacrifices for the sake of the company. From the company's point of view this reduces recruitment costs and makes manpower planning and control easier. The Japanese approach to human resource management tends to be more accommodational than confrontational (which is more typical of American management).

It is important to point out that the Japanese companies are able to produce a much more combat ready workforce by their exemplary management style as well. For example, Japanese managers wear the same uniform as the workers, do not have reserved space in the parking lot, eat the same food and use the same washroom as the rank and file. In this way they are able to identify with their workforce and can appeal to issues pertaining to their stomachs, minds and hearts. Interestingly, they have achieved higher efficiency in productivity among a disciplined and loyal workforce not just in Japan, but also in their plants in the US, and even in depressed areas in Britain. In short, they are able to achieve more than American and British managements because they know what will make a workforce tick.

In general, while good physical conditions and the adoption of a rational approach to the recruitment and retention of employees in order to boost their morale are fairly easy to establish, the inculcation of loyalty is not that simple. Competing companies can easily match one another's conditions of work but corporate loyalty is unique to the company. In addition, loyalty lasts while the other two aspects of employment change according to the economic, competitive and market environments. This makes policies aimed at increasing corporate loyalty vital.

7 Implementation of strategies: The operational factor

7.1 Swiftness in execution
7.2 Adaptability in maneuvers
7.3 Deceptiveness in actions and strategies
7.4 Capitalizing on available means
7.5 Anticipation of the enemy's reactions and changes in environment
7.6 Deception, fraud, and corruption in business and politics

As mentioned at the beginning of Chapter 6, the human factor (as discussed thus far) involves a clear understanding of the roles and responsibilities of the various parties involved in the combat mission. The operational factor, on the other hand, relates to certain principles that are required to ensure the successful accomplishment of the mission. In other words, the performance of the combat mission depends to a large extent on whether certain principles of implementation are adhered to. Among others, three major principles of implementation by Sun Tzu deserve special mention and discussion. These are:

- Swiftness in execution
- Adaptability in maneuvers
- Deceptiveness in actions and strategies

Besides these three major principles, there are also two other aspects that affect the implementation of strategies. These are the need to capitalize on available means and the anticipation of enemy's reactions. Figure 7.1 summarizes the various points that were discussed in

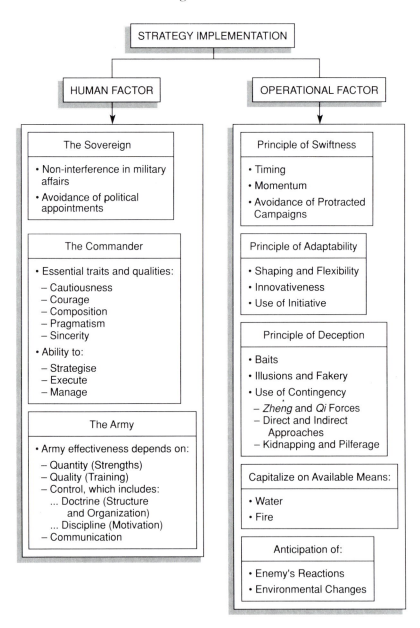

Figure 7.1 Strategy Implementation

the previous chapter on the human factor underlying implementation of strategies, as well as highlights the salient points to be discussed in this chapter.

7.1 Swiftness in execution

A plan is useless unless it is executed. However, how the plan is executed is equally important. Among other principles in executing the war plan, Sun Tzu advocated swiftness. This is, of course, in sharp contrast to his views on planning, where, he says, the thoroughness and attention to detail would necessitate that the process will take much longer. However, once the plan is decided on and formalized, it has to be executed expediently. Underlying such a policy is the recognition that if execution is delayed there could be leakages of the plan, as well as opportunities for the enemy to read the various maneuvers in the plan. Thus, speed in execution will deny the enemy the advantage of time to prepare his defenses against the attacking force. Speed also gives the element of surprise, as it makes use of the unpreparedness of the enemy. To quote Sun Tzu:

> "Speed is the essence of war. Capitalize on the unpreparedness of the enemy; travel by the unexpected routes; and attack those places where he does not take precautions."

兵之情主速，乘人之不及，由不虞之道，攻其所不戒也。

There are three dimensions to the principle of swiftness – timing, momentum, and avoidance of protracted campaigns.

7.1.1 Timing

By timing, Sun Tzu meant attacking at the most appropriate and suitable moment:

> "When the strike of the falcon breaks the body of its prey, it is because of correct timing."

鸷鸟之疾，至于毁折者，节也。

Note that a falcon is known to be able to strike, immobilize, and fatally wound its prey precisely because of accurate timing. Moreover, it is capable of overcoming a prey much larger than itself, through the sheer speed and accuracy of its strike. Thus, at the moment of engagement, it is able to attain relative superiority because it uses its strengths (advantages) against its victim's weaknesses (disadvantages).

Besides catching the unpreparedness of the enemy, correct timing can also allow one's force to exploit the advantages of the situation:

"Generally, those who reach and occupy the battleground early will have time to rest and wait for the enemy. Those who arrive at the battleground late will have to rush into action when they are already tired and exhausted."

凡先处战地而待敌者佚，后处战地而趋战者劳。

As pointed out in Chapter 5, it is important to strike at the most opportune time, neither too early, nor too late, but at the exact moment. Unfortunately, unlike some other concepts in war, it is not easy to teach someone the application of timing. This is because it is very much an art rather than a science, and a lot depends on the judgment of the commander(s) on the ground, as well as the strategists. This is true in the case of war as well as in business.

While timing cannot be taught like a science, the art of applying it can be improved when one has a better feel of the situation. In other words, while it cannot be imparted like a set of strategic tools such as the Boston Consulting Groups's Product Portfolio Matrix, or the Experience Curve, it can be acquired indirectly by the individual. For example, in the case of a company, the CEO's sense of timing in various types of decision-making and implementation of strategies would be greatly improved if he had a better understanding of the following:

- the environment in which he operates, including the political, legal, social, cultural, physical, and infrastructural factors;
- the nature of competition, including the market structure, the number and types of competitors, the methods of competition, and the types of strategies used;
- the characteristics of the target audience and market segments that his company is serving, including consumers' changing levels of affluence, education, lifestyles, tastes and preferences, attitudes toward new products/services, the rate of adoption of innovation, and so on.
- the strengths and weaknesses of the company relative to the competitors, including both human and non-human resources, tangible and intangible assets.
- the experiences of the company in similar situations in the past, including the experiences in other products/services, and markets if applicable.

A few examples will illustrate the importance of the need to have this feel or sense for timing in business operations. In Singapore, the first Western fast food restaurant to start operations was A&W. It was set up before 1970. Unfortunately, it was established at a time when the standard of living of the average Singaporean was relatively low, and Western fast food was not yet well-received. At that time, A&W positioned itself correctly in the middle and upper income segments of the market. It was a place for treats and special occasions and having few outlets seemed logical.

The situation changed very quickly in the late 1970s and 1980s. Consumers' affluence increased tremendously, lifestyles were changing and there was increasing preference for Western fast food and better eating places. A&W should have been aware of the changing trends of the consumers, but it did not. Instead, it was the other Western fast food chains like McDonald's, Kentucky Fried Chicken, and Burger King that realized the tremendous potential provided by the new Singapore consumers. They came in a big way in the late 1970s and early 1980s and expanded and marketed themselves very aggressively. Currently chains like McDonald's, Kentucky Fried Chicken, and Burger King are all big players in an industry with annual sales fast exceeding US$100 million. In contrast, although A&W was the first to be in the Singaporean market, it failed to sense the right time to change and capitalize on the market. Today, it is struggling against high odds in the industry.

Another good example of timing is the case of Kentucky Fried Chicken's operations in Hong Kong. The company tried to penetrate the Hong Kong market in the 1970s but failed badly and pulled out for several years. The reason for its failure was that it went in too early, as Hong Kong consumers at that time were simply not ready for Western fast food. Nonetheless, Kentucky Fried Chicken learned their lesson and were able to use the experience to their benefit in subsequent years and in other countries. For example, they succeeded in establishing themselves in Singapore and Malaysia. More remarkably, they have also succeeded in establishing very credible footholds in the Chinese markets in the mid-1980s. Among other reasons for the success of Kentucky Fried Chicken in these areas was their ability to avoid the mistakes they made in Hong Kong and acquire a better sense of timing by understanding the environment, the competitors, the consumers and themselves better.

In the area of investment, timing is by far the key success factor. No one can say there is anything wrong with carpets, paintings, coins, gold bars or shares. The harsh reality is that good timing can make a person rich overnight, or bankrupt next morning. Failing to sell a good investment at the right time can result in losses. For example, General Motors shares cost less than US$30 in early 1986 and rose to US$70 subsequently. However, in early 1990, it dropped again to about US$46. With inflation, the value was definitely a loss to any investor who held the share for too long. Similarly, shares like IBM used to be very attractive for many years. In the mid-1980s, IBM stock was worth well over US$120. However, in 1990, it had even fallen below US$100. By the same token, anyone who missed the chance to liquidate their portfolio of shares prior to Saddam Hussein's invasion of Kuwait in August 1990, would probably be regretting and lamenting at how fast profits can wither away. The key in successful investment is not so much when to buy, but knowing the right time to sell. It is an art that few can master.

7.1.2 Momentum

While timing is used to catch the unpreparedness of the enemy, or to exploit the situation to one's advantage, momentum is used to achieve synergy of actions to overwhelm the enemy and to deny the enemy the benefit of time to develop effective defenses and retaliatory measures. The impact of momentum is best illustrated by Sun Tzu:

> "When torrential water pushes boulders, it is because of its momentum."

> 激水之疾，至于漂石者，势也；

Water is by nature a very soft medium yet, owing to its momentum, it is able to push boulders and, for that matter, to cut valleys and gorges. The sheer advantage achieved through momentum of large numbers can be quite overwhelming. The Chinese army, for example, was known to use this concept of momentum in some of their ancient wars.

Besides war, momentum is easily applicable in other areas as well. For example, in sports such as basketball or volleyball, no sensible coach would call for a time-out when his team is riding a momentum during a game. On the contrary, the opposing team's coach must call for a time-out under such a situation in order to disrupt the momentum and take some of the wind out of the winning side. It is not uncommon for a relatively weaker team to win when it has found the right momentum.

In business, momentum applies as well. One situation in which momentum is critical to a firm's ability to succeed is when it is in frontier ground as described in Chapter 3. When a company has captured only a very small percentage of the total market share, it is very important that it maintains its momentum in order to secure a larger share. This is to enable the company to benefit from economies of scale. Similarly, when introducing a new product, it is important to go for more converts after the initial acceptance.

Japanese manufacturers tend to go after larger market shares as opposed to higher profit margins in their marketing strategies and this approach has resulted in their deliberate lower pricing strategy in order to gain the extra share of the market. Now, such a share-driven strategy is very much premised on the concept of momentum – that through lower pricing, consumers will become more price sensitive and consequently more willing to try the product; and as more consumers purchase the product, a certain momentum is created to carry the product through to many other consumers. In other words, the adoption process of the new product will be speeded up once a critical mass is generated and momentum developed.

The effects of momentum must not be discounted in business. In fact, to some extent, the success of many Japanese products and services in the world market today can be attributed to the momentum factor. For example, once a Japanese manufacturer manages to establish a foothold in a foreign market, he will seek to expand as quickly as possible. As mentioned earlier in this book, this was the case of their penetration into the automobile industry in the United States. Once a Japanese product is accepted, more and more brands, models and styles would follow suit, to the extent of overwhelming the other brands in the market. This is how they succeed in products like cameras, refrigerators, photocopiers, cars, hi-fi and stereo equipment, radios, television sets, and so on. Today, the effects of the momentum created are quite telling. For example, if you want to buy a camera for normal use, what brands can you choose from? Your choice is likely to be a Japanese brand, as many other brands are almost non-existent. Many other products are facing the effects of the Japanese momentum.

7.1.3 *Avoidance of protracted campaigns*

Besides timing and momentum, the third aspect of swiftness in execution is the avoidance of protracted campaigns. According to Sun Tzu:

> "When victory is long delayed, the ardor and morale of the army will be depressed.
> When the siege of a city is prolonged, the army will be exhausted.
> When the army engages in protracted campaigns, the resources of the state will be impoverished."

久则钝兵挫锐，攻城则力屈，
久暴师则国用不足。

In general, it is true that while troops are trained for battles, no soldier likes to go to war, nor yearns for it. Thus, when war begins, it is important not to prolong it. Any delay would definitely affect the morale of the troops and deplete the resources of the state. Early completion of the war also allows the state to conserve and consolidate resources and so deny the enemy the opportunity for retaliation and prevent third parties from interfering or taking advantage of the situation.

Similarly, a business firm should not be engaged in protracted campaigns against its competitor(s). For example, a protracted price war is bound to hurt all parties concerned, except the consumer. This is because the discounts are bound to erode the profits of the companies that are engaged in the battles. Similarly, if companies are involved in long promotional wars, the effects can be equally damaging. First, each company will have to develop new and creative ways of promoting their products or services. Over a long period of time, such demands can have a demoralizing impact on the employees. Second, promotions, like price discounts, will also affect the company's bottom line profit margins. Third, continuous promotions may also create a negative image of the industry. Finally, when such promotions are extended over long periods of time, it may be difficult to revert back to normalcy. This is because consumers may treat the promotions as norms over time and would be very upset when such expected benefits are suddenly taken away.

In summary, in the execution of the mission, one must wait for the most opportune time to strike at every stage of the battle. When the attack is launched, a continuous bombardment in terms of effort and actions flows. Momentum is thus created, sustained, and if possible, further amplified. Finally, one should aim to complete the whole campaign within the shortest time possible.

7.2 Adaptability in maneuvers

While swiftness in execution allows one to gain time, momentum and quick results, as well as providing the element of surprise, should not be construed as blind assaults. In fact, Sun Tzu forbade this. Rather, he advocated that swiftness in execution must be accompanied by the consciousness of the need to be adaptable. These two principles seem to be in opposition and they are not easy to apply together. Yet to win the war, there is a need to recognize and be conscious of the fact that despite all the detailed planning, something can still go wrong, and the commander on the ground must be smart enough to recognize this, and change his plans accordingly. He must not be carried away by the fast moving events, and be overwhelmed by the various changing situations. Rather, he must adapt to the ground conditions once war begins. There are at least three aspects to the principle of adaptability – shaping and flexibility, innovativeness and the use of initiative. Just like the three aspects of swiftness, they serve to reinforce each other in the use and application of the principle of adaptability.

7.2.1 *Shaping and flexibility*

The conduct of war can be a very complicated matter. Yet Sun Tzu used a simple and common medium, water, to illustrate the need to be flexible when fighting battles:

> "The guiding principle in military tactics may be likened to water. Just as flowing water avoids the heights and hastens to the lowlands, an army should avoid strengths and strike weaknesses."

夫兵形象水，水之形，避高而趋下；兵之形，避实而击虚。

> "Just as water shapes itself according to the ground, an army should manage its victory in accordance with the situation of the enemy. Just as water has no constant shape, so in warfare there are no fixed rules and regulations."

水因地而制流，兵因敌而制胜。故兵无常势，水无常形；

The above statements suggest that the general must be flexible in his actions with respect to strategic and tactical variations in order to gain maximum advantage of the changing circumstances. Note that one of the most startling remarks is that there are no fixed rules and regulations in execution. In other words, the general has almost the ultimate discretion to decide what he deems best, depending on the situation of the war.

To exercise flexibility, the general must adopt strategies that are fluid enough to be able to change instantaneously in response to the situation. At the same time, the troops on the ground must also be able to perform, if required, more than one role. In fact, this is the idea underlying both the direct and indirect forces:

> "In battle there are only the direct and indirect forces, yet their combinations are limitless and beyond comprehension."

战势不过奇正，奇正之变，不可胜穷也。

> "For these two forces are mutually reproductive; their interactions are endless like those of interlocking rings. Indeed, who can tell where the variations begin and end?"

奇正相生，如循环之无端，孰能穷之？

Note that both the direct and indirect forces can switch roles anytime, and either one force can hold the trump card for victory. At the same time, both forces create a lot of flexibility and variations in which the general can fight out his battles. In essence, this fluidity also renders one's force unpredictable to the enemy and more capable of generating the element of surprise. In the same way, fluidity is very important in business. For example, contingency planning is a must in all planning exercises, and sensitivity analysis (with high, low, and most likely estimates) is very much part of business forecasts. The company must build enough leverage within its planning and operating systems so that it can react accordingly to the changes in the environment, and the competition. It must not rigidly stick to one plan or course of action. Alternatives must always be available.

There is no doubt that among other principles, adaptability probably has the most varied applications to business. However, one must also be cautious about some of the possible dangers and negative applications. To begin with, if one were to treat business as war and subscribe to the idea of no fixed rules and regulations in execution, and shaping plans according to the circumstances on the ground, the results can be quite frightening. The following are some examples:

(1) Bribery. A company may resort to bribery, if necessary, all the way up to the highest level of government, in order to solicit key or additional business, without any corporate conscience. Moreover, in countries where the practice is rife, it may not hesitate to use it as a competitive tool. While this may seem irksome, Sun Tzu, in fact, advocated it in war:

> "The enemy's agents who are sent to spy on us must be sought out, bribed, guided and cared for, so that they can be converted into double agents to work for us."

必索敌人之间来间我者，因而利之，
导而舍之，故反间可得而用也。

While bribery is an expected practice and the norm in war and politics, there is no doubt that it is an unethical practice in business, and should be eradicated if possible. Unfortunately, it has existed since business transactions first took place. Even in countries where there are very strict laws against this practice, such as Britain, Canada, and the United States, bribery exists. Some recent examples can be found in Japan. On 9 December 1988, Japanese Finance Minister, Kiichi Miyazawa was forced to resign over his alleged involvement in receiving unlisted shares from Recruit Cosmos, a real estate company. A few days later, on 14 December 1988, Hisashi Shinto, chairman of Nippon Telegraph and Telephone Corporation (NTT), the country's largest corporation, also resigned over alleged involvement in insider trading on the stock market. Mr. Shinto quitted after admitting that he had received 9 million yen (over US$70,000) in profits from the sale of unlisted shares of Recruit Cosmos. Japanese newspapers also accused NTT of purchasing sophisticated computers from the Cray Corporation of the United States, later selling them to Recruit Cosmos at lower prices.

The resignation of Mr Miyazawa and Mr Shinto represented only the tip of the iceberg. In fact, the seriousness and widespread nature of the Recruit shares-for-favors scandal is something worth documenting. Table 7.1 shows the chronology of the main events that were unfurled, and culminated in the resignation of the Japanese Prime Minister, Noboru Takeshita on April 25, 1989. In making his resignation announcement, Mr Takeshita also apologized to the nation and took responsibility for a spreading influence-peddling scandal that involved some 160 prominent Japanese personalities – the Prime Minister, cabinet ministers, bureaucrats, government officials, and leading businessmen.

It was very interesting to note that Prime Minister Takeshita had initially tried to prevent the scandal from blowing out of proportion by reshuffling and appointing new faces into his cabinet so as not to tarnish the image of Japan's ruling LDP party. Unfortunately for the Prime Minister, even his newly appointed Minister of Justice at that time, Takashi Hasegawa, who was to conduct the investigations, was also involved in the scandal-ridden real estate company. Mr Hasegawa resigned on 30 December 1988, barely 60 hours after his appointment, when newspapers uncovered that his supporters had received over US$40,000 from Recruit.

While many Japanese will wrestle and grapple with the moral issues underlying the Recruit scandal, it is also important to point out that it was not an isolated incident. In fact, it is of no comfort to point out that the last corruption scandal that engulfed the Japanese government and the LDP was in 1974. It was another well publicized case concerning Lockheed's payment to the then Prime Minister Kakuei Tanaka – again for favors.

At this juncture, it may be appropriate to highlight that among the developed countries, Japan seems more susceptible to the practice of gifts-for-favor. Indeed, gift-giving (which could easily be termed bribery by Western definition) is a perfected art in Japanese culture,

Table 7.1 The Recruit Scandal

Date	Event
1986	Recruit Company, a rapidly growing information and publishing conglomerate, sold large numbers of unlisted shares in its subsidiary, Recruit Cosmos, at low prices to about 160 influential politicians, government officials and businessmen. This was done in order to solicit favors.
June 1988	Major newspapers reported that senior members of the ruling Liberal Democratic Party (LDP) were given Recruit Cosmos shares before they were listed on the stock market. The allegations were that the holders were able to capitalize on profit opportunities once the shares were listed on the exchange.
July 1988	Various Japanese newspapers alleged that Recruit also sold shares to Cabinet ministers and their aides, including Prime Minister Noboru Takeshita and Finance Minister Kiichi Miyazawa. These allegations were denied.
July 1988	The Chairman of Recruit, Hiromasa Ezoe, and Ko Morita, president of Japan's top financial newspaper, the Nihon Keizai Shimbun, resigned when their share purchases were discovered.
November 1988	Japan Socialist Party member of parliament (MP) Takumi Ueda resigned after admitting that he had received Recruit shares. Ueda was the first political victim of the scandal. Many would follow suit. The former Recruit chairman, Ezoe, was summoned to Parliament to help investigations and to testify on the affair.
December 1988	Finance Minister Miyazawa was forced to resign in the face of questions about his purchase of Recruit shares. The Chairman of telecommunications giant NTT, Hisashi Shinto, resigned over share purchase by his secretary. Justice Minister Takashi Hasegawa also resigned when he was implicated. Miyazawa was the first cabinet minister to resign, while Hasegawa's resignation came barely 60 hours after his appointment. These developments suggested the seriousness of the whole affair and placed tremendous pressure on the ruling LDP and Prime Minister Takeshita.
January 1989	Economic Planning Minister Ken Harada resigned when he too was implicated in the scandal.

Table 7.1 (Cont.)

Date	Event
February 1989	The scandal claimed another prominent victim. Democratic Socialist Party Chairman Saburo Tsukamoto had to step down over his involvement in the Recruit-share affair. In the same month, four prominent businessmen, and a former Labor Ministry official were arrested on suspicion of corruption.
March 1989	Former NTT chairman Hasashi Shinto was arrested. He was formally charged with accepting shares as bribes from Recruit.
April 1989	The Japanese Prime Minister, Noboru Takeshita, told Parliament that he had received large donations from Recruit. He had earlier tried to deny his involvement. Increasing number of LDP members, business leaders and the general public called for him to step down. Mr Takeshita obtained approval from the party leadership for his resignation.
June 2, 1989	Sosuke Uno was chosen as new Prime Minister. He too, resigned over his involvement with a geisha girl, and over the crushing defeat of the LDP in the Upper House, in late July 1989.

and is rife among businessmen. Thus, while to one culture gift-giving may be considered a deliberate, unethical attempt to peddle influence, the same perception may not apply in another culture where it may be perceived as one of many ways to win (that is, there are no fixed rules in business warfare). It is, therefore, no surprise that bribery has taken on so many disguised methods of payment that at times it can be very difficult to discern. The following are some examples:

- Direct cash payment or deposits in numbered foreign bank accounts;
- Overbilling of sales with kickbacks (such as commission) to the buyer;
- Payments through a third party;
- Free gifts such as houses, watches, paintings, including samples of the product, etc.;
- Provision of free services and perks such as holidays, club mem-

bership, travel and entertainment;

- Granting unsecured loans that are never collected;
- Putting "suspicious" people on payroll, or appointing unnecessary consultants;
- Providing free training programs or consulting services;
- Providing scholarships and educational expenses for children of interested parties;
- Making contributions to organizations of payee's choice, including even to charitable causes;
- Buying properties from payee at inflated prices or selling properties at deflated prices;
- Share rights for business associates to be decided strictly by directors of the company.

While bribery should never be encouraged as a way to do business – whether it is meant to obtain or retain business, to reduce political risks, to avoid harassment, to reduce taxes, or to induce official action – as it can increase dramatically the costs of operations, and even breeds further bribery and corruption, it is important to recognize that it exists, and companies must learn to manage it. It would be too naive to assume that it does not exist, and that it can be eradicated.

Rather than avoid the problem of bribery, companies should actively confront the challenge. Companies that do not have a counter-bribery policy will always end up paying the wrong person, the wrong source, or under/over paying, resulting in frustrations and disappointment. At the same time, as pointed out earlier, it can lead to internal corruption and increase the costs of doing business. Here it is important to point out that we are against bribery as a means of doing business and do not tolerate its existence. However, bribery exists, and is actively practiced by many businessmen in various countries as a competitive tool to gain strategic or unfair advantage. Such practices are especially rife in countries where there are no fixed rules and regulations governing the conduct of business, or where rules are very relaxed and vague.

It is also very important to point out that even when one has a well defined set of rules and regulations, it is not sufficient. This is especially so in the conduct of international business. What is considered as totally unacceptable and illegal in one's country (like bribery and gift-giving) may be viewed as acceptable in another country. Thus, it is essential that a company operating overseas must pay close attention to the local customs, practices, and even government policies. In essence, understanding the local culture in which the company operates. This, in fact, is the major thrust of any textbook on international business or international marketing.

(2) Unscrupulous business practices. There are many inherent dangers if businesses do not adhere to rules and regulations. For example, while discounting and pricing in relation to market forces are acceptable practices, deliberate attempts to use price as a weapon to squeeze out competitors can become questionable. In fact, some countries have been accused of subsidizing their exports in order to penetrate overseas markets. Companies have been charged with dumping excess production capacity at the expense of other competitors.

The over-emphasis on eliminating competitors by all-means philosophy may also lead companies to manufacture defective or lower quality products in order to capture a bigger market share. In fact, one of the main reasons for the emergence of the consumer movement is to counter the malpractices of business. In Europe and North America, increasing consumer movements have resulted in various changes in regulations by government and other agencies to ensure product safety, improved product quality and durability, information on product usage, disclosure of product contents, and so on – all designed to protect the interests of consumers.

There is growing concern for consumer protection in the less developed countries as well. One of the noteworthy efforts was launched against Nestle Corporation which was alleged to have sold sub-standard baby formulae to some less developed countries. In fact, several worldwide consumer groups were successful in getting the World Health Organisation to issue a code regulating worldwide advertising and the marketing of baby formulae.

In sum, it is to the interest of every company to seek competitive advantages in order to survive and be more profitable. Indeed, the mere justification for the existence of a company is, by and large, to make money. It would be unthinkable not to make money. However, the moral issue is not how much money the company is capable of making, but rather how it goes about making the money – is it the straight or crooked way. Unlike wars where rules are rarely enforced and policed (even so, there is the Geneva Convention), there are very explicit rules and regulations, legal systems, and codes of conduct that govern how businesses should operate. In addition, there are well-established penalties for breaches of the law, and the policing system is fairly rigorous. Firms should therefore be constantly reminded of such consequences.

Besides the negative aspects of issues pertaining to non-adherence to fixed rules and regulations, there are many positive business lessons that can be learnt from the concept of flexibility and shaping. In fact, we will argue that the large Japanese manufacturers have probably mastered this concept best. Let us illustrate with some commonly known examples.

The Japanese are known to be very detailed in planning. In fact, the process can be very long. One would therefore expect that if the Japanese take such a long time to plan, it must be very thorough, and they would be more rigid in sticking to their plans. However, while being detailed and thorough in planning, they are surprisingly very flexible when it comes to the execution of the plan. To quote Kotler *et al* (1985, p. 254):

> "Flexibility has been the visible trademark of the Japanese. They
> have not engraved their strategies in stone. They have not
> become so committed to a specific strategy that they have been
> blinded by it. Rather, they have remained committed to broad
> strategic thrusts, and they have demonstrated tremendous
> flexibility in pursuing these thrusts. This is reflected in both
> their incremental behaviors and their revolutionary outbursts.
> They have continually adapted to the market and competitive
> environment and their evolving position within it."

The commitment to flexibility is seen not just in the implementation of plans. The Japanese production system is known to be very flexible. To begin with, they rely heavily on sub-contracting systems which are geared towards flexibility in many ways. First, it cushions the impact of falling demand and orders, as the burden (such as problems of re-trenchment of workers) is passed to the sub-contractors. Second, it allows the buyer to source from multiple suppliers. Third, it creates competition among sub-contractors, which inevitably pushes up quality. Finally, competition among the various suppliers also tends to push down costs.

Going beyond purchasing, the Japanese shop floor is organized in a very flexible manner so as to capitalize on changes in product designs, order sizes, and so on. To complement such a system, Japanese workers are trained to perform more than one function and their job rotation system ensures that their level of competency is not affected.

At the final product stage, Japanese products are known to be shaped according to the demands of the markets that they are selling to, even though the market size may seem small. For example, while the United States largely ignored the markets in South-east Asia in the 1960s and 1970s, the Japanese courted this part of the world enthusiastically with products that were designed specifically for them. Today, the Japanese are reaping the rewards of their early investments as these markets have become increasingly important.

The flexibility of Japanese marketing is also illustrated by their penetration of the US market. The following comments from Kotler *et al* (1985, p. 121) are very illuminating:

"The Japanese have not used any one approach to extend their presence in US markets…. The Japanese improve, extend, and proliferate their product lines and they engage in market segmentation, sequencing, and flexibility….

In short, the Japanese learn by doing. They develop and modify products, introduce them, and then watch how the market reacts. This observation or learning provides the basis for the next round of product development or modification, introduction, and further learning."

It is important to note that Japanese market flexibility even goes beyond the concern with product development and adaptation. It extends to the individual marketing variables. For example, in the area of pricing, the typical approach adopted by Japanese manufacturers is that of a low-price, penetration strategy. This strategy applies when they first started attacking the world market in the 1960s with low-technology products, and applies today even with their high-technology products like computers and medical equipment. Once their products have gained acceptance, or when they have eliminated their key competitors, prices are then raised gradually. For example, when Japanese television sets were first sold in the US, their prices were kept very low. Once they gained acceptance in the 1970s, prices were raised closer to the American models. When they began to dominate the US market by the 1980s, Japanese brands like Sony were already commanding price premiums. This same pattern of development is also beginning to take shape in the automobile industry. Japanese imported cars were sold very cheaply when they first penetrated the US market. Today, this is no longer the case. Japanese cars are sold at comparable prices with American-made models. This is because the Japanese have captured a sizeable share of the US automobile market, and their cars are now widely accepted by consumers. For some brands (like the Mazda RX-7 sports car), their prices even command a premium over comparable American models.

In essence, Japanese successes in the world market can be attributed largely to their ability to practice the concept of flexibility and shaping. This fact has been widely acknowledged by many Western scholars (e.g. Kotler *et al* 1985, Abernathy *et al* 1981, and Drucker 1971) who even argue that Americans stand to gain by learning from the Japanese.

7.2.2 Innovativeness

Another very interesting concept related to the principle of adaptability, as advocated by Sun Tzu, is that of innovativeness. This can be illustrated by the following remarks:

> "Therefore, do not repeat the tactics that won you a victory, but vary them according to the circumstances."

故其战胜不复，而应形于无穷。

> "He must be able to change his methods and schemes so that no one can know his intentions.
> He must be able to alter his camp-sites and marching routes so that no one can predict his movements."

易其事，革其谋，使人无识；
易其居，迂其途，使人不得虑。

This non-repetitiveness of tactics implies a constant search for new and innovative ways of meeting the challenges offered by the ever-changing circumstances. In addition, the use of new approaches will also prevent the enemy from anticipating one's plans, as one becomes unpredictable through continual innovation. In essence, the strategy to be adopted should be novel and situation dependent, rather than relying on seemingly proven strategies.

It is important to note that while shaping and flexibility are more reactive in that they flow according to the situation, innovativeness is more proactive in that it attempts to dictate the situation:

> "Thus, those skilled in manipulating the enemy do so by creating a situation to which he must conform."

故善动敌者，形之，敌必从之；

Innovativeness is also very much desired in business. This is especially so in the present environment where technology is becoming more and more important as a competitive edge. Here again, the Japanese firms are adepts in this area. In fact, there are sharp contrasts between the ways in which Japan and Western countries put high technology into use. In Japan, owing to the limited demand for military applications, technology is always first used in the private sector for products that are easiest to manufacture. Only later are applications extended to include the more difficult areas. In other words, Japan uses a bottom-up approach – from the easiest to the most difficult applications.

The Western countries, on the other hand, tend to adopt a top-down approach – that is, technology is typically first applied in the most difficult areas such as space exploration or military systems. There are significant differences and results between these two approaches. In the Japanese bottom-up approach of using technology for business applications, the product is targeted at the consumer and the manufacturing process is relatively simple. As Japan has a large domestic market, consumption is on a massive scale. This enables economies of scale to be achieved quickly and costs of production as well as prices can be lowered accordingly. In turn, more funds can be generated and invested in more plant and equipment and product quality can be quickly established and raised.

In the Western top-down approach of using technology for sophisticated and difficult military applications, there is always a scarcity of facilities because production is on a small scale, and quality is difficult to stabilize. Thus, costs also tend to be very high which also hampers further investments. The following are some examples of the differences of the two approaches:

(1) When large-scale integrated circuits (LSIs) first appeared, they were quickly explored for usage in the Western countries for missile and space development. Japan, however, saw the potential of LSIs very differently. They used them in the production of pocket calculators and watches. Several hundred thousand units of LSI for the private sector were produced in Japan, so there was no hesitation nor reservation about investing in facilities. The result was that the price of an LSI circuit dropped very quickly to only a few hundred yen. This was much cheaper than anywhere else and product quality was also stabilized.

(2) Several years ago, while American defense officials were still experimenting with the automatic gyro-computer system to fly missiles, the Japanese had already successfully used it to fly model toy aeroplanes. At a model airplane competition held in a Florida city, a radio-controlled model plane from Japan contained an automatic pilot operated by a gyroscope exactly as in a real aircraft. By programming a micro computer, the plane could be controlled from the ground to do all kinds of flying maneuvers by simply pushing a button. There was no longer any need for the operator to observe the flight patterns in order to control the plane. The Japanese were able to overcome the application problem of the technology because they chose to use it on simpler products.

(3) When carbon fiber, a medium that has an exceptionally high tensile strength of 200 kg per sq mm, which is three times the tensile strength of regular steel and is also lighter than aluminium, first appeared, European and American companies immediately considered it for potential application in the aircraft industry (a difficult area). In Japan, the companies used this new material to manufacture golf clubs and fishing rods (an easy application). In doing so, mass-production technology was established and quality was achieved before using the material for larger and more difficult products. This bottom-up approach resulted in Japan claiming some 70% of the world production of this new carbon fiber today. In fact, the top two manufacturers, Toray Industries and Toho Rayon Co., are Japanese.

(4) When shape-memory alloys, which are made mainly of titanium and nickel, first appeared American and European companies considered the technology for difficult applications such as the assembly of missiles and satellites. In contrast, Japanese companies first used the alloy in the manufacture of coffee makers, which is a very simple undertaking that can be mass-produced economically and at a consistent high quality. It was then used for making the materials for the automatic control of the direction of air flow from the outlet of air conditioners. Then it hit on a gem application – a brassiere (made by Wacoal, Inc., of Kyoto) which can return to the shape of the user no matter how often it is washed and stretched! By 1988, the demand for such a brassiere was so great from the United States and some European countries that the company was having problems increasing its production capacity.

(5) While the United States and other Western countries confined the use of an extremely sophisticated semiconductor called a CCD image sensor to military purposes, the Japanese used it to mass produce the camcorder, a compact, single-body camera and video cassette recorder. By 1988, the silicon CCD chip contained in the camcorder was being produced at a rate of several hundred thousand per month, and exported to various places of the world.

From the above examples, it can be seen that the Japanese use technology very differently from Western countries. In particular, they are able to use something designed for military purposes for economic gain. In addition, their successful innovative adaptations allow them to manufacture a continuous stream of new and commercially valuable products. What is more intriguing is that the basic technology involved was largely discovered or invented by scientists in the Western countries. The Japanese, however, managed to get hold of the technology and then cleverly adapt it for commercial purposes.

Two recent examples will illustrate this. Photonics, which is an emerging technology that uses light instead of electricity to process and transmit information, was invented by the Americans. In fact the Americans are still the leaders in basic photonics research. However it is in the application area, an industry worth at least US$100 billion by the end of the century, with widespread usage in telecommunications (optical fibers), fiber optic cameras for surgery, gyroscopes, sensors, data storage, optical computing etc, that the Americans are lagging behind the Japanese. Fuzzy logic is another technology invented by the Americans. Unfortunately, they failed to take its application into the commercial realm. Meanwhile many Japanese companies have used fuzzy logic in the manufacture of air-conditioners, vacuum cleaners, washing machines and other consumer durables. In fact, as of early 1990, one Japanese stockbroking company even applied fuzzy logic in its share investment strategy that resulted in an excess return of over 20% when compared to conventional, binary logic.

Some clever acts of pilfering technology from others has brought some embarassment to the Japanese. In December 1988, the American Arbitration Association ordered Fujitsu Ltd to pay International Business Machines (IBM) Corporation a sum of US$237 million to settle a bitter software copyright dispute. IBM claimed that Japan's largest manufacturer of robots and computers had simply borrowed and adapted basic software programs which were developed by American scientists. The ruling appeared to substantiate accusations that the Japanese are brilliant when it comes to adapting a scientific breakthrough for commercial use, but contribute very little in the field of original thinking and pure research.

While it is true that in the past Japanese firms have been able to churn out superior commercial products built on basic research developed in the West, the trend may not continue. Today, Japan has been propelled into a new era of high technology and both Japanese industrialists and scientists are becoming increasingly aware that they cannot continue to borrow, purchase or steal the building blocks necessary for technology in the 21st century. They have also recognized that the era where intellectual property can be used freely is over. Consequently, the Japanese government's science and technology agency has drawn up very ambitious plans so that, within the next 23 years, Japanese scientists will hope to develop:

- artificial eyes, ears and organs which will not be rejected by the human body;
- techniques for removing underwater sludge from the sea;
- an artificial intelligence which will be capable of making decisions like a human, including the ability to control aircraft;
- the means of preventing cancer; and
- space robots with high levels of artificial intelligence which will be capable of performing dangerous and difficult tasks.

As a nation, the Japanese have demonstrated that innovative behavior can be planned systematically and proactively. Despite their traditional handicaps such as teamwork (which might stimulate productivity, but is unlikely to stimulate the individual thinking necessary to basic research), the seniority system (which tends to muffle and muzzle debate and free expression) and general lack of individual creativity (the lack of free thought in Japanese laboratories and universities is best reflected by the fact that up to 1988, only five Japanese scientists won Nobel prizes as compared to 20 Frenchmen and 14 Americans), they have decided to switch gear and have taken positive steps to dictate the future. As a demonstration of such efforts, over US$40 billion (5 trillion yen) were already invested in R&D within a mere 4-year period (1985 to 1988).

However, Japanese innovativeness is not confined to technology and product development. In fact, Kotler *et al* (1985, p. 115) comment:

> "... Japanese firms are adept at using a multiplicity of competitive weapons with varying degrees of emphasis – price, promotion, product quality, product features, service, distribution, product line stretching and proliferation – to penetrate and win markets."

The same authors in their concluding chapter (p. 254) also remark:

> "Creativity has increasingly become a feature of Japanese strategy. Indeed, without creativity, strategic entrepreneurship is difficult, if not impossible. Strategic initiatives, competitive advantages and distinctive competences must be created. Moreover, as market, competitive and environmental conditions change, these initiatives, advantages and competences must be challenged and reshaped – in short, recreated."

Japanese innovative behavior is not confined to the manufacturing and design of products and services. It has now gone beyond the laboratory and the production room. Innovation, as demonstrated by the Japanese, must be present in the strategic and marketing dimensions as well. Thus, a firm must never be satisfied with the ways things are done. Rather, it should constantly seek new product ideas, improve customer services, create better advertising and promotional methods, develop innovative distribution systems and find cost-cutting methods. In essence, there is a constant need to create new customer values in order to sustain and increase a firm's market share and profits.

Fortunately for firms, there are many tools and methods to help them become more innovative in their thinking and behavior. Michael

Porter's (1985) value chain concept is one such tool. Basically, the value chain disaggregates a firm into its strategically relevant activities in order to understand the behavior of costs and the existing and potential sources of differentiation. A firm then tries to gain advantage by performing these strategically important activities more cheaply or better than its competitors.

Besides Michael Porter's value chain concept, there are other techniques that have been advocated for development of new and creative ideas. For example, brainstorming is often used by groups of individual to develop ideas and find creative solutions. Role playing is also used by some companies to generate competitive strategies, or develop counter-actions against competitors.

Perhaps the best known person today who has developed various techniques and methods to help individuals think creatively and innovatively is Edward De Bono. His concept of lateral thinking is well known and his books such as *Lateral Thinking for Management* (1971) and *Opportunities* (1978) are very well received. Thus, there is no shortage of opportunities for firms to pursue innovative behavior. What is perhaps needed more is the willingness of companies to take the opportunities.

It is very significant to note that many American firms are now becoming more innovative in their ways of doing business, especially in product design. They have learned from the Japanese that they can no longer rely solely on price and other marketing gimmicks to sell their products. In fact, Stanford Design Forum was set up in early 1990 by a group of Americans to promote design management among companies. In addition, Harvard Business School has also added design management into its curriculum. So far, several companies have begun to reap rewards as a result of their innovative product designs. For example, Black and Decker managed to grab 20% of the electric mixer market in 1990 with the new *Handymixer*. Unlike conventional mixers which have to be stored in a drawer, it could be mounted on a wall. This innovation put a US$20 premium on the price. Sunbeam Appliance Co produced a mini food processor (called Oskar) designed to look good and save countertop space. Within two years, the company took 30% of the market. Other companies like Xerox, IBM and Apple have all incorporated design innovation as part of the overall corporate and manufacturing strategy.

Unfortunately there are also some other American companies which have yet to wake up and take concrete innovative actions. The automobile industry is one such example. Instead of improving their product quality and paying more attention to product innovation and design, Detroit's largest car manufacturers have hired the top advertising agencies in Madison Avenue to invoke anti-Japanese feelings through disparaging commercials. The approach is not only xenophobic, but also demeaning and unethical. So long as the American car manufacturers cannot match up to the innovative and high quality Japanese imports, they will continue to lose market share. Ironically, the same innovative and high quality Japanese cars are now manufactured and assembled in the US by the Americans themselves. Toyota and Honda plants in the US, for example have outperformed their American counterparts. In the final analysis, for manufactured goods, it is innovation and product quality that matter. Strong advertising can only invoke temporary feelings if it cannot be backed up by product claims. This, unfortunately, is what is plaguing the US automobile makers.

7.2.3 *Use of initiative*

The third aspect of the principle of adaptability is the use of initiative. While innovativeness is a proactive, deliberate and systematic approach to problem-solving, the use of initiative requires both the proactive and reactive dimensions. In other words, it requires the individual to be very responsive to changes in situations, as well as able to take pre-emptive action. Thus, resourcefulness at the point of decision-making is essential. In addition, the exercise of initiative is often instantaneous and an intuitive act of the individual who is faced with the decision.

Sun Tzu recognized the use of initiative when he said:

"There are situations when the orders of the ruler need not be obeyed."

君命有所不受。

And he gave an example of a situation when orders could be disobeyed and initiative used:

"If the situation is one of victory, the general must fight even though the ruler may have issued orders not to engage. If the situation is one of defeat, the general must not fight even though the ruler may have issued orders to do so."

故战道必胜，主曰：无战，必战可也；
战道不胜，主曰：必战，无战可也。

Thus, the use of initiative requires the general to make decisions at the point of battle as there is hardly any time for him to consult and discuss with the ruler (who is often away from the battlefield). He must decide on the spot what his next move is. If the situation dictates that he should attack, he must do so, even if he had prior orders not to engage. This is because there are so many variations and changes at each step of the battle. If the general cannot exercise initiative under such circumstances and must await the orders of the ruler for each move, it is like telling your superior that you would like to put out a fire. By the time the order to do so is approved, the ashes would have turned cold!

As discussed earlier in this chapter, the general must advance without seeking personal fame and glory and must retreat without fear of being punished. At all times, he must have the welfare of the people and the interests of the ruler at heart. Thus, in exercising his initiative under such conscience-clear circumstances, he has not betrayed the trust given to him, nor should his loyalty be questioned.

Initiative also extends beyond pragmatism. This is because pragmatism, to a large extent, is reactive in nature. Initiative, however, encompasses both the reactive and proactive dimensions. Other than reacting very expediently and effectively to changes in the environment, it also involves constantly looking for better ways to win:

> "If the enemy provides an opportunity, quickly capitalize on it. Forestall your enemy by capturing something he treasures most, but do not easily agree with him on fixed dates for battles."

敌人开阖，必亟入之。先其所爱，微与之期。

> "Effective strategies must constantly change according to the situation of the enemy."

践墨随敌，以决战事。

However, it is important to recognize that Sun Tzu did not advocate the use of initiative at all levels. In fact, it is confined to the highest level of command only:

> "He must be capable of keeping his officers and men ignorant of his battle plans."

能愚士卒之耳目，使之无知。

> "He only assigns tasks to his soldiers, but does not explain the purpose; he tells them to gain advantages, but does not divulge the dangers."

犯之以事，勿告以言；犯之以利，勿告以害。

In business, there is an increasing need for the exercise of initiative, especially when competition is getting tougher and technology is fast changing. This mental agility in decision-making is very important. In applying initiative in strategy implementation, one tries to control the time and place of action and attempts to dominate both the business situations and the competitors. When confronted with difficulty, a solution is quickly found, even if it is a temporary measure, until a better and longer-term answer is found. For example, what should a company do when its competitor suddenly starts a promotion such as a sale or price discount? If the promotion is very attractive, the company's market share can be quickly eroded. There is an obvious need to react immediately and, if possible, not to imitate the gimmick of the competitor because following the competitor with the same offer can only check the erosion of share, but not regain it. Thus, it is necessary to produce something different. Initiative and innovativeness are needed.

In industries where competition is rife and where the product is not highly differentiated, initiative is almost a necessary trait required of managers. In the fast food industry, some companies even provide emergency kits to restaurant managers to cushion any sudden promotional onslaught by competitors. In these kits are various promotional items and give-aways like balloons, pencils and other small gifts. They are used as temporary buffers against the competitors until the management produces more viable solutions.

However, the exercise of initiative in business must be properly controlled and monitored, just as in war. While there are merits in allowing the exercise of initiative throughout an organization, management must also ensure that corporate policies and guidelines are not breached and that corporate law and order must still prevail. For example, there could be tremendous chaos if every salesperson were to decide at what price he/she wishes to sell a product, or a factory operator refuses to follow the established procedure for assembling a product. Quality control circles and work improvement teams require leadership and proper management for them to be effective and successful.

Before going on to discuss the principle of deception, it is important to reiterate that the three aspects of adaptability – shaping and flexibility, innovativeness and the use of initiative – are very much inter-related. They must be carefully studied and understood. At the expense of idolizing the Japanese, it may be necessary to refer to them once again as the gurus of the art of adaptation. For example, over the last few years when the Japanese yen was appreciating remarkably against the American dollar and other European currencies and the country was facing an aging population with severe labor shortages, many American leaders and scholars argued that such problems would greatly undermine the Japanese manufacturing sector. In making the judgment, these leaders failed to recognize the tremendous resilience of Japanese corporations (*Kaisha*) in adapting to a changing trading environment. Instead of throwing up their arms in despair, Japanese companies took very concrete steps to adjust. The following are some examples:

(1) The depressed shipbuilding and steel industries diversified into new lines of business. The Nippon Steel Corporation, for instance, gave top priority to newly-established interests in electronics, new materials and information systems. It also used its redundant engineers to form a construction and development company, instead of retrenching them.

(2) Many large manufacturers weathered the crisis by moving production operations overseas. They also sought various ways to increase the level of productivity at home. In March 1987, the Honda Motor Company established new headquarters in the United States to expand its production operations in North America. Its huge plant in Marysville had assembled 363,668 Honda Accord and Civic cars in 1989. This figure was the highest of all single auto factories in the US. More importantly, the Accord became the best selling car in the US in 1989. Besides Honda Motor Company, Nissan Motor Company had drawn up long-term plans to move its operations overseas if the exchange rate reached 100 yen to the US dollar. Other Japanese auto makers had also entered into joint-ventures with the American Big Three automakers.

(3) Electric machinery manufacturers, such as Hitachi, overcame the strong yen problem by transferring workers from their affected consumer electronics division, where profits had been eroded by the exchange rate and strong competition from cheaper products made in the newly industrialized countries like Taiwan, South Korea, Hong Kong and Singapore, to the growing computer-related sections. Another company, Matsushita, Japan's largest manufacturer of consumer electronics, sought ways to reduce costs and increase productivity. The result was that it was still able to provide Japanese consumers with low-cost electronic goods, including the world's cheapest microwave oven.

In fact, in the longest run of growth since the five year *Izangi* boom of the 1960s, Japanese companies have, in the late 1980s, drawn on enormous capital pools to finance a whole range of strategic expansion overseas while investing heavily in productivity at home. Fixed investments increased by more than 16% in Japan in 1989 to more than US$340 billion, an amount comparable to Japan's expenditure on capital investment in the 1960s. At the same time Japan's direct foreign investments increased to over US$41 billion in 1989, with the bulk going to only 11 countries in North America, Europe, and East Asia. These were done mainly to protect its market share and increase its competitive advantage. More significantly, with a chronic labor shortage even the small and medium sized companies were forced to expand overseas and invest in a new wave of labor-cost rationalization that resulted in an even higher value-added and efficient economy.

These stories show that Japanese companies were very flexible and adaptable in adjusting to the sharp decline of the US dollar and the chronic labor shortage especially during the period 1987 to 1988. Various combinations of measures were taken. Nonetheless, there were some commonalities among the measures. Japanese manufacturers accepted short-term reductions in their profits, invested in cost-reducing programs, shifted production operations offshore and improved productivity at home. In addition, they took advantage of the strong yen by importing cheaper materials and energy. In contrast to measures typically adopted by Western managers in a crisis, retrenchment was kept to a minimum so as not to create a morale problem, assets were not sold off for short-term gains and R&D programs were not abandoned. In many instances, personnel costs were reduced by cuts in the salaries of managers and executives.

The results of Japanese policies of adaptation are already being felt. During 1988, Japanese manufacturers increased productivity by an average of 14.8%, while wages rose only 4.2%. The result was that Japan's factories effectively slashed their production costs by 10.2% in 1988. Similar patterns of growth are expected for 1989 and 1990. At the macro level, the effects are also showing.

Despite a doubling of the value of the yen against the US dollar over a three year period (1986 to 1988), Japan's exports rose an estimated 14% during 1988, leading the economy to an overall growth rate of 4.8%. The trend is almost certain to continue into 1989, with exports likely to grow between 6 to 8%, and an economic growth rate of between 3.5 to 5.0% – possibly the highest of any OECD countries. Thus, it appears that as a result of taking various economic restructuring policies and investing for higher efficiency at home and abroad, the Japanese have managed to adapt to the labor shortage and the stronger yen. They are poised for another economic miracle of an export boom that may refuse to die. This is because the increasing exports are also in highly profitable products and markets. For example, in 1988, exports of computers were up by 31%, semi-conductors rose 18%, and machine tools were higher by 17%. In sum, recent statistics have shown how effective the restructuring has been. Prior to the restructuring,

Japanese companies could be considered dangerous. After the restructuring, they are becoming lethal.

A further result of the success is that on the last day of 1988, the Japanese government paid off the last of its foreign debt. With a payment of US$3.6 million to British investors, Japan retired a loan dating back to the early 1950s, when the country was struggling to rebuild an economy left in ruins by World War II. Moreover, Japan has become the world's lender and Tokyo is home to the world's ten richest banks. The Tokyo stock market is bigger than New York, London, Paris and Frankfurt combined. The depth of the Tokyo stock market is reflected by its over 1,640 listings, with capitalization of over US$3.5 trillion. By contrast, although the New York Exchange has an almost equal number of listings, its capitalization is only US$2.2 trillion.

As a result of the stronger yen, many Japanese corporations have also started on an acquisition spree in overseas markets that includes not only factories and businesses, but also commercial and residential properties. With this move, Japan is almost untouchable as it now has its fingers in every economic pie – from banks to commodities, to metals, to service industries, to property and the like. Thus, Japan can no longer be labeled as a single-country, export-only economy. Rather, it is now a global conglomerate that operates from every conceivable base.

It is worthwhile to note the contrast between the way the Japanese handle their stronger currency and the way Western countries, say the United States, has handled its problems. For example, prior to 1985 the yen was greatly undervalued (which helped to push their products into world markets) and the US dollar was over-valued. However, the United States did not pursue any of the strategies used by the Japanese. The Americans could have used their artificially over-valued currency to build and buy factories and businesses overseas abroad. They could have acquired all these cheaply with their inflated currency. For that matter, they could have pursued many of the other policies that the Japanese did. Instead, the Americans wasted the money and opportunities on controversial defense spending, increased bureaucratic wastages and other unnecessary programs. In essence, the Americans wasted the excess resources on consumption. In contrast, the Japanese could easily have fallen victim to their own success like the Americans. However, they spent wisely on investment overseas. The Japanese were able to do it very successfully because its system is premised on adaptability, and changes can be made quickly and expediently. The American system – with its sectoral and partisan politics – is, in contrast, very rigid and resistant to change. The result is that the contrasting rewards and costs in both societies are very significant.

7.3 Deceptiveness in actions and strategies

Among various principles advocated by Sun Tzu, the principle of deception is probably one of the most thorny and sensitive concepts, especially when applied to business. This is because the word deception, involves ethical issues. In addition, if the concept is not clearly understood, its application to business can be easily abused, although we do not dispute that there could already be many abuses of this principle already.

Deception was briefly mentioned in Chapter 4. It will be further elaborated upon here. First of all, there is no doubt that Sun Tzu advocated the principle of deception explicitly as one of the key principles in war:

> "All warfare is based on deception."

> 兵者，诡道也。

> "War is based on deception. Whether to concentrate or divide the forces, or when changes should be made to gain advantages, must depend on the circumstances."

> 故兵以诈立，以利动，
> 以分合为变者也。

From the above quotations, it is important to note that deception, as advocated by Sun Tzu, is designed to gain strategic advantages. In war, it is very important to have relative superiority of forces and equipment at the point of engagement. This is clearly stated by Sun Tzu:

> "The enemy must not know where I intend to attack. For if he does not know where I intend to attack, he must defend in many places. The more places he defends, the more scattered are his forces and the weaker is his force at any one point."

> 吾所与战之地不可知；不可知，则敌所备者多；
> 敌所备者多，则吾所与战者，寡矣。

Now, there are basically two ways to achieve relative superiority once the battle begins. The first way is to conceal one's intention and keep the enemy guessing where you are attacking/defending. As stated in the above quotation, when the enemy does not know where you are going to attack, his forces will be depleted as a result of trying to defend too many places.

The second way is to use deceptive tactics so as to deliberately mislead the enemy. For example, the enemy may be misguided into maneuvering his troops and resources in anticipation of one's apparent designs which are actually contrary to one's true intention. The successful use of deception would cause the enemy to misdirect his combat power and hence reduce his focus on the true target. With the enemy's combat power diverted, one can then seize the opportunity to attack a weakened enemy at the point of engagement. Thus, the use of deception is a necessary part of one's combat strategy if relative superiority at the point of engagement is to be achieved. For example, it makes it possible for a smaller force to handle a bigger force and allows for speedier completion of the combat mission.

A good example of the application of Sun Tzu's principle of deception could be cited from the period of the Three Kingdoms in China (around A.D. 220 to 265). It concerned the episode commonly known as the Empty Castle. The enemy forces were fast approaching and Liu-Pei was totally unprepared to engage them. His military advisor at that time was the well-known Zhu Ke-liang. Zhu proposed an unusual method of deceiving the enemy. While asking Liu Pei's troops to withdraw quickly, Zhu had the castle gates opened wide. In addition, he ordered some old and seasoned soldiers, dressed in civilian clothing, to casually sweep the streets leading to the castle gates. At the same time, Zhu sat at the top of the castle, sipping Chinese tea and playing a Chinese classical instrument. When the enemy forces came, they were taken by complete surprise by what they saw and hesitated to rush through the empty and wide open castle gates. To them, it was apparently a ploy. The enemy's superior commander, Sun Chian, had to come forward to assess the situation more clearly. Now, Zhu Ke-liang was known to be a very cautious and detailed strategist who seldom took chances. In order to determine if Zhu was trying to apply deception, Sun Chian strained his ears to listen to the musical chords played from the instrument. If Zhu was faking, his music was bound to reflect signs of nervousness. Unfortunately for Sun, the musical chords from Zhu's instrument were steady and firm. Thus, Sun concluded that Zhu must be laying traps behind the castle gates. Instead of ordering his troops to march through a totally undefended castle in pursuit of his enemy, Sun Chian ordered a withdrawal to encamp so as to allow him more time to assess the situation. This mistake in judgment allowed more time for Zhu and his forces to escape.

It is important to realize that the principle of deception is not unique to the era of Sun Tzu. It was pointed out in Chapter 1 of this book that the Japanese applied this principle in the bombing of Pearl Harbour during World War II. It is a war principle that is entrenched in almost every culture. For example, when the British army commanded by Lord Chelmsford invaded Zululand in southern Africa in 1879, the Zulus proved to be no easy prey through their use of various deceptive tactics. One such deception was their use of an *impi* (the equivalent of a division) to condense its formations so that the enemy could not estimate its regiments or actual strength. Another tactic that they used was to have small, diversionary groups of soldiers drive herds of cattle around the countryside, raising dust and deceiving the enemy as to the actual size and location of the main Zulu force.

Using such deceptive tactics, the Zulus misled Lord Chelmsford into splitting his army and taking half the force on a wild goose chase to the southeast. Meanwhile, the main Zulu impi of 20,000 attacked the remainder of the British force that was relaxing at the base camp at Isandhlwana. This attack from the north took the British soldiers by complete surprise, resulting in a massacre. With such a disaster, Lord Chelmsford was forced to retreat to Natal.

The Zulus were applying a timeless principle of warfare – deception as advocated by Sun Tzu. Deception is indeed a definite sin in everyday life, but in time of war, it is a necessary evil. Some people even argue that it is a virtue in war. In modern warfare, deception has become an integral part of both strategic planning and hardware development. In fact, the primary realm of deceptive warfare today is heavily electronic-based. Planes, tanks, ships, and helicopters all have electronic means of finding the enemy or preventing him from finding them. Various jamming devices and anti-jamming devices are created to deceive the enemy. Modern battles, more than ever before, favor the side with the most effective electronic technology. Ironically, it is such technology, with its full complement of deceptive means and hardware, that compels potential enemies to seek ways to become friends.

It is interesting to point out that the use of deception is not something that is confined to war alone. In fact, in the noble game of sports, deception is very much the core of many winning strategies. For example, in the game of volleyball, the setter will often try to deceive the opponents by the way he sets the ball, while several potential spikers would be leaping in the air concurrently. More often than not, it is not easy to detect who the actual spiker will be. In many other games like soccer, American football, basketball, and so on, various strategies are often used to deceive the opponents into making the wrong move. In world class long distance running, there is often a runner called a "rabbit" – who is deliberately included to disrupt the momentum of the potential winners. His job is basically to deceive the lead runners into believing that he is a potential threat and make them run at his unrealistic pace. Even in table-tennis, the service itself is the beginning of deception. The use of deceptive tactics in war and sports is thus not a deliberate attempt to cheat, but rather a conscious effort to gain strategic advantage over the opponents. The ultimate goal is to win, and to win decisively.

Viewed from a strategic angle, deception also complements the principle of adaptability. While the principle of adaptability seeks to exploit opportunities provided by the enemy and the ground situation, the purpose of deception is distract the enemy and disperse his combat power. In addition, deception also helps to generate surprises, so that the enemy can be caught off-guard. It enables the one using it to attain relative superiority when engaging the enemy.

There are many ways to employ deception, and Sun Tzu gave several examples including baits, illusions and fakery, and use of multiple courses of action to generate surprises.

7.3.1 Baits

One of the ways to achieve distinct advantages in combat, as discussed in Chapter 3, is to choose a battleground that is more advantageous to oneself than to the enemy. For this reason, Sun Tzu mentions that the adepts in warfare will always bring the enemy to where they want to fight and are not brought there by the enemy. One way to bring the enemy to where you want to fight is through the use of baits as deception:

> "Thus, those skilled in manipulating the enemy do so by creating a situation to which he must conform. They deliberately give away something that the enemy will take. They entice the enemy to leave his position with baits so that their men could ambush him."

故善动敌者，形之，敌必从之；
予之，敌必取之；以利动之，以卒待之。

> "By enticing the enemy with some baits, one can make him come on his accord."

能使敌人自至者，利之也；

Sun Tzu even went as far as saying:

> "Offer the enemy a bait to lure him; when he is in disorder, strike him."

利而诱之，乱而取之，

From the above statements, we can see that there are several uses of baits. First, baits are used to lure the enemy out of their strongholds to pursue the attacking troops and then force them to fight in an unfamiliar terrain. More often than not, the pursuing troops will also encounter ambushes. In fact, this is the typical guerrilla tactic of hit-and-run that was used very successfully by the Vietcong against the American soldiers during the Vietnam war.

Secondly, baits in the form of give-aways are designed to generate complacency of the enemy, and to lower his defenses. The baits are used to give him a false sense of achievement and when he is overly elated and least prepared, he becomes most vulnerable to sudden attacks.

Finally, baits can also be used offensively to distract the enemy's forces. For example, by holding out various baits in different directions, the enemy's forces may be divided in pursuit of them. Thus, even if the enemy is numerically superior initially, his strength at any one point is weaker as a result of this dispersion. This provides opportunities for the smaller but concentrated force to attack a larger force. Besides this spatial advantage (achieved through dispersing the enemy's forces), baits can also allow the smaller force to achieve temporal advantage in that when the enemy's forces are widely dispersed, it takes some time for them to re-gather and re-organize to be effective again.

The seriousness of falling into traps created by baits led Sun Tzu to provide the following warnings:

"Do not pursue an enemy who pretends to flee."

佯北勿从

"Do not succumb to enemy's baits."

饵兵勿食

While the term *deceptive tactics* seems very unethical, the truth is that baits are used in the business world. The following are some examples:

(1) A company may enter a market where the supposedly large demand, as originally conceived, never materializes. Often, the company is lured by the successes of its competitors who are earlier entrants. Unfortunately, much of the goodies are gone by the time the company enters the competition.

(2) In mergers and acquisitions, baits are used to lure more prospective acquiring companies so as to increase the acquisition price. The baits may take various forms – potential future earnings, cash reserves, capital appreciation of assets, opportunity for diversification, entrance to foreign markets, and so on.

(3) To attract investors, companies often resort to using sweeteners like bonus issues, rights and warrants. However, these financial instruments are no different from baits in that they are used to lure more investors' funds into the company. In fact, in the late 1980s, many unwary investors were conned by junk bonds in the United States. What were supposedly high yield financial instruments, turned out to be scandalous tools to deceive investors' money.

(4) In an attempt to lure high caliber and/or top personnel who are currently employed by their competitors, many companies often resort to head-hunting firms to do the assignment. One of the possible reasons for using head-hunting firms is to camouflage the identity of the recruiting firm, and hence reduce the sensitivity. While one may view this as a professional approach to recruiting staff, it is nonetheless, a rather deceptive tactic. Moreover, tremendous baits or heavy incentives are often used to lure the wanted person.

(5) One of the commonly used methods for less developing countries to attract foreign investments is the offer of incentives, such as exemption from taxes through pioneer status, unlimited repatriation of earnings, liberal foreign exchange controls, abundant supply of low cost labor and utilities, accelerated depreciation, and so on. Such incentives are obviously used as baits. Unfortunately, there are instances whereby companies simply gobble such proferred baits without careful consideration of other factors, such as the political, cultural, social, economic and religious conditions of the country. The result is that they face constant dilemma after putting in large investments.

(6) Even among developed countries, baits have been used for economic and political purposes. For example, in the recently concluded US-Canada Free-Trade Agreement, Canada is now able to use, as a bait, security of access to the US market, to persuade offshore investors like Japanese and West German automakers to build manufacturing plants in Canada. In turn, these will attract more investment and provide more employment for Canada.

Perhaps the greatest and most widespread use of baits by companies could be seen in their attempts to attract more customers. While these efforts are directed at the consumers and not the competitors, their widespread usage deserves mention. The following are some examples:

(1) The use of some items as **loss leaders** in order to attract more shoppers to a store. Such a practice has been in existence for umpteen years!

(2) The use of various sales gimmicks like, "While Stocks Last", "Mystery Gifts for First 100 Customers," "Mammoth Reductions," and "Chance to Win a Free Trip to America", and many others to lure and entice the unwary shoppers.

(3) The waiving of an entrance fee to join an exclusive club, to be followed by a subtle, but increasing annual fee. There are many variants of such tricks. For example, the giving away of a free shaver (main product) so that the consumer will be hooked on to the continuous use and purchase of the blades (supplies). Such a pricing strategy is what is called two-part pricing or complementary pricing.

(4) The waiving of legal fees, processing fees and other administrative charges in order to entice consumers to borrow larger home mortgages.

(5) Provision of interest-free loans in order to attract more buyers of high ticket items, such as new cars, appliances and boats.

(6) Free delivery, after-sales service and warranties (apparently, these are costs to be recovered).

(7) The addition of free gifts to entice buyers of high ticket items like cars and houses. For example, property developers lure prospective home buyers with items like built-in bedroom wardrobes and kitchen cabinets, kitchen appliances, water heaters, concealed air-conditioning, a security alarm system, and so on. Car dealers offer items like free radio and cassette player, anti-rust treatment, food hampers, and even holidays to entice buyers!

Indeed, there are countless examples of deceptive techniques used by marketers and business firms as baits to lure the unwary consumers. The above examples probably represent only the tip of the iceberg. Many of us may even refuse to acknowledge that such tactics are deceptive and may even argue that they are great incentives!

Unfortunately, the truth is that such tactics are indeed baits used to attract customers. This is because nothing is free! The so-called free incentives must be recovered by the sellers and are camouflaged in the prices of the products. However, companies have been so successful through their advertising and promotional efforts that they have made us think of such gifts as incentives rather than baits. Most of us even view them as highly desirable and necessary!

7.3.2 *Illusions and fakery*

Another way to achieve deception is through the practice of illusions and fakery. In the words of Sun Tzu:

> "Therefore, when capable, feign incapability; when active, feign
> inactivity. When near to the objective, feign that you are far away;
> when far away, make it appear that you are near."

故能而示之不能，用而示之不用，近而示之远，远而示之近。

Illusions and fakery, therefore, serve several purposes. First, illusions serve to confuse the enemy about your real intention. They will make you become more unpredictable in the eyes of the enemy, and hence affect his judgement of you. Thus, although you may engage the same enemy each time, he has to do a new and thorough assessment of you. In this way, you wear him down in terms of time and resources needed for the assessment.

Second, faking – especially through false pretence of incapability, vulnerability, humility and weakness – serves to lower the defenses of the enemy and indirectly encourage his arrogance. Thus, like the use of baits, when the enemy is elated and least prepared, it is the best time to strike him. This is illustrated by the following:

> "In the beginning of battle, be as shy as a young maiden to entice
> the enemy and lower his defenses. When the battle progresses,
> be as swift as a hare so as to catch the unpreparedness of the
> enemy."

是故始如处女，敌人开户，
后如脱兔，敌不及拒。

Thus, by pretending to be inferior initially (like a young maiden who is demure, helpless and vulnerable), the enemy is likely to ignore you. This gives you the opportunity and time to assess the enemy, to gather and organize your troops and resources and to plan your strategy and line of attack. When you launch the attack, be like the hare – alert, quiet, swift and sudden – that the enemy is caught totally off-guard. This is also consistent with the principle of swiftness in execution.

The pretence of inferiority even extends to accommodating one's plans within the designs of the enemy:

> "Therefore, the crux of military operations is to pretend to accommodate one's plan to the designs of the enemy. Once an opportunity arises, concentrate your forces against the enemy, and no matter how distant the enemy, you can kill his general and defeat his army. This is what it means to achieve success in a crafty and ingenious way."

故为兵之事，在于顺详敌之意，
并敌一向，千里杀将，此谓巧能成事者也。

This seemingly accommodating the enemy's design is, in fact, cleverly orchestrated so as to lure him to play into one's hands instead. It is an art and requires the highest level of skills. It is no wonder that Sun Tzu commented:

> "To feign confusion, one must possess discipline; to feign cowardice, one must possess courage; to feign weakness, one must possess superiority of forces."

乱生于治，怯生于勇，弱生于强。

and he said of the guru of warfare:

> "Therefore, the victories won by a master of war never gain him reputation for wisdom or courage."

故善战者之胜也，无智名，无勇功。

The reason – the master of war wins it so swiftly, sneakily and expediently that when the enemy realizes it, he is already defeated! Finally, illusions and fakery are used to generate surprise at the point of engagement. This sudden change of stance, from incapability to capability, from weakness to strength, from vulnerability to aggression will so shock the enemy that he may be incapable of reacting for a while. As illustrated by Sun Tzu, it is unthinkable that like a young maiden who is demure and weak, you can suddenly strike like a swift hare. Such a drastic change can have an immobilizing and stunning impact that cripples the enemy.

When Japanese companies first made their moves on the world markets, they were like the young maidens. They kept a very low profile and there was little fanfare about how they went about their silent conquests. Few competitors paid any attention to their efforts. Japanese products were ridiculed as toys of inferior quality that were unlikely to affect the products of the Western world. In fact, in the earlier years, the Americans even helped the Japanese to develop economically (especially after World World II). There was no hesitancy about transferring technology to the Japanese. When the Japanese did borrow, rob or steal Western technology, they were, until recently, quickly pardoned and forgotten. In essence, even as late as the early 1970s, Japan was regarded as a nation with little potential for economic threat or significance – only a young, demure, and vulnerable maiden who should be helped at all times. However, in the 1970s, the Japanese lady grew up quite suddenly and began to demonstrate a big appetite. She moved so swiftly and quietly, that is, quite unnoticably for a long while and started to carve out very large market shares in various areas in the world market before she was finally noticed. By then, the impact, as is now experienced by many countries, is so sizeable and momentous that it is quite impossible to dislodge her.

While the suddenness and unabated increase of Japanese overseas investments in the 1980s was very well received by some countries, it also brought tensions and embarassment to others. Among ASEAN countries (which include Brunei, Indonesia, Malaysia, the Philippines, Singapore, and Thailand), Japanese investments were generally welcomed, as they provided a healthy balance to the traditional American and British investments. The same sentiments were shared by people in Hong Kong who did not seem to mind what passports foreign investors carried, so long as they pumped in cash to the local economy.

The reverse sentiments, however, were strongly felt in Australia, the United States, and Britain. As Japanese investors bought up huge chunks of land and properties in these countries, local resentment was provoked and a lot of negative publicity was generated against the Japanese. For example, in Australia, within a 12-month period (1987 to 1988), Japan overtook the United States and Britain as the largest foreign investor, with 12% of all foreign investments, totalling US$16.5 billion as of June 1988. In addition, by May 1989, the Japanese controlled close to 70% of tourist facilities in the Australian Gold Coast. It was estimated that a quarter to a third of ongoing commercial projects in the Sydney and Melbourne central business districts were backed by Japanese money and the amount involved was in excess of A$4.0 billion (*Straits Times*, 12 May 1989). More significantly, Australian farmers were up in arms in early 1989 because Japanese firms were buying up leading cattle stations, and using them to export Australian beef to Japan! Following a wave of protests about too much Japanese presence, the Australian government was forced to contemplate ways to restrict foreign real estate investment and acquisitions – although admittedly, such actions might come a little too late, as much damage was already done. So severe was the anti-Japanese feeling that a Mr Bruce Ruxton, head of the Victorian state branch of the Retired Serviceman's League – a politically powerful veterans' organization was quoted as saying that Australian feeling against the Japanese was the "worst since World World II" (Singapore *Straits Times*, July 8, 1988). In Britain, the great Japanese passion for golf saw them acquiring, by the late 1980s, three courses – including Turnberry, scene of the 1986 British Open – for about US$25.0 million by leisure group Nitto Kogyo. Offers were also made for several other British golf courses in 1989. During the same period, Kajima Coporation was also financing the development of a new championship course in Buckinghamshire. The acquisition of British golf courses by the Japanese reflected a very interesting phenomenon. In Britain, it was difficult, if not impossible, for foreigners to become members of traditionally snooty British golf clubs. The Japanese therefore adopted the strategy that if you could not join them, buy them!

This "buying up" philosophy extended to other properties as well. The Japanese, as of late 1980s, were busily buying up what was left of Fleet Street. Rupert Murdoch's newspaper empire in Fleet Street was to become the London headquarters of yet another Japanese bank by 1990, and the Daily Express' famous black-fronted building was sold in 1989 to trading house C. Itoh. In addition, six Japanese companies, led by construction giant, Shimizu, took a 50% stake in a US$1.67 billion redevelopment of the Greater London Council's former headquarters on London's South Bank. Other acquisitions made by the Japanese in the 1980s included the headquarters of the Financial Times (bought by construction group Ohbayashi) for about US$239 million, and a US$334 million newsprint plant in Kent.

As of late 1989, Britain was attracting some 40% of all Japanese investments in Europe. Since YKK Fasteners set up the first Japanese factory in Runcorn in 1972, the trickle had become a flood. The number of Japanese residing in London .exceeded 50,000 by 1989 and the Nippon Club, a social organization for Japanese expatriates, had grown from 500 members in 1962 to more than 16,000 in early 1989. Thus far, the Japanese had managed to bring with them decorum, dignity, jobs, and what was called "Nippon know-how" to Britain. However, in a tradition-steeped and snooty society, it is likely that the "bubble" might burst anytime, and anti-Japanese feelings would surface, as in Australia.

In the United States, Japanesè acquisitions were increasingly characterized as an invasion of the yellow hordes and concern was growing in the late 1980s over the leverage that the Japanese were gaining in America. There was awe, envy and resentment, as well as exasperation that whatever Americans did, the Japanese could do better – including the business of buying businesses. Such mixed feelings were even echoed by prominent businessmen like Lee Iacocca. The chairman of Chrysler, in a 1989 visit to Tokyo stated that the Japanese presence could be felt on almost every street corner in the United States. He cited examples of Japanese real estate holdings – six of California's top 12 banks, six of Chicago's 10 leading banks, one quarter of all land-mark buildings in Los Angeles, a large section of New York, including Tiffany's, most of Hawaii's top hotels and a host of resorts and golf courses across the country.

In fact, apocryphal comments like: "Why should the Japanese attack Pearl Harbour again? They now own it," and "Japan buying up America," had become reflective of the resentful feelings that were brewing among Americans. In order to cushion any further negative publicity, Toyoo Gyohten, Japan's Deputy Minister of Finance for International Affairs, had to publicly deny the "Japan buying up US theory" as absurd and without basis (*Straits Times*, 21 February 1989). However, if Japanese foreign acquisitions continue without restraint, increased anti-Japanese resentment would be inevitable.

Such anti-Japanese feelings were further fueled by the Japanese writer and politician Shintaro Ishihara who, in a series of articles in early 1990, argued that Japan should be more assertive toward the Americans. His views generated so much controversy that many Japanese politicians and intellectuals had to publicly reject them in order to cushion further Japan bashing.

Owing to high property prices, Japan's total land assets were worth 403.4 trillion yen (US$3.2 trillion) at the end of 1987, 4.1 times the total value of all land in the United States. In short, Japanese land prices would purchase the whole of the United States – which is 25 times larger than Japan – plus all of the companies listed on the New York Stock Exchange! It is no wonder that the "Japan buying up US theory" found much credibility among many Americans. Despite such "wealth", it is very significant to note that the Japanese, even up to today, do not feel the sense of prosperity. If anything, the nation and the people have constantly projected an image of vulnerability, a quality of life, and standard of living far behind that of the Western world. Many Westerners, including some scholars, seem to fall prey to such a line of argument. This "still lacking" stance was, in fact, the position adopted by the Japanese Economic Planning Agency's 1988 White Paper. In the report, it stated that while Japan is now a rich nation, most Japanese would be considered poor by the standards of other industrialized countries. Thus, despite their phenomenal achievements, the Japanese still choose to portray an image of humility and inferiority!

Moving beyond the Japanese example, it is very interesting to note that while companies may not deliberately adopt faking or illusionary strategies to deceive their competitors, there are however, many companies who manufacture counterfeit products and services that attempt to short-change the consumers. In fact, currency forgery is a rampant business practiced in many countries.

For example, there are many fake watches, designer leather goods, clothing, computer software, books, video cassettes, and so on, that are now widely available. The manufacture and sales of counterfeit products have become so severe and rampant – their sales are in the multi-billions – that manufacturers of the original products have begun to make concerted efforts to curb the growth and wipe out the menace. They have lobbied their respective governments for tougher action against countries where the pirated products are manufactured, distributed or originated.

The problems created by fake products are real and serious. Fake products not only erode the sales and profits of the original manufacturers, but also retard them from engaging in R&D, product improvement and design, and marketing and promotion. More seriously, counterfeits also affect the image of the original products in that they are extremely damaging to the trademarks of the original manufacturers and destroy the high reputation that the original products enjoy in the eyes of consumers. This point can be illustrated by a recent example. According to a report in the Singapore *Straits Times* (26 August 1988), Singapore was identified as a distribution centre for the re-export of fake top-grade perfumes, bearing names like Opium, Rive Gauche, Poison, Diorissimo and Coco – to the Middle-East, Africa and other parts of Asia. Apparently, Singapore's strategic position as a leading international port and transshipment center was being exploited by the counterfeit syndicates. Some 20,000 pieces of fake perfumes, amounting to more than US$1 million was seized in a single day – obviously only reflecting the tip of the iceberg. Investigations showed that the components were believed to have been manufactured in Taiwan, the final products assembled in Malaysia, and finally shipped through Singapore to undeveloped markets where the consumers are less sophisticated and unable to discern the difference.

Besides the problems relating to counterfeits, it is important to recognize that some companies also engage in the art of faking or bluffing. In fact, rumors on corporate takeovers, new products, special new formulae, and other juicy corporate news could very well be leaked deliberately with the intention of throwing the competitors off-guard. At other times, such rumors are used to push up the prices of the companies' shares so as to facilitate some other corporate purposes.

In the area of accounting, companies are known to window-dress their accounts so as to create a favorable impression with their investors and financiers – an art of illusion! Such illusionary exercises are done at various times – for example, before the company goes public, issues new shares or rights, or even before closing the books for the financial year.

7.3.3 Use of unpredictable or multiple courses of action to generate surprises

The third way to achieve deception is to rely on unpredictable or multiple courses of action to generate surprises. As mentioned by Sun Tzu, *surprise* is very much needed in war so as to catch the enemy off-guard and unprepared. For this reason, Sun Tzu advocated the flexible employment of the *zheng* (direct) and *qi* (indirect or unexpected) forces in attack. At any one point in time, either one of the two forces could be the decoy, while the other could be the main attacking force. Thus, the enemy is always kept guessing about the real versus the fake, and it is definitely harder to defend one's territory under such circumstances as the attack could come from any direction. Since the principle of the *zheng* and *qi* forces have been discussed extensively in Chapter 4 of this book, they will not be elaborated here.

In addition to the flexible use of the *zheng* and *qi* forces to confuse the enemy (or create deception), Sun Tzu also advocated many other methods that could be used to deceive the enemy, as well as create the element of surprise. The basic idea is that in war, one must not be confined to one particular course of action. Rather, various options must be explored so that the enemy will be more easily deceived as he has to do a thorough assessment of each course of action that one takes – since each one is new and unpredictable. For this reason, Sun Tzu went further to emphasize the need to use both direct and indirect approaches (as opposed to forces):

> "He who knows how to use the direct and indirect approaches
> will win. Such is the art of maneuvering."

先知迂直之计者胜，此军争之法也。

While the use of direct and indirect forces concern the deployment of troops, the use of direct and indirect approaches concerns the use of strategies. For example, if one's troops are quantitatively and qualitatively inferior to those of the enemy, it would be suicidal to encounter the enemy head-on. Rather, a nicheing strategy must be sought in order to attain relative superiority at the point of contact. Thus, the use of indirect approaches also led Sun Tzu to advocate acts of sabotage to harass the enemy. This is because when the enemy is under constant harassment, his judgement will be impaired and he is likely to commit errors.

The use of varied and unpredictable courses of action is very similar to contingency planning in business. As mentioned in Chapter 4, contingency planning must be part and parcel of any good corporate planning practice. Such contingency plans must take into account the alternative employment of corporate resources as well as alternative strategies. More importantly, the contingency plan must be equally effective.

In essence, any company must be prepared to have a turnaround strategy if the master plan fails. One classic example of how a company successfully managed itself out of near disaster was that of the Coca-cola company's decision to drop the old Coke and introduce the new Coke in April 1985. The century-old old Coke was perceived to be losing its market presence. For example, in the United States, for the 14-year period from 1971 to 1984, Pepsi-Cola had outperformed the old Coca-Cola dramatically. The share of Pepsi increased from 15% of the US market in 1971 to 19% in 1984. During the same period, the market share of the old Coke dropped from 25% to 22%. Effectively, Pepsi had narrowed Coke's 10% lead to a mere 3% by the end of 1984. The new Coke was launched specifically to turn the situation around – that is, to recapture Coca-Cola's lost market share.

Unfortunately, the market response to the new Coke was very unexpected. In the US consumer rebellion against the decision to drop the old Coke reached such frantic heights that the company and distributors were bombarded with unpleasant, threatening calls and letters. Fortunately for the company, it reacted very quickly to the market responses and introduced the old Coke as Classic Coke. While many critics viewed the whole episode as a big oversight on the part of Coca-Cola, there was no doubt that the company would not have turned the situation around if not for one important factor – **contingency planning**. The company lost no time in bringing back the old Coke as Classic Coke, literally within weeks of launching the new Coke. The result – Coca-Cola not only got back their market share, but also had another product successfully introduced into the market. In the process of doing so, they probably scored one of the biggest publicity successes of all time – the whole episode made headlines in many countries, and Coca-Cola became the first consumer product ever to be featured on the cover of *Time* magazine – an acknowledgement that Coke had become the world's favorite soft drink. From a brand name and trademark, Coca-Cola became an inherent part of people's lives and habits – thanks to the ability of the company to manage in a contingency situation. It was indeed very remarkable that Coca-Cola was able to find opportunities amidst a crisis situation. In fact, the Chinese characters for crisis (危机) actually consist of two words that impart very interesting meanings. The word 危 means danger (危险), while the other word 机 means opportunity (机会). In other words, in every crisis situation, there exists an opportunity to be exploited. Such an opportunity, as in the case of the Coca-Cola company, can sometimes create surprises for the competitors.

Besides using direct and indirect forces and approaches, another way to surprise the enemy is to capture something of value to him. Sun Tzu said:

"If someone asks: 'What should I do when faced with a large and well-organized enemy troop about to invade my territory?' My reply is, "First capture something that he treasures most, and he will conform to your desires."

敢问: 敌众整而将来，待之若何? 曰: 先夺其所爱，则听矣。

From the above remarks, the capture of something of value to the enemy would include both people and things. Thus, the concepts of **kidnapping** of people and **pilferage** of things (which may include hardware like equipment and software like strategic plans) as we commonly know them were advocated centuries ago by Sun Tzu. One of the main purposes of capturing something treasured by the enemy is to put him on the defensive so that he will be kept guessing what your next move will be. This also facilitates the use of deceptive tactics, and strategic advantage is gained. While kidnapping of people occurs more in the political and military realms today, there is a parallel practice in business called **head-hunting**. One certain way to paralyze a competitor is to kidnap its key executives through head hunters. Indeed, head-hunting is a big business today, and firms like Egon Zehnder International and Korn/Ferry International are well established names in this business. Interestingly, few people question the moral and ethical practices of staff-pilfering or kidnapping, even if such executives are recruited from direct competitors. While no ethically minded CEO would publicly advocate stealing staff from competitors, yet privately such practices are perhaps condoned and encouraged.

Similarly, no company would ever admit stealing patents, copyrights or technology from its competitors. Yet industrial espionage is known to exist and companies' secrets do get stolen. Few advocates would be as candid as the influential Indonesian business leader (mentioned earlier in Chapter 4) who encouraged Indonesian firms to steal Japanese technology if necessary because Japanese companies are reluctant to transfer technology (Singapore *Straits Times*, 22 July 1987).

Interestingly, in the 1960s, 1970s, and even up to the early 1980s, Japanese companies were often accused by their American and European counterparts of pilfering their technologies. Today, however, the Japanese have become victims of their own economic success. According to one source (*Straits Times*, 10 January 1989), Japan has become a center for industrial espionage for Western technology to the communist and socialist countries. This issue of industrial espionage will be discussed in greater detail in the next chapter.

It is important to point out that even with winning strategies, one must avoid repeating them. In this way, the enemy will always be kept guessing on your next move, and you always have the upper-hand in creating surprises. Thus, Sun Tzu said:

> "Therefore, do not repeat the tactics that won you a victory, but vary them according to the circumstances."

故其战胜不复，而应形于无穷。

It is equally important not to repeat tactics too often in business. In fact, this is the reason behind the quest for creativity in strategy development. Perhaps one of the areas in which creativity is commonly found and desired is in advertising. One good example of such advertising creativity in Singapore was when Ogilvy & Mather came out with two very attention catching phrases that helped to make FinnAir famous almost overnight. Capitalizing on the abbreviated names of the capitals of both countries, Ogilvy & Mather came out with the words "Go to Hell" and "From Sin to Hell" in their advertisements for launching the airline in Singapore. The two advertisements created quite a stir among the audience. Prior to this, few people could connect Singapore (abbreviated to Sin) to Helsinki (abbreviated as Hell)!

7.4 Capitalizing on available means

Besides the three major principles – swiftness in execution, adaptability in maneuvers, and deceptiveness in actions and strategies – underlying the operational factor in implementation of strategies, there are two other aspects that affect the implementation of strategies. They include the need to capitalize on available means, and anticipation of enemy's reactions.

Sun Tzu clearly understood the need to capitalize on terrain and weather in order to secure strategic advantages in war. In fact, he devoted much discussion to terrain, weather and types of battleground. These aspects have also been dealt with extensively in the earlier chapters of this book in terms of their business applications. There were two other elements of nature during Sun Tzu's time that were heavily exploited by the capable general in war – *water* and *fire*. In Chapter XII he said:

"Those who use fire in their attacks are wise. Those who use water in their attacks are powerful. Water can isolate an enemy, but cannot rob his supplies and equipment."

故以火佐攻者明，以水佐攻者强。
水可以绝，不可以夺。

Fire is used to reduce the enemy's strengths before the actual engagement in combat. Hence, one's relative strength is improved. In the same way, water can also be used as a medium to achieve advantage. However, there are subtle differences between the use of water and fire.

In the case of using water as inundations for attack, one must have superiority of forces. This is because to cause a flood, one needs greater resources than to perform arson. In addition, since water can only isolate the enemy but may not destroy supplies and equipment (and possibly not even the men if they can swim), there is still a need for superiority of forces in the event of direct combat. This is necessary to ensure victory.

The use of fire, however, does not require superiority of forces. This is because, to perform arson, one needs only minimal resources, especially if one is able to capitalize on the advantages conferred by the weather.

"To use fire attacks, the means must be available, and the materials for setting fire must be always ready."

行火必有因，烟火必素具。

"There are appropriate times and suitable days for launching attacks with fire."

发火有时，起火有日。

Moreover, the successful use of fire will reduce the strengths of the enemy. Thus, a significantly smaller force can engage a larger force and cause a weakened enemy as a result of destruction by fire. Hence, Sun Tzu viewed those who use fire as intelligent. He also went into some details on the use of fire in attack:

> "There are five ways of attacking with fire. The first is to burn personnel; the second, to burn stores; the third, to burn equipment; the fourth, to burn arsenals; and the fifth, to burn supply routes."

凡火攻有五：一曰火人，二曰火积，三曰火辎，四曰火库，五曰火队。

Thus the targets for destruction by fire include personnel (in those days, this would also include the horses), provisions and food for survival, the logistic support necessary for movement of supplies, weaponry and ammunition for combat and supply routes for re-stocking of troops, food, equipment and weapons. It is important to note that the use of fire in attacks is also a form of sabotage. This is because it can inflict heavy damages with minimal resources and can be carried out by using traitors within the enemy's camp as well.

While it is uncommon that fire is used literally as a form of competitive weapon in business, it would be too naive to assume that it does not exist. Arson does happen in the business world and, at times, it even causes serious damage to commercial and industrial properties. The possibility that acts of arson may be instigated by vicious competitors should never be ruled out.

Besides the direct interpretation of the use of fire and water in business, it is important to recognize that such media during the times of Sun Tzu (around 400 B.C.) were actually available means that could be capitalized for purpose of gaining advantage in war. In fact, they represented the state of the art in technology at that time. Water is a resource made available by nature, while fire involves using man-made materials as well. To use them effectively, the commander must exploit the opportunities conferred by the weather and terrain. In the same way, the CEO in business must attempt to exploit whatever available means are at his disposal to build advantages in competition. This would include exploiting available technology, automation techniques, management skills and production facilities. For example, with the advent of the computer, it has become much easier to manage and analyze information. The market is flooded with all kinds of computer software – on marketing, finance, accounting, production scheduling, forecasting, data management systems and so on – that can be purchased easily. These are available means to the business firm and it would be foolish not to capitalize on them.

To have the competitive edge in business, the company must adopt a proactive attitude to scan the environment for available means and resources to exploit in order to improve its operations. It is true that many companies do not have their own research and development (R&D) department, nor do they have departments whose tasks are to develop better management tools or production techniques. More often than not, they have to acquire such productivity tools from the open market. Thus, it is essential that companies pay close attention to what is new and available for purchase. Such means are readily available today. Companies only need to learn how to capitalize on them so that strategies can be more effectively implemented.

When the Japanese managed their economic recovery after World War II they realized that they could not compete head-on against Western companies. Instead they went about identifying areas where they could compete, focusing on their core strengths rather than just the products themselves. Small cars and motorcycles were the best that they could produce at the time and so the first Honda motorcycles to arrive in the US markets created no sense of threat to their American competitors. Today, 80% of motorcycles sold in the US are made in Japan.

Similarly, Japanese watchmakers were able to overwhelm their Swiss competitors by focusing on their core competence. In the early 1970s electronics technology was readily available in Japan and Casio focused its efforts on producing basic digital watches which sold for half the price of Swiss mechanical watches. The onslaught, begun in 1974, almost wiped out the Swiss watchmaking industry. Only the invention of the *Swatch* salvaged a credible market share for Swiss industry.

The lesson for the world is a thought provoking one. It is not enough to concentrate on what others do, or what is available in the market place since these may not be easy to reproduce. Focusing on one's own available resources and developing core competence and strengths around the available means is far more important. In this way it is possible to break out of the trap of competition.

7.5 Anticipation of the enemy's reactions and changes in environment

It will be naive to assume that when one embarks on an offensive, the enemy will not react. In other words, it is dangerous to assume that the enemy is not capable of strategizing nor developing effective responses. In fact, Sun Tzu's works are full of strategies and counter-strategies which can be used effectively by either side. Thus, as stated by Sun Tzu, it is very important to ensure one's invincibility by creating strong defenses before going on the offensive. In addition, contingency plans must be developed. However, contingency plans are actually measures of the last resort and are used only when the original plan fails. It is definitely better to succeed the first time around. To achieve this, it becomes very important that one must anticipate accurately the likely enemy responses to one's attacks. One way is to use spies. However, to begin with, it is useful to know the types of reactions that the enemy can take.

First, the enemy can always launch a counter-offensive. Second, the enemy may develop strong lines of defense. Finally, the enemy can also use deception. Whatever the reaction may be, anticipation of the reaction is very important so that men and resources could be accurately deployed for the decisive win. However, while every effort is made for an accurate assessment of the enemy's reaction, it is important to ensure that in the implementation of strategies, flexibility and variation are still maintained. As mentioned earlier, one of the doctrines of war, as advocated by Sun Tzu, is to follow the enemy's situation in order to decide on the battle plan. The idea is that while attempting to predict what the enemy will do, it is important that victory can still be gained by being able to modify one's tactics in accordance to the enemy's situation:

> "Thus, the one who is capable of gaining victories by modifying his tactics according to the changes in the enemy's situation can be considered as divine."

能因敌变化而取胜者，谓之神。

There is an important element that the general must anticipate in trying to predict enemy's reactions – whether there are changes in the chain of command in the enemy's camp. This is because with a change of leadership, strategies may be altered drastically. In war, it is not uncommon for the commander of the army to be changed mid-way through the campaign, and this factor must be taken into consideration. It is therefore not surprising that Sun Tzu made a lot of references to the character of the general, profiling his desirable traits and weaknesses that should be avoided.

Besides being able to anticipate correctly the enemy's likely reactions, the general in war must also be concerned about changes in the environment in the implementation of strategies. This is because war situations are never static. For example, as the troops move across different types of terrain, different types of battlegrounds are created and the strategy might have to change. At the same time, weather conditions may also change as the battle progresses. Such changes can create both opportunities and threats. For example, adverse weather conditions may affect the advance of troops, the date and mode for the final assault. If the temperature is very hot and the wind direction favorable, then fire attack may become a very desirable and effective tactic to use. As stated by Sun Tzu, to use fire as a means of assault:

> "The best time is when the weather is scorching hot. The best day is when there is a strong wind caused by the alignment of the moon with the positions of the four stars."

时者，天之燥也；日者，月在箕、壁、翼、轸也。

In essence, there is a need to modify a strategy that may be carefully evaluated and implemented because of the reactions of the enemy and the changes in the environment. In doing so, the general is applying the principle of adaptability and will be in a better position to ensure success.

In business it is important to anticipate correctly competitors' reactions, and monitor changes in the environment once a strategy is implemented. Accurate forecasts of competitive reactions and the environment will necessitate changes in the strategy that is implemented. However, it is not possible to be 100% accurate in forecasting. The CEO of a competitive firm may be changed and a new assessment would have to be made on what actions the new challenger would take. The government may impose new regulations or change its policy as it deems fit. Such changes are not easy to forecast. For example, to capitalize on the "flee Hong Kong" mentality as a result of the Tiananmen incident in China in May/June 1989 and to help overcome labor shortage, the government of Singapore decided to liberalize its immigration policy in early July 1989. This liberalization created both opportunities and threats to different companies, depending on the nature of their business. Nonetheless, it is a factor that must be considered quickly and decisively for those companies affected. As an illustration, the Ngee Ann Polytechnic, the National University Hospital, and the Singapore General Hospital viewed the liberalization as new opportunities, and took decisive steps to recruit lecturers, nurses, and medical specialists from Hong Kong within days of the government announcement. In doing so, such organizations would be able to implement even faster their expansion plans and goals.

It is very heartening to note that some American companies have today responded very well to the Japanese challenge by paying more attention to competition and environment. Two companies deserving special attention are Hartley Davidson and Motorola.

Hartley Davidson's turnaround was very remarkable. In the early 1980s it was dying as its share of the motorcycle market in the US had dwindled from 75% in 1973 to less than 25% by the early 1980s as a result of losing out to Japanese imports. However, under the leadership of Vaughn Beals, the company took drastic and decisive steps to improve by studying and understanding the competitors and the environment. For example, the company visited Japanese plants in 1980 and even toured Honda's assembly plant in Marysville, Ohio to understand how the Japanese do it. They learned that robotics, corporate culture and songs, morning exercise, and modern equipment were not enough without the professional managers who understood the business and paid attention to detail. Hartley followed and improved on what they learned from their competitors. The company even introduced the "just-in-time" manufacturing system in order to eliminate inventory and so cut costs. Employees were involved in the planning and implementation of changes in the production system and no changes were implemented without total acceptance from every group involved, from engineering to the factory floor and to management. In addition the company assessed the environment in detail and decided to throw its resources into establishing a strong niche in the big bike market. It paid off. Today, Hartley has regained more than 50% of the big bike market, has created a high quality, committed and thinking workforce and has forged a strong alliance with its dealers.

Motorola is another company that has done well. Its approach, which includes competing aggressively with Japanese companies in their home market, is fast becoming a model for other American companies. It realized that in the wireless-communication business, investment in research and development, attention to quality control, the need to focus on manufacturing details and technical advances are crucial for success. Thus it spent heavily on R&D. For example, in 1989, it spent US$784 million or 8.2% of the company's US$9.6 billion in sales, way above the norm of 4–5% for the industry as a whole. In addition, like Hartley Davidson, it lobbied for protective levy barriers against Japanese imports in order to have competitive price advantages and prevent dumping. Such efforts helped to open up the Japanese market for Motorola. Today it is highly profitable and in 1989 earned about US$500 million on its US$9.6 billion.

7.6 Deception, fraud, and corruption in business and politics

Before leaving this chapter, the authors feel very strongly that they must make some comments on the issue of deception, fraud and corruption in business and politics. There is no denial that business and politics are closely related. More often than not, one is used to exchange for favors with the other. Thus, it is difficult to divorce the discussion of one from the other.

7.6.1 *Recent examples of fraudulent practices*

The Recruit scandal in Japan, highlighted earlier in this chapter, is a good example of how a company tried to hand out cheap stocks in exchange for political favors. While many people have argued that the Recruit scandal will bring about fundamental changes in the practice of influence-peddling in Japan, the authors are of the view that significant changes are not likely to happen. If any changes do occur, they will be fairly cosmetic in nature. Indeed, in the aftermath of the scandal, some major business groups began discussion about establishing a code of ethics, and in typical Japanese fashion, had formed endless committees to study the issue. However, to the authors, such exercises are merely academic. Little, if any, will change. This is very much supported by Professor Masayuki Fukuoda of Tokyo's Komazawa University who quoted the common Japanese saying that "trying to have ethics in Japan is like trying to buy fish at greengrocer" (*Straits Times*, 6 January 1989). In fact, Professor Fukuoda has developed the "Japanese Rules of Morality," which certainly seem to apply to the Recruit scandal:

> "If it does not come out, it is okay. If it comes out, blame it on
> an aide. If that does not work, say everyone does it – that
> always works."

Some scholars and Japanese observers argue that a shocking turn of events can move the Japanese into action. For example, they cited the oil crisis of the 1970s, the doubling of the value of the yen in 1986 and 1987 and the awakening of security threats as a result of some Japanese companies selling restricted high technology items to the Russians in 1988, as events that propelled Japan into action. Similarly, they argued that the Recruit scandal will hasten reforms. Unfortunately, when it comes to influence-peddling, it may not be as simple.

Ethics in Japan is a very tricky issue. Japan is a gift-giving nation. Gifts cement relationships of all kinds – political, business, social and personal. Renting an apartment requires a gift of cash, Japanese reporters have to pay their interviewees, market researchers end their interview with small gifts, Diet members require gifts for every favor asked, and so on. Thus, the Recruit scandal could be very much like a storm in a teacup. The only exciting thing about the scandal is not its presumptive corruption, but rather how high and how extensive the peddling went.

Cultural interpretation of the ethical issues of corruption is very important. When the Watergate scandal happened, it surprised most Americans with its revelations of corruption in high places. To the Japanese, payoffs are but a way of life. In fact, the average Japanese businessman views corruption like the weather. Everybody talks about it, but nobody can do anything about it. Even the Lockheed scandal (also mentioned earlier) did not have much impact on the Japanese. This is because after the Lockheed scandal, only limits on corporate contributions to politicians were set. These limits are largely ignored in practice. If any lessons were learned from all these scandals, a cynic critic of Japanese management practices, Makoto Sataka aptly commented (*Straits Times*, 6 January 1989):

> "If there was a lesson learned, it was don't use cash. It is too direct. Use stocks."

To be fair to the Japanese, deception, fraud and corruption are universal problems that plague many countries, including the Western world. For example, Giulio Andreotti, Italy's Prime Minister, called for a crackdown on tax dodgers immediately when he resumed office in July 1989. Interestingly, the Italians are known to have the propensity to avoid the tax collector. It was estimated that if Italians reported all of their income, there would be enough tax revenue to eliminate 75% of their budget deficit of US$100 billion for 1989 (*Straits Times*, 4 August 1989). What was even more interesting was that in order to encourage tax-paying, Andreotti's hapless predecessor, Ciriaco De Mita, tried unsuccessfully to introduce a form of amnesty that critics, especially unions, protested as amounting to rewarding people for their past crimes. Moreover, some Italian economists argue that a measure of tax evasion is healthy, for it gives the people money to pay for private schools, messengers, and facsimile machines that are increasingly needed as alternatives to hopeless public services. Thus, in Italy, just as in Japan, some fraudulent practices are not necessarily condemned by society.

There is no doubt that deception, fraud, and corruption do exist, despite efforts to stamp them out. And they will continue to exist so long as individuals and organizations are gaining from such practices. Even in the United States where tight rules exist to penalize the culprits, there is no shortage of offenders. The recent FBI indictments against 46 Chicago futures traders in August 1989 is a good example. On 2 August 1989, US Attorney-General Richard Thornburgh announced that federal indictments had been laid against 46 Chicago futures traders as part of a crackdown on white-collar crime in all its various guises. Citing violations of the new US Racketeering Influenced and Corrupt Organizations Act, such as insider trading, altering trading records, tax frauds, racketeering and withholding customer orders from the market in order to dole them out to compatriots, the US government intended to send the strong signal that fraudulent practices cannot and must not be permitted to flourish. Specifically, the following are some examples of the fraudulent practices that led the futures traders into trouble with the law:

- **Front-running**. This involves exploiting the knowledge of a client's incoming order by arranging other deals that will make a profit when the client's order is placed. Front-running is typically carried out by a broker informing a trader, known as a "local" or someone who trades only for himself, that a big order is about to arrive. The local then buys a futures contract. When the customer's order comes into the trading pit, the price of the futures contract is likely to go up. Thus, the local enjoys a profit, which is split between the conspiring broker and the local.

- **Cuffing**. This involves holding to a client's order until the price of the commodity falls, and then executing it at the higher price it had traded at previously. For example, when a broker gets a client's order, the price may be, say, US$50. Seconds later, it drops to US$45. The broker conspires with a local to buy a contract for the client at US$50. The local then makes a profit of US$5 by buying another contract for US$45.

- **Bagging**. This involves using a conspiring local to mark up the price of a futures contract, and thus giving the local a profit. For example, a broker might buy a contract at, say, US$40, and sell it to a conspirator (the local) at that price. He then buys it back at US$45 for the customer. The profit of US$5 is again shared between the broker and his conspirator.

- **Giving Up the Edge**. This is selling futures contracts at the low end of the price range to ingratiate oneself with a corrupt broker who then bestows favors in return.

In a separate case, the Securities and Exchange Commission (SEC) of New York announced in early August 1989 that it had settled an insider trading case that was filed against a businessman, Fred C. Lee, from Taiwan for US$25 million. The agreement marked the end to one of the largest insider trading cases brought by the SEC. As part of the settlement, Lee neither admitted nor denied the allegations that he used privileged information to execute illegal trades in 25 publicly traded securities.

Around the same period, on 3 August 1989, the SEC also charged two New York investors, Jury Matt Hansen and Fergus M. Sloan Jr., with participating in a scheme to defraud more than 100 brokerage firms. In a civil lawsuit, the SEC said that the two men, together with their firm, Fermat Associates in New York, committed fraud by buying millions of dollars worth of securities without having sufficient money to pay for them and selling them later the same day at a profit to cover their cost.

It is even more frightening to note that companies are even willing to take chances on the safety of their customers in order to save costs. In late July 1990, Eastern Airlines was indicted on criminal charges by the US government for compromising safety standards. Among other charges, the airline was accused of coercing its maintenance personnel to falsify aircraft maintenance records to show that scheduled but incompleted maintenance and repair had been carried out over a period lasting from 1985 to 1989. This was done to avoid flight delays and cancellations, completely ignoring the importance of safety. Expectedly, Eastern Airlines was investigated and that the charges were made is sufficient indication of the severity of fraudulent practices in business.

The above are but a small sample of the seriousness of white-collar crimes. The good thing about them all is that in the case of the US, the government is taking active and swift steps to stamp out the practice. For example, the Chicago Mercantile Exchange (CME) responded swiftly on 3 August 1989, only a day later, to the indictment of 24 of its members, with an array of new rules to fight trading abuses. The new rules include curtailing the controversial practice of **dual trading** which allows a member to trade for himself as well as execute customer orders, and further restricts trade among members of so-called broker associations. In addition, other measures were also introduced. These include stepping up electronic and manual trade-tracking and surveillance practices, stiffer disciplinary procedures and penalties and implementing ethics training for CME members. In the words of Leo Melamed, the Chairman of CME Executive Committee, "If that means we must instil the fear of God in any wrongdoers, we will do that." Thus, no effort will be spared to restore the CME's image as an honest marketplace. In the same way the Eastern Airlines case, at the point of writing, has been actively investigated.

7.5.1 The price for honesty

The prevalent and persistent occurrence of fraud seems to create the impression that crime pays, or rather that honesty leads nowhere. Indeed, the research done by a Dr Don Soeken, an American psychologist, provided very intriguing findings on the price that people had to pay for trying to stay honest. According to Dr Soemen (*Straits Times*,

August 10 1988), many bosses had tried to get rid of their subordinates who reported on their fraudulent acts by having them certified as insane. These **whistleblowers**, as they are commonly known, were American civil servants who had uncovered fraud, corruption and iniquity. Their bosses were senior officials with secrets to hide, and they came from various State Departments. The findings on 233 whistleblowers conducted by Soeken and his academician wife showed that:

- 90% of them lost their jobs or were demoted;
- 27% of them faced lawsuits;
- 26% of them faced psychiatric and medical referral;
- 25% of them became alcoholics;
- 17% of them lost their homes;
- 15% of them were divorced during the aftermath;
- 15% of them attempted suicide; and
- 8% of them became bankrupts.

According to the findings, the overwhelming majority spoke about unbearable stress and depression. Almost two-thirds of them failed, after five years, to be vindicated for their disclosures. What is heartening, however, was that the majority of them said they would do it all again, even though they would warn others to be more cautious. This is because most whistleblowers were found to be highly moral people. When they saw something that bothered their conscience, they simply had to tell somebody. Unfortunately, when discovered by their organizations, they were quickly dismissed as dead beats or insane people and every attempt would be used to prevent them from further disclosure.

From Soeken's study, it is obvious that to be a whistleblower requires an extraordinary tenacity and courage to uncover secrets that governments and corporations are determined to hide. Thus, not many people are able to play such roles. Indeed, the price of remaining clean, honest and decent is very high indeed. In fact, even in Britain, the Official Secrets Act and the Law of Confidence make whistleblowing an extremely risky affair. British civil servants would still be bound by the Law of Confidence even if the Official Secrets Act is reformed to take into account public interest.

In the United States, the situation is slightly better. There, civil servants take an oath to serve not the government but the people. In addition, there is the Freedom of Information Act that enshrines openness, and government and corporate agencies have been set up to help the little guy reform his own organization from within. This system has

worked quite well and has served to protect whistleblowers. For example, two senior executives of Ashland Oil were awarded US$69
million by a federal jury in Kentucky in July 1988 after they were
sacked for exposing bribes which the company offered to officials in
Oman.

In consolation, it is comforting to note that honesty does pay.
Besides, there are sufficient rules and regulations to ensure that the
majority of individuals and corporations abide by them. In addition,
people and corporations do care about their image, and offenders
belong to the minority.

7.5.2 The case against corrupt practices

In the final analysis, restraints must come from the organization itself.
No amount of laws and penalties would prevent the practice of corruption, and the use of deceptive techniques. The organization must realize that it has a moral responsibility to society, without which there can
only be chaos and disaster, especially when such effects are aggre-
gated. Take the case of the Philippines. According to a *Business World*
journal report (*Straits Times*, 25 July 1989), some 40% to 50% of the
Philippines' Gross National Product (GNP) could be lost yearly to graft
and corruption in the bureaucracy and private sector and Philippines'
GNP in 1988 was estimated to be US$37 billion. The same journal also
reported that a study by the Philippines' Economic Intelligence Investigation Bureau (EIIB), an arm of the Finance Department, showed that
the country was losing US$4.25 billion annually to various forms of
"economic subversion." This figure only covered measurable losses like
smuggling and illegal dollar transfers abroad. Outright theft of public
funds and bribery were excluded.

Besides such "losses" the EIIB also estimated annual leakages of
US$1.55 billion to illegal logging and harvests of natural resources,
US$1.23 billion to "dollar salting," or unlawfully stashing export earn-
ings abroad, US$0.93 billion to tax evasion, and US$0.57 billion to
smugggling.

The Philippines is not an isolated case. China, after her
opendoor policy, was also infested with widespread corruption. In
Guangzhou, tobacco factory director Zhang Ying was sentenced to
death for accepting US$20,000 bribe from a Hong Kong businessman
(*Straits Times*, July 20 1988). Besides Zhang Ying, the vice-director of a
state-run electronics company was also given a suspended death sentence for taking a US$120,000 commission from a Hong Kong business
partner. These are but two of the more than 1200 cases that Guangzhou
prosecutors took to court between 1982 and 1987. In fact, the economic

reforms of China provided numerous opportunities and loopholes for more than 40 million party officials to make illicit profits. The problems relating to graft and corruption were so serious that local courts adopted a policy whereby officials might receive up to US$540 worth of financial gains before charges could be filed. However, corrupt practices became more sophisticated over time. For example, cash demands were substituted for benefits in kind, gifts and even requests for funding of children's education abroad. Recognizing the seriousness of the problem, the Chinese official newspaper, The People's Daily, commented in one of its 1988 editorials that if corruption within the Communist Party of China remained out of control, it would endanger the economic reform and touch off disturbances in the country. Thus, true enough, in May 1989, students in China began to demonstrate. The series of events climaxed with the now well-known June 1989 Tiananmen episode in which thousands of students were reportedly shot dead. This incident would not have happened if the Chinese government had taken more concrete steps to curb corruption and the buying of favors or "*quansi*."

7.5.3 *The onus on individuals, corporations, and governments*

In a nutshell, there is no denial that corruption, if left unchecked, can have dire consequences. It only makes sense that all organizations and individuals recognize their moral obligations and responsibilities and take collective efforts to prevent the spread of corruption. To begin with, there is no reason to believe that a Code of Conduct, similar to that shown in Table 7.2, cannot be drawn up for organizations. Such a code will go a long way to guide the senior managers and those who have contact with outside bodies, on how to behave ethically.

For organizations operating in different countries and cultures, there is a greater need to decide what is an acceptable code of conduct for the managers. For example, should they buy or pay for favors? IBM (International Business Machines), for example, does not believe in engaging directly in political contributions to other countries, or other influence-peddling techniques. However, it does allow its dealers or agents to do so – an indirect, but above-board way of doing the same thing.

In the final analysis, there is nothing like doing things the "clean" way. To the authors' knowledge, there has never been an organization nor nation that could survive the tests of time as a result of engaging in corrupt and deceptive practices. Ultimately, the truth must triumph.

Table 7.2 Code of conduct for Singapore Government Ministers

Among other things, the rules require that a Minister:

- must disclose to the President his sources of income, his holdings of stocks and shares, as well as interests in any professional practice.

- must use strictest discretion in deciding, where there is a clash of private and public interest, if he should hold on to his stocks and shares.

- must not hold directorships in public companies, take part actively in any professional practice, be associated in a formal or advisory capacity with commercial bodies or receive any payment from them.

- may be honorary directors or directors in philanthropic bodies or private companies where public duty and private interests are unlikely to conflict. These directorships must be announced in the Government Gazette.

- ought not to enter into any deal where his private interests might conflict with his public duty.

- must not use official information to profit himself or his friends.

- ought not to put himself or allow himself to be put in a position where he would be tempted to use his official influence to promote any scheme or help any company in which he has a stake.

- should not use his official influence to get someone admitted to or promoted in the Civil Service. He can, however, give a testimonial supporting the person if he knows him personally.

- ought not to accept any kind of favour from those who are negotiating business or seeking to do business with the Government.

- should scrupulously avoid speculative investments and securities over which he will have inside information by virtue of his position as a Minister.

- should carefully avoid accepting valuable gifts from members of the public so that there would be no suspicion that he is not observing the "Rules of Obligations."

Source: Singapore Code of Conduct for Ministers *The Straits Times*, 4 August 1989

8 *Strategic controls*

8.1 The principle of intelligence
8.2 The principle of security

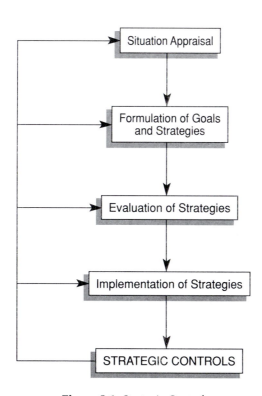

Figure 8.1 Strategic Controls

The final aspect of the Sun Tzu model is that of strategic control (see Figure 8.1). When a strategy is developed and implemented, it is also subjected to change. This is because in war, both the enemy and the environment are never static. Thus, a strategy will have to be refined as a result of the reactions and counter-strategy of the enemy and how the environment evolves. Strategic controls act as the feedback mechanism to the earlier stages of the strategic planning process as well.

Control is an essential part of any strategy. However, to effect control, one must collect, collate and analyse information on the enemy and the environment. Sun Tzu addressed this in his principle of intelligence. In addition, there is an equally important need to prevent the leakage of information to the enemy. Sun Tzu discussed this in his principle of security. To a large extent, the principle of intelligence represents the offensive dimension of strategic controls, in that information must be acquired so that effective strategies can be developed. On the other hand, the principle of security represents the defensive dimension, in that there is a need to protect information. Otherwise, if they were stolen by the enemy, the strategies would be rendered ineffective.

8.1 The principle of intelligence

The need to gather information on the various factors that can affect the outcome of a war has been clearly stated by Sun Tzu:

> "One must not enter into any alliance with the rulers of neighboring states without knowing their military motives and designs. One must not move troops without being familiar with the conditions of mountains, forests, passes, swamps, marshes, and so on."

是故不知诸侯之谋者，不能预交；
不知山林、险阻、沮泽之形者，不能行军；

Clearly, Sun Tzu recognizes the role of military intelligence for purposes of war. In fact, he says:

> "The reason why the enlightened ruler and the wise general are able to conquer the enemy whenever they lead the army and can achieve victories that surpass those of others is because of foreknowledge."

故明君贤将，所以动而胜人，成功出于众者，先知也。

Thus, foreknowledge or military intelligence is necessary for the development of superior war strategies. What is interesting is the means which Sun Tzu advocated for the acquisition of such foreknowledge. In contrast to what is commonly believed about the Chinese being superstitious and having the tendency to consult their ancestors or all kinds of gods for their decision-making, Sun Tzu says:

> "This foreknowledge cannot be elicited from spirits nor from the
> gods; nor by inductive thinking; nor by deductive calculations.
> It can only be obtained from men who have knowledge on the
> enemy's situation."

先知者不可取于鬼神，不可象于事，
不可验于度，必取于人，知敌之情者也。

Note that the statement clearly focuses on the significant role of human intelligence as a means for information acquisition. Sun Tzu did not believe in chance, fate, intelligent guesses, arm-chair theorizing, speculating or forecasting based on past events. He believed in the active mode of collecting data through the use of men who know the enemy's situation. This clearly indicates the use of human beings for espionage. Such activities may include the use of spies to acquire information about the enemy's plans and other information such as observation of enemy activities, its position in battle, the locations of ammunition dumps, supplies, troops, and so on. It can also include an assessment of the enemy's state of morale and the leadership qualities of the enemy's generals.

From the sayings of Sun Tzu, it is important to point out that he does not rule out other methods for collecting information. However, he suggests that the most effective means is through the use of spies. Sun Tzu is widely acknowledged as the first person to provide perhaps an exhaustive classification of spies. According to him there are basically five different types of spies:

> "Thus, there are five types of secret agents that can be used.
> They are local agents, inside agents, double agents, doomed
> agents, and living agents."

故用间有五：有因间，有内间，有反间，有死间，有生间。

8.1.1 *Local agents*

> "Local agents are ordinary people recruited from the enemy's country."

因间者，因其乡人而用之。

In war, the use of local agents is very important. These are the ordinary inhabitants of the country which one intends to conquer. Often, they can be easily recruited with some enticement of benefits or favors. Being natives of the country, they are also not likely to arouse suspicion and can gather information very easily. However, being ordinary people, their access to privileged or high level information will be very limited. Thus, they are relied upon to provide very basic information such as the state of morale of troops, the attitude and behavior of the local citizens toward their own government and the general state of affairs within that country. At times, they may also be used to spy on limited activities of some other locals that the conquering force may be interested in. In fact, one of the handy roles that local agents can play would be to provide information on the characteristics of their homeland. While such information may be common knowledge to the locals, it is vital to the attacking forces who are unfamiliar with the terrain:

> "One cannot gain the advantages of terrain without the use of local guides."

不用乡导者，不能得地利。

In war, refugees and prisoners-of-war (POWs) provide a rich source for recruitment of local spies. It is no surprise that one of the main tasks of any military intelligence is to question the POWs and treat them well:

> "Captured soldiers should be treated well and cared for."

卒善而养之

In this way, some of them may be used subsequently. For example, if convinced and converted, they could be sent back to their homeland and become local spies. Besides refugees and POWs, another way to recruit local spies is through the double agent who will be discussed later.

While local spies seem to play a relatively minor role individually, their aggregate role should not be underestimated. They could be used to spread and confirm rumors and as channels of communication with the local people. In aggregate, they can play a stabilizing or destabilizing role. The Israelis, for example, are known to employ local spies extensively in governing their conquered territories in the Middle-East. Their roles include, among others, the provision of information on dissenting members and their organizations and helping the locals to secure employment passes to work in Israel.

In business, what is the equivalent of the local spy? This can be viewed at both the **macro** and **micro** level. At the macro level, when a country wants to export or penetrate a foreign market, it can conduct intensive studies on the needs and preferences of that market by interviewing and surveying their potential consumers and/or customers. The Japanese are known to conduct very detailed and intensive studies on the markets that they intend to penetrate. Where does this information or intelligence come from? The locals, of course!

At a micro level, a company can also survey consumers on competitive products, and their respective strengths and weaknesses. Such surveys can even extend to cover other marketing aspects such as pricing, distribution, advertising and promotion, and strategies. Conducting investigations on the users or consumers of competitors' products is almost equivalent to employing local agents! Alternatively, the company can also employ some locals to gather information on competitors' products and other related market information. To some extent, market research and survey companies are taking part in espionage activities whenever they are paid by their clients to conduct investigations.

8.1.2 *Inside agents*

"Inside agents are the enemy's officials whom we recruit."

内间者，因其官人而用之。

One of the important aspects of espionage work is to identify discontented officials of the enemy. Such officials may include those who consider themselves worthy but who are deprived of office or given low level jobs; those who have committed errors and have been punished or demoted; those who have not been progressing in their careers; those who are opportunistic and willing to capitalize on gains in times of trouble; those whose loyalty is suspect; and those who are always sitting on the fence with no opinions of their own. These officials are frequently sought out discreetly and bribed to work against their own country. They are relied upon to spy on the state of affairs of their country and to sow discord among loyal officials, as well as between such officials and the ruler. At times, they can even smuggle out secrets relating to the army and security of the country.

In business, inside agents exist too. For example, in Singapore, there were reported instances of bosses who complained that their own private secretaries had been leaking valuable information to their competitors. Inside agents, to a large extent, are also those very much responsible for leaking privileged information on the company to outside parties. In fact, it is precisely to curtail and curb such agents that in many countries there are elaborate laws that regulate insider trading on stocks and shares! Those caught doing so are severely punished.

It is also interesting to note that an employee who is planning to join a competitor's firm often turns unknowingly, or even deliberately, into an inside agent just before he or she leaves. One might even suppose that such a person would probably be frantically gathering information to benefit the new employer.

It is interesting to note that in recent years Japanese corporations and agencies have been actively recruiting American scholars and "think tanks" to be their agents in defending the widening trade deficits that the US has with Japan. The purpose is to influence these opinion leaders to blame the trade deficit on American fiscal or corporate policies, rather than on unfair Japanese export strategies or trade practices. In fact, in 1988 various Japanese agencies invested US$150 million in these efforts. In 1989 the amount was increased to US$250 million. These figures exclude the hundreds of millions spent in hiring lawyers, lobbyists and public relations experts. They have even hired prestigious former US legislators, congressmen and government officials to influence the US Congress and White House policies on trade and investment. While they might not have significantly altered the positions of the major decision makers in the US, they could, nonetheless, tilt the nature of debate and cause discord among policy makers. Unknowingly, many American think tanks (such as the Brookings Institute), scholars and lobbyists have become inside agents for the Japanese. Indeed, by accepting Japanese sponsorship, their positions have been greatly compromised.

8.1.3 Double agents

Among the five types of spies, the double agent could possibly be the most important of them all. By definition:

> "Double agents are enemy spies whom we recruit."

> 反间者，因其敌间而用之。

The importance of double agents can be shown by the fact that Sun Tzu advocated that they must be actively sought out and cultivated:

"The enemy agents who are sent to spy on us must be sought out, bribed, guided and cared for, so that they can be converted into double agents to work for us."

必索敌人之间来间我者，因而利之，导而舍之，故反间可得而用也。

The value of double agents becomes very apparent when their varied services are taken into consideration. In fact, Sun Tzu gives the impression that the double agents provide pivotal functions to all the other four types of agents:

"It is through such means (the double agents) that the enemy's situation is known, and hence local and inside agents can be recruited and used."

因是而知之，故乡间、内间可得而使也；

"And it is through this medium (the double agents) that we know the enemy's situation, and hence are able to use doomed agents to spread false information to the enemy."

因是而知之，故死间为诳事，可使告敌；

"It is through information provided by such a medium (the double agents) that the living agents can return at the opportune time with reports on the enemy."

因是而知之，故生间可使如期。

In fact, Sun Tzu even goes as far as saying:

"The ruler must have complete knowledge of the activities of the five types of agents. This information must come from the double agents, and thus it is essential that double agents be treated very generously."

五间之事，主必知之，知之必在于反间，故反间不可不厚也。

Thus, double agents play "the linking pin" role for the other types of agents. Hence, among the three types of agents recruited from the enemy's territory, they are probably the most valuable and treasured. This is because double agents have the confidence of the enemy, have access to enemy secrets, are able to recruit and communicate with the other types of agents and can assist in the infiltration of the enemy with other spies. It is no wonder that they are to be treated generously and delicately.

While the use of double agents seems to be a remote phenomenon in business, the fact is that they exist. In various lectures on this subject conducted by the senior author, many chief executive officers (CEOs) divulged that they had personally experienced double agents in their lines of business.

One area in which double agents may occur is the private investigation business. At times, instead of working for the client, the commercial private investigator might be bought over by the competitor and work for the latter instead. Another group of people who are vulnerable to double spying activities are business consultants and market researchers. Often, the priviledged information that they have access to on one client might be used for the benefit of another. Thus, a high level of professsional ethics is needed for the conduct of such businesses.

8.1.4 Doomed agents

While local, inside and double agents are recruited from the ranks of the enemy, doomed agents belong to one's own country. By definition:

> "Doomed agents are those of our own spies who are deliberately given falsified information to deceive the enemy."

死间者，为诳事于外，令吾间知之，而传于敌间也。

These are agents who can be expended or disposed of without any serious consequences. Thus, information which is actually false is deliberately leaked out to our own agents. These "weak" spies, when captured by the enemy, are bound to volunteer such information in an attempt to save their own lives. Such fabricated information becomes bait that will deceive the enemy, and tempt him to take the wrong course of action. When we score the decisive victory, the doomed spies might be put to death by the enemy. However, as doomed agents are classified as weak and disposable, their deaths are of no loss to us.

In business, doomed agents are those of our employees to whom we deliberately give fabricated information on the company which they would leak out to the competitors to mislead them. These are the "bigmouth" employees, who, after a few rounds of beer or liquor at the local bar, would volunteer information willingly. The key is that such employees may even be fairly senior in the organization, but they are of no value. When they get into trouble with the competitors for providing the wrong information, the company is unlikely to be sympathetic to them. The consequences for them are of no concern to the company.

8.1.5 Living agents

Besides doomed agents, living agents are another type of spy from one's own country. According to Sun Tzu:

> "Living agents are those of our own spies who return safely from the enemy's territory with information."

生间者, 反报也。

Living agents have to be specially selected and trained. To begin with, they must be intelligent and wise, yet appear stupid so as not to arouse suspicion; they must be strong at heart, yet dull so as not to attract attention; they must be talented, full of initiative, agile, vigorous and brave, so as to adapt to changing situations; they must be down-to-earth and able to endure hunger and hardship so as to survive in the harshest conditions; and they must be able to withstand humiliation and torture in order not to give away their mission and betray their nation. These attributes are necessary because living agents are normally sent deep into hostile enemy territory with specific missions. They have to gain access into the organization and power hierarchy of the enemy, become intimate with the ruler, members related to the ruler and high level officials. Their objectives include observing the enemy's movements, understanding their strengths and weaknesses, pilfering their plans and state secrets and smuggling relevant information out of the enemy's territory. The reason why they are called living agents is because these are people who can come and go and communicate reports without arousing suspicion nor being caught.

In business, a living agent is a person who leaves the organization, goes to work for the competitor for a number of years, then returns to work with his original organization again. Such a person is very valuable as he knows the competitor's organization well. Again, it is not surprising that living agents exist in the business world. In Singapore, the senior author knows of a case of a very senior marketing research person who left to work for a major competitor for a

period of time, but subsequently returned to the original employer –
after having learned much about the competitor! Besides this individual, there must be many other cases of living agents in business. While
such people may not be deliberately planted into competitors' firms,
they can, nonetheless, be lured back to their original employers by
more attractive salaries and perks.

At a macro level, when a nation actively seeks to find its former
citizens to return to their home country to work, it is to a large extent,
sourcing and using living agents. For example, in the early 1980s,
Taiwan deliberately pursued an active policy of trying to attract returning nationals to work in her newly developed Science Park. Various
generous incentives were offered to lure these overseas Taiwanese to
return. In fact, quite a few American Chinese (Taiwanese) were lured
back and became living agents.

8.1.6 *Military espionage and business intelligence*

The use of spies in military and political operations has never been
questioned. In fact, it is both an important and crucial arm of the
military/political intelligence machinery of any nation. Sun Tzu made
the following comments about the significant positions of spies:

> "Thus, among all military matters, none can be compared to the
> intimate relations to be maintained with spies; none can be more
> liberally rewarded than spies; and none can be more secretive
> than matters pertaining to espionage."

故三军之事，莫亲于间，赏莫厚于间，事莫密于间。

The importance of spies in war can be further supported by the following statement:

> "Generally, before attacking any army, occupying any city, and killing
> any enemy personnel, it is necessary to gather information such as
> the names of the commanding general, his attendants, aides-de-camp,
> gatekeepers, and bodyguards. Spies must be instructed to gather such
> information in detail."

凡军之所欲击，城之所欲攻，人之所欲杀，必先知其守将、左右、
谒者、门者、舍人之姓名，令吾间必索知之。

However, the use of spies is not an easy matter:

"Only those who are sagacious and wise can successfully use espionage. Only those who are benevolent and just can direct and manage spies. Only those who are detailed and subtle can obtain and decipher the truth in espionage."

非圣智不能用间，非仁义不能使间，非微妙不能得间之实。

It is not surprising that Sun Tzu considered the use of spies a very delicate matter. Yet, according to him:

"There is no place where espionage cannot be used."

无所不用间也！

From the various statements by Sun Tzu, several comments can be made about the use of spies. First, it is a key and pivotal function of the military and the government. To a large extent, any military organization without the espionage arm is like a body without ears and eyes. Second, there are different types of spies for different missions, with some being more important than others. Third, spies – especially living agents – should generally be well trained and well treated. Fourth, spies could be recruited from the enemy, and even other countries. In fact, Sun Tzu's classification showed that three out of the five types of spies come from the enemy. Fifth, the control and management of spies must be done at the highest level, even up to that of the ruler. Finally, espionage is an offensive "weapon" for war, and is a very delicate operation. Interestingly, the world of business is also filled with espionage. Ironically, while military espionage is considered necessary, normal and acceptable, business espionage is looked upon with scorn. Many people condemn it as unethical, despicable and unacceptable. Yet, the fact remains that it exists. However, business espionage – the deliberate attempts to steal or pilfer industrial or trade secrets – must not be confused with market intelligence.

In market intelligence, a company actively seeks information from the market place using "above-board" methods to improve its ways of doing business. Thus, there is nothing unethical about market intelligence. In fact, owing to the massive amount of information that must be processed in today's competitive business world, many top corporations in the United States have someone performing the functions of a Chief Information Officer (CIO). Specifically, the CIO oversees the actual operations of the company's MIS (management information system) department, links information technology (IT) to the company's business strategies, and ensures that all parts of the organization can absorb and use IT effectively.

While the CIO is performing a very credible role, there is scope for a large corporation to have another type of CIO, a Chief Intelligence Officer, to complement the other. Besides working closely with the Information Officer, this new CIO will perform functions beyond those commonly done by the marketing research department. For example, he will be responsible for gathering, analyzing and interpreting information pertaining to the market, the environment and the consumers. In addition, he is expected to profile the personalities of key competitors so that detailed analysis can be done on their likely actions and reactions. Thus, he would have to work very closely with staff of the corporate planning department as well. In view of the increasingly competitive environment of the future, the company that is likely to get ahead of the others must excel in market research (intelligence), management of information, technology and marketing. Thus, the two types of CIOs would be essential for ensuring the success of the company.

On a macro level, the success of the Japanese can be attributed to some extent to their market intelligence systems. Over the years, Japan has created a massive institutional infrastructure that is geared to collecting information on various world markets. For example, the Japanese general trading companies (GTC), the Ministry of International Trade and Industry (MITI) and the Japan External Trade Organisation (JETRO) have each established worldwide networks of intelligence systems. These organizations conduct all kinds of market-related research and information gathering and compile, collate and compose them for use by Japanese companies. For example, JETRO could provide detailed market information, analyze competitors' activities, diagnose the political and legal conditions, project the market trends, and make meaningful suggestions on product and marketing strategies for its clients.

MITI, on the other hand, would sponsor huge R&D projects, protect Japan's strategic technologies and underwrite any research costs if necessary. For example, it acts as an insurer against catastrophic failures when it comes to pursuing new technologies or abandoning old ones. A recent critical role it played was when it guided the country's steel companies through a painful retrenchment in the early 1980s. In addition, it also charts the research agenda for Japanese firms, advises them on what products to focus on and which markets to enter. At times, it also act as a power-broker when conflicts among Japanese companies arise.

Finally, the GTCs have worldwide product divisions with skills to provide in-depth knowledge about a particular country and products. Their staff are well trained in language, culture and market conditions of the countries that they work in. These GTCs constantly update their information and databanks, and are known to trade and share information with one another. In fact, the volume of messages transacted by the GTCs is known to exceed that of their country's Ministry of Foreign Affairs.

Together, the JETRO, MITI and the GTCs of Japan form a formidable market intelligence force unrivalled by any other country in the world. Many of the Western countries, including the US, pale in comparison with Japan in terms of understanding foreign products, markets and culture. There can be no doubt that among other reasons for her success, the sophisticated market intelligence systems must be one of the major contributors.

Besides being known for market intelligence, Japan is equally known as a place where spies converge to pilfer business technology for military purposes. In the 1940s, Japan was controlled by a ruthless security force called the *Kempeitai*. In order to curtail any further military ambitions of the Japanese, the Americans literally demolished the Japanese security force after the war. In addition, the American legal experts also purged all kinds of Japanese laws that could encourage militarism, including laws pertaining to espionage, intelligence and security.

Unfortunately for the Americans, such past actions are now taking a serious toll on them in a different way. This is because post-war Japan has developed very quickly into a major industrial nation. Today, it is the centre of some of the latest industrial technology and is also fast becoming a paradise for spies from the Soviet Bloc. In fact, the US is now extremely concerned over the leakage of classified technology from Japan to the Soviet Bloc. The irony is, owing to the efforts done by the US after the war, Japan today is not equipped with laws to combat spying. For example, Japan has no law that penalises the leaking of military or strategic secrets by private citizens. At present, the statutory protection against espionage is a clause in the civil service law which prevents government employees from revealing official secrets. The penalty is also not a deterrent since the maximum penalty is one year's imprisonment and a fine of US$200. In the absence of any anti-espionage law, spies who are caught in Japan are usually charged with minor theft or dealing in stolen goods.

The issue of cracking down on espionage activities has been receiving increasing attention for several reasons. First, post-war industrial Japan has become a centre for high technology. While such technology has largely been used for business applications in Japan, the Soviet Bloc will not hesitate to steal it for military purposes. For example, in May 1988, a Japanese firm, Toshiba Machine, was found to have provided the Soviet navy with Western technology.

Second, Japan has a lot of industrial and technological co-operation and joint research with the Western world. Often, there is tremendous transfer of technology across national borders. However, if such technology falls into the hands of the wrong parties, the results can be quite undesirable.

Finally, Japan has been found to be incapable of dealing with espionage. In addition, the general public, spearheaded by the Japan Bar Association, is opposed to enacting anti-espionage laws for fear that such laws may infringe civil rights.

In summary, it is important to acknowledge that business espionage exists and companies must make conscious attempts to protect their corporate secrets. While, it is important to condemn business espionage, it is equally important to face the issue squarely. In other words, you may not engage in stealing technology from others, but you cannot stop others from trying to steal your technology. In addition, you must recognize that business espionage, like military espionage, has been used actively by some companies as an offensive arm to augment their market intelligence activities. Thus, defensive strategies are needed, and this leads us to discuss the **principle of security**, which deals with the protection of information.

It is very interesting to note that there is an area of espionage in business that is very difficult to prevent or condemn as unethical: the stealing of ideas. For example, it is well known that the administrators of five star hospitals have stolen many ideas and concepts from other industries, such as the airlines and hotel businesses. Today, the food served in a high class hospital is presented in a manner similar to that on airlines. The standard of room service is comparable to the in-flight service on an airline. At the same time, the patient's ward is equipped very much in the manner of a deluxe room in a hotel, complete with television and in-house videos, well decorated walls, classy furniture, self controlled airconditioning and so on. Some hospitals even provide daily newspapers of the patient's choice and the food is presented *à la carte*. In addition the lobby and grounds of a top class hotel would make it in no way inferior to those of a resort hotel.

In marketing, even non-profit making organizations such as zoos, universities and political parties have stolen marketing concepts and principles for application in their own areas. Today in the US political campaigns are run like major commercial ventures, full of media hype and fanfare.

Besides stealing ideas and concepts, the advent of technology has also to some extent, facilitated business espionage. For example, with the escalating use of facsimile machines, one of the biggest challenges facing companies is how to curb "faxpionage". Information can now be intercepted in the process of transmission. In the same way, computer sabotage has become an increasing problem today as more and more security codes are breached.

8.2 The principle of security

While the principle of intelligence represents the offensive arm of strategic controls, the principle of security represents the defensive arm. It is important to recognize that, in war, while you may be conducting espionage against the enemy, he is doing the same to you. In the same way, while a company is finding out more information about its competitors, the environment, the market and the consumers, the competitors are most probably doing the same thing. Hence, it is necessary to keep plans secret and prevent information from leaking out. Among other measures, Sun Tzu suggested five main ways of maintaining secrecy.

8.2.1 *Withholding strategic plans*

One of the key aspects of maintaining secrecy is to ensure that strategic plans are never divulged. In fact, they should be kept top secret at the highest level. Sun Tzu said:

> "He (the general) must be capable of keeping his officers and men ignorant of his battle plans."

能愚士卒之耳目，使之无知。

> "He only assigns tasks to his soldiers, but does not explain the purpose; he tells them to gain advantages, but does not divulge the dangers."

犯之以事，勿告以言；犯之以利，勿告以害。

The rationale behind not divulging strategic plans to the rank-and-file is a very simple one – prevention of leakage. At the same time, when plans are made known and the dangers highlighted, no one may be willing to carry out the mission. In the same way, it is difficult for the chief executive officer (CEO) to disclose his strategic plans to all members of the organization. Such plans should be confined to those few on a "need to know" basis. This is because strategic plans, like those in war, are those that determine the long term success or viability of the business. As such, they could be "sabotaged" by competitors once the latter come to know about the plans. It must be emphasized that at a strategic level, whether in war or business, it is the one or two major decisions that make or break the organization. Such plans should therefore be guarded with utmost security.

This need to maintain secrecy at the strategic level must not be confused with planning at the operational level. At the operational level, it is the attention to details and execution that determine winners from losers. Thus, for operational planning, it is important to make known the contents to the rank and file so that the plan can be carried out effectively.

8.2.2 Adopting tight security measures

Confining strategic plans to a "need-to-know" basis is not sufficient. Sun Tzu also advocated the need to adopt tight security measures:

> "When war actions are decided upon, block all possible passages of communications and prohibit any dialogue with emissaries."

是故政举之日，夷关折符，无通其使；

> "Tight security measures must be taken when war plans are being deliberated in the ancestral temple to ensure successful execution."

厉于廊庙之上，以诛其事。

Security measures to prevent leakage of information may include installation of check points, posting of sentries, classification and control of secret documents, inspection of articles and belongings and so on. Today, many armies use a very broad spectrum of means to help them do the surveillance – ranging from animals like dogs to very sophisticated electronic systems. In addition, they have also developed very sophisticated ways of coding and sending messages so as to prevent the enemy from intercepting and interpreting them. All these measures – directed at both people and objects – are necessary as it is through people and objects that information can be leaked. As pointed out earlier, whatever espionage we conduct on the enemy, he will probably be doing the same to us. Thus, there could also be local agents, inside agents, double agents, and living agents of the enemy amongst our ranks. It is, thus, not surprising that Sun Tzu said:

"The enemy's agents who are sent to spy on us must be sought out, ..."

必索敌人之间来间我者，

While in war, the adoption of tight security measures is a common and necessary practice within the army, the same cannot be said about companies in the handling of business secrets. In fact, companies tend to be rather lax about security measures, and when attempts are made to tighten security, they are often resisted, or never taken seriously. Even for companies relying on R&D as a means to compete, security measures are often lacking. As a result, it is no surprise that corporate secrets are easily stolen or leaked to competitors.

In general, companies tend to push the responsibility of protection to the macro level of the government. This is evidenced by the enactment of various copyright laws to protect intellectual property, and the institutionalization of various bodies for registering of patents, trademarks, and inventions. In addition, companies and countries also rely on some loosely structured international organizations to do the policing and regimentation. While such measures are applaudable, they are nonetheless reactive in nature – they are designed to catch the culprit who attempts to violate the rule. Besides, when the violater is caught, much damage could already have been done.

The better method to tackle the issue of leakages of corporate secrets is perhaps to deal with it at source and this requires measures at the micro level of the company or organization. This is very much in line with the thoughts of Sun Tzu. Note that from the quotations cited earlier, the onus of preventing the leakage of information lies at the level of the general in war, or the CEO in business. He must take active measures to protect secrets and not leave them to some third party! This is because in the final analysis, he will be held responsible.

8.2.3 *Punitive deterrents*

Besides taking preventive measures, Sun Tzu did not rule out the need to use strong and punitive deterrents for those who are caught in the act of espionage. He says:

"If espionage operations are divulged before they are implemented, the agent and those whom he divulged information to should all be put to death."

间事未发，而先闻者，间与所告者皆死。

It is thus not surprising that many countries consider the leaking of state secrets as acts of treason and will not hesitate to mete out the death sentence. In addition, they also enact various laws like the Official Secrets Act in Britain as a medium for them to carry out tough action against violators and traitors.

While the use of the death sentence as an extreme form of punishment may seem harsh and inhumane in a modern, civilized and democratic society, there is no doubt about its effectiveness. An example from the laws pertaining to the abuse and trafficking of drugs provide a meaningful illustration. In many Western countries and in some states of the US, there is no death penalty for drug trafficking, possession or abuse – the maximum sentence is life imprisonment. The result of such leniency is that the various problems relating to drugs have been on the increase in such countries and drug trafficking never ceases. In contrast, countries like Malaysia and Singapore impose the death penalty for drug trafficking and possession of drugs (in excess of a certain amount). The result of such a strong and punitive measure is that drug trafficking and possession have never become a major problem in such countries. Those who want to take chances would have to risk losing their lives.

In business, violators are never sentenced to death, nor can they be made to face the death penalty for disclosing corporate secrets. However, the harshest punishments should be meted out against employees who betray the company. This would mean outright sacking as well as laying charges in court wherever possible. Punitive deterrents should complement tight security measures. The former are aimed at making offenders realize the dire consequences of being caught, while the latter are designed to discourage the thought of even trying. When used together, they can be very effective in maintaining secrecy for any organization. Thus, one should not be implemented in the absence of the other.

8.2.4 Creation of unpredictability

Besides the more direct measures discusssed, there are also indirect ways to maintain secrecy. One of these indirect means is the creation of unpredictability in planning and strategy development. For example, the general can alter and/or constantly vary his plans so as to confuse the enemy.

The enemy will face greater difficulty in carrying out espionage and intelligence activities because the general's intentions have become difficult to guess. With every change of pattern in operation, there is no previous experience to rely upon. The enemy's intelligence work will have to start from "square one" again. Thus, Sun Tzu advocated that:

"He must be able to change his methods and schemes so that no one can know his intentions."

易其事，革其谋，使人无识；

"He must be able to alter his campsites and marching routes so that no one can predict his movements."

易其居，迁其途，使人不得虑。

Besides changing strategies, altering campsites and marching routes, Sun Tzu also suggested **shaping** as another way to create unpredictability:

"The ultimate in deploying one's troops is to be without ascertainable shape. Thus even the ablest spies cannot detect anything, nor are the wisest men able to develop counterstrategies."

故形兵之极，至于无形；无形，则深间不能窥，智者不能谋。

Note that when one can achieve unascertainable shape in the deployment of troops, security is maintained. This is because the enemy will have great difficulty in deciphering the deployment and will have to commit lots of effort and time before any headway can be made.

The same principle applies to business. By being adaptable and flexible in the use of strategies, including the employment of various types of resources, the company will put its competitors into a more difficult guessing game. This is because, each time, they would have to contend with new and different situations. What they have acquired or learnt previously may not be applicable. Thus, through variation and shaping, a company can put its competitors on the defensive and cause them to expend large amounts of resources and time in trying to guess the actions of the company. Thus, creation of unpredictability is an indirect and defensive measure designed to confuse the opponents and, in the process, gain the advantage of time for oneself.

8.2.5 Use of deception

Another indirect way to preserve secrecy is to use means to deliberately throw the enemy off-guard. This is achieved through the use of deception. For example, under the principle of intelligence, doomed agents were highlighted as spies who are used for purpose of deceiving the enemy into taking the wrong course of action. When the enemy is

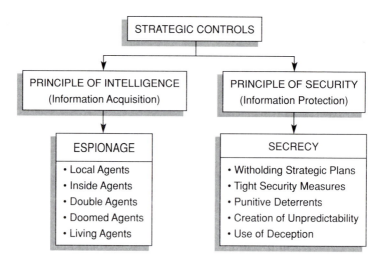

Figure 8.2 Strategic Controls

lured into believing the fabricated information, he will be diverted from the actual course of action. Thus, secrecy will not be threatened, at least for a while.

Deception has been discussed in much detail in the previous chapter. What needs to be emphasized here is that it could also be used as a means for maintaining secrecy for a company. When used appropriately and viewed in a correct perspective, it has a definite place in the strategy development of a company.

Figure 8.2 summarizes the key points that have been discussed in this chapter. Note that strategic controls, as mentioned, involve both information acquisition and information protection.

8.2.6 Security in Business

The need to adopt tighter security in business is becoming more and more important and urgent today. This is because, with the advent of computers and technology, it is becoming easier to pilfer information. For example, it was mentioned earlier that "faxpionage" is now been practiced. Thus, in an effort to curb "faxpionage", counter-faxpionage facilities such as secret codes (which prevent the machine from printing messages unless the user punches in the correct code) have been incorporated. In the same way, the computer industry is investing millions of dollars to develop tighter security measures to prevent hackers from breaking through the security codes of various data/information banks.

Besides data banks and research institutions, the bank industry is another vulnerable target for computer hackers. For example, in June 1990, a Malaysian young executive successfully cracked his bank's computer security code and transferred money from various customers to his account. The total amount of the electronic robbery amounted to over US$1.3 million. There is, therefore, an urgent need to employ stringent control measures to prevent such crimes. These measures may include:

1. Changing passwords regularly. This can also include intruder detection feature passwords that lock the account after several abortive attempts to gain access. In addition, the password can be encrypted.

2. Having the computer call back the account holder after being logged on. This would prevent unauthorized access.

3. Having different personnel to counter-check fund movements and having regular auditing.

4. Programming the computer to alert staff of abnormal transactions such as excessive amounts.

In the final analysis, however, the backing of top management is crucial in the adoption and implementation of all these security measures.

As mentioned earlier, the problem of security would be best tackled at source. A good example is the continual efforts put in by various government agencies that are involved in the printing of money. To prevent forgery state-of-the-art technology has to be used so that counterfeiting is practically impossible. For example, some of these anti-tampering measures include:

1. The method of production. In the production of the steel plate for printing of the notes, as many 30,000 lines and dots can be painstakingly carved by experienced engravers. Such complex design, after aided by computers and lasers make it difficult for anyone to imitate.

2. The quality of paper. The paper itself can be a security test as it must withstand the tests of folding, abrasion, rubbing, flexing, scratching, ageing, scrubbing, etc. In addition, if it has to contain other security features, it has to be of even higher quality, and hence tends to be very expensive. This addds to the costs of production which few forgers would dare venture.

3. The watermark. This is a unique feature that can only be incor- porated during the manufacturing process of the paper. If the

paper texture is high quality, it is possible to include more details through having a larger watermark. This in turn adds to the security.

4. The security thread. It is possible to weave various types of security threads – flourescent, photosensitive or microprinted – within the paper note. These threads provide added security and in many instances, the absence of them can be easily detected by the naked eye of any ordinary person handling the note.

5. The ink. The inks that are used in the printing are formulated in such a way that make it difficult to copy. In addition, various special effects are incorporated so that forgery can easily be detected. For example, the intaglio process (which leaves a raised design) makes it difficult for the printing to be duplicated by any photographic means.

The reason why so much effort is put into ensuring a security-tight process in the printing of bank notes is very obvious – it has serious repercussions in any money economy.

Besides the bank note industry, there is a definite need to step up security to protect one's business. Today's business world is getting more and more dependent on strategic information systems, that is, more information is stored, analyzed, transmitted and received through the computer and its related technology. Unfortunately, the reliance on information technology itself becomes a weakness by itself – it provides opportunities for more and unexpected competitors and third parties to access the information. More seriously, there is a risk of information not only being stolen, but being destroyed completely as well. In fact, this is what is happening with the recent rampant occurrences of computer virus. The result is that computer virus warfare is now openly acknowledged and declared by many companies. The unfortunate thing about the bouts of computer viruses is that they were started by some mischievous computer buffs who unknowingly caused massive destruction of data and information that took much effort to create.

With greater advances in computer technology and reliance on information for decision-making, there must be concerted efforts by all parties to develop strong security measures against the hackers, and the need to establish strong and punitive measures against the violators.

9 The art of strategic management and thinking

As stated at the beginning of this book, we are not concerned with presenting a strategic management tool. Rather, we have attempted to systematically relate the works of Sun Tzu's *Art of War* to business practices, especially in the areas of strategic management and thinking. Apart from its relevance to business practices, we have also cited the opening of China and the possible influence on Japanese strategic thinking as other important reasons for studying this book.

The model, as illustrated through the chapters, consists of five basic stages that are typical of the strategic planning process. This is shown in Figure 9.1. It begins with situation appraisal and ends with strategic controls. However, the strategic controls act as feedback mechanisms to the earlier stages of the strategic planning process. For example, when new information is acquired through the active arm of intelligence, it affects situation appraisal, or the formulation of goals and strategies, or the evaluation of strategies, or the implementation of strategies, or a combination of any of these earlier stages of the planning process. Thus, fine-tuning and adjustments may have to be made in order to capitalize on the new information. This applies to planning of strategies in war and business.

Conversely, if information is leaked out owing to lapses of security measures, it can also affect one or more, or all the earlier stages of the planning process. Again, re-assessment will have to be made, and

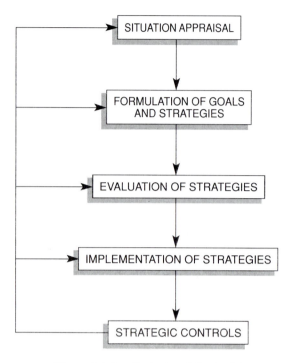

Figure 9.1 Sun Tzu's *Art of War* Model

adjustments, modifications or complete changes to the original strategies might have to be carried out.

Each stage of the planning model had been illustrated in the earlier chapters. Figure 9.2 provides a comprehensive overview of the full model. While each stage has various factors, elements, principles and other dimensions, there are some basic and fundamental principles that can be drawn from the comprehensive model. These basic principles also form the basic thrust or central theme of Sun Tzu's *Art of War.* They are important for the development of strategies in war as well as in business. Together, they form what we call the *Art of Strategic Management.*

9.1 The art of strategic management

The art of strategic management consists of seven key concepts that are embedded in the model as shown in Figure 9.2. These concepts are:

- detailed planning

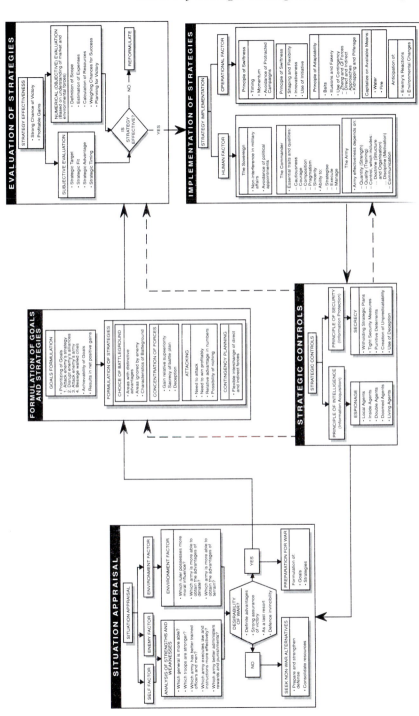

Figure 9.2 Sun Tzu's *Art of War*: The Comprehensive Model
(Larger print of this figure can be found at the back of this book.)

- market intelligence
- choice of battleground
- swiftness in execution of plans
- adaptability in maneuvers
- creation of strategic advantages through deception
- attack, if one has to fight in the open

9.1.1 Detailed planning

Any strategic management must begin with detailed planning. Note that the focus is not whether a company plans or does not plan. Rather, it is how detailed the planning is. It is not about what strategic planning tools must be used or how scientific those tools should be. Instead, it is simply the recognition that planning must be detailed. Once a CEO recognizes that there is a need for detailed planning, he will ensure that the necessary tools will be employed. When he knows that planning must be thorough, he will not hesitate to use whatever means are at his disposal to ensure the accomplishment of those plans. This acknowledgement of detailed planning is an art, not a science. It is so simple, yet many CEOs often forget to practice it, despite the availability of scientific planning tools.

No matter what planning tools or methods are used, thoroughness of planning would entail the inclusion of the 8 factors as discussed in Chapter 2. These 8 factors – political leadership (moral influence), corporate leadership (generalship), external factor (climate), physical or infrastructural factor (terrain), corporate structure and organization (doctrine or law), competitive edges (strengths), human resource development (training) and motivation (discipline) – would encompass considerations from the micro to the macro level, the inclusion of both the controllable and uncontrollable aspects, the internal and external dimensions, the human and non-human components, the static and dynamic forces and the tangible and intangible matters. In short, detailed planning has to be exhaustive in coverage and considerations.

9.1.2 Market intelligence

Detailed planning cannot be carried out on the basis of intuition, gut-feeling, calculated guesses or other subjective means. It must be based on intelligence. According to Sun Tzu, this intelligence cannot be obtained from spirits nor from the gods; nor by inductive thinking; nor by deductive calculations. It can only be obtained by men who have knowledge of the enemy's situation. Thus, there is a need to actively collect, store, analyze and utilize information for the development of more effective strategies.

As mentioned in Chapter 8, the time has come for the institution-alization of not only the position of the Chief Information Officer, but also that of the Chief Intelligence Officer. The successful acquisition and utilization of information for strategic purposes will definitely be one of the factors that determines the competitiveness of organizations in the future.

9.1.3 Choice of battleground

In military combat, one of the important factors to ensure success is to choose battlegrounds carefully. This same logic applies to business. Choosing the right battleground will enable the company to exhibit its strengths better, and camouflage its weaknesses. In addition, it will also enable the firm to exploit opportunities in the market place – for example, through nicheing strategies – and cushion the effects of threats in the environment.

In choosing a battleground to compete, a company should opt for one in which it has distinct advantages over its competitors. It can also look for areas ignored by the competitors. Finally, an understand-ing and appreciation of the characteristics of different battlegrounds will help decide what kind of strategies would be appropriate and effective.

9.1.4 Swiftness in execution of plans

Once a detailed plan is developed based on information gathered through intelligence and the battleground chosen, it is important that the plan be executed swiftly. Swiftness includes perfect timing (as it catches others off-guard, and hence minimizes opposition), the mainte-nance of momentum and the avoidance of protracted campaigns. It also demands that coordination be perfect.

There are several advantages inherent in executing plans swiftly. First, it has that element of surprise, especially when momentum is also maintained. When events move quickly, it has a mesmerizing effect. Second, as plans are executed quickly, it does not allow the competi-tors much time to react, and their defense strategies can be threatened. In addition, it also denies competitors time to read the various strate-gies and maneuvers in the plan, and hence makes it difficult for them to develop counter-strategies. Finally, swiftness in execution minimizes the likelihood that the contents of the plan would be leaked or spied upon. It has that counter-espionage effect.

9.1.5 Adaptability in maneuvers

Swiftness in execution does not mean charging blindly and brutally. Rather, throughout the implementation process, there is a need to maintain adaptability in maneuvers. This requires the practice of shaping and flexibility, as battle conditions in war are never static. In the same way, business situations are always very dynamic as they are affected by various factors – the consumers, the competitors, the government, the general public, the state of technology, the state of the economy and so on.

Adaptability in maneuvers also entails the provision for innovation and the exercise of initiatives. To move ahead of competitors, a company must encourage the flow of innovative ideas on all fronts – from the conception of product/service ideas to the actual implementation of marketing strategies. More importantly, at any time when opportunities arise as a result of the changing environment or other factors, the company must be capable of capitalizing on them. It must not shy away, even though the execution process may have to be modified. At times, it may also entail changes to plans that are already made.

In short, while plans should be adhered to as much as possible, bearing in mind the principle of detailed planning, and should be executed as swiftly as possible, bearing in mind the principle of security, a company must still be bold and flexible enough to deviate when necessary.

9.1.6 Creation of strategic advantages through deception

In war, the creation of strategic advantages is very important to winning. Besides exploiting the advantages provided by weather and terrain, another important means is the use of deceptive strategies. The use of deception – such as baits, illusions and fakery, and the use of contingency planning are all designed to gain strategic advantages and the morality behind their use in war has seldom been questioned. However, the use of deceptive strategies in business in order to create strategic advantages does create many ethical and moral problems. Yet, it is impossible to deny that deceptive strategies are being used in business, especially in the area of negotiation, and it is almost imposssible to eradicate such practices.

The concern for ethics in business has in fact been growing stronger in recent years. Without doubt, more companies are realizing that in the long run, deceptive strategies and fraudulent practices can harm their reputations and market shares. In today's highly competitive business climate, unethical practices can also hurt both dishonest and honest companies and could even threaten the economic stability of whole industries. For example, a series of procurement scandals in the 1980s within the Pentagon of the United States adversely affected the whole defense industry in America. To protect the industry, the Defence Industry Initiatives on Business Ethics and Conduct, a corporate ethics project representing nearly every large US contractor, was set up in 1989 to issue internal ethics codes, conduct ethics training sessions and make available company hot lines for employees to report suspected abuses. Within several months, the project turned in over 100 fraud cases to the Pentagon and recovered US$43 million of government money.

In America, the concern for ethics has grown phenomenally. Many companies, for example IBM, Hewlett-Packard, and General Dynamics and professional bodies such as the American Institute of Public Accountants have developed various ethics initiatives, ranging from ethics manuals and workshops to policing and surveillance methods, to protect their corporate image. Even business schools such as Harvard, Stanford, Columbia, Northwestern and many others have included the teaching of ethics in their management curriculum. However, at the end of the day, it still depends very much on the moral standards of the individual and the company that he is operating in and the code of conduct of the competitors, both domestic and international. Inevitably, the rules governing honesty are like those of cartel arrangement; the first party that departs from the pack gains tremendous advantage. Strong policing and heavy penalties must be imposed to make the system work, which ironically, pushes up the price of doing business anyway! The consolation is a simple one: if nothing is done, it may lead to total decay and destruction of societies. Thus, even if the price is high, it is worth paying, as it serves to preserve the survival and continuity of commercial transactions and hence societies at large.

While outright attempts to cheat are easier to classify as fraud and deliberate efforts to short-change the consumers can be considered deception, there are many other cases and instances that do not fall neatly into the black area. Such grey areas which unfortunately may form the bulk of decision-making processes in the corporate boardroom, are difficult to handle. Without doubt, most companies would want to develop and create strategic advantages over their competitors. They would like to throw the competitors off-guard and, if possible, even to mislead them. Thus, strategies are sometimes even designed to deceive the competitors as well as to wipe out any gains (such as market share) made by competitors. Herein lies the dilemma: how much of such strategies are ethical?

In sum, the authors condemn deception and fraud in business. Yet, we must also acknowledge and caution that fraudulent practices do exist in business and companies do use deceptive strategies to gain advantages over their competitors. While one company may not practice them, it alone cannot prevent its competitors from doing so. Similarly, while a country may have rigorous and strict rules governing and policing fraudulent practices, it cannot dictate that other nations follow suit. What is more important and useful is to tackle them head-on. It is better to face such problems squarely and objectively, than to pretend that they do not exist.

9.1.7 Attack when in combat

Finally, when in combat, or when faced with open competition, the most viable way to win is to go on the offensive. If possible, it is even desirable to attack the competitor's plan at the inception stage. The need to be on the offensive in open confrontation is premised on the assumption that the alternative to it – defense – can only result in a non-lose situation. As we have seen, defense can prevent failure but cannot guarantee success. At best, it can only result in a draw. At worst, it can even lead to "self-choking" and isolation. Indeed, the focus on attack has led to the development of nicheing strategies for those with smaller forces and weaker equipment. To achieve success with nicheing, one must constantly keep in mind that in direct confrontation, it is the relative superiority of forces at the point of contact that matters most. Thus, absolute superiority alone in numbers and resources are not sufficient in winning. What is more important is to develop and use strategies that allow the achievement of relative superiority.

9.2 The gurus of the art of war

It is very interesting to note that when one examines the seven basic concepts underlying the art of war – detailed planning, market intelligence, choice of battleground, swiftness in execution of plans, adaptability in maneuvers, creation of strategic advantages through deception and attack when in open confrontation – one cannot help but think of the very similar ways in which Japanese companies go about in their strategic planning process. Knowingly or otherwise, Japanese companies have been practicing many of the military-like strategies of Sun Tzu in business. We are not alone in holding this view. Scholars like Philip Kotler, Kenichi Ohmae and many others have often described the Japanese economic conquest of the world as a militaristic campaign. To this, we might add that the Japanese campaign is not only militaristic, but based very much on Sun Tzu's type of strategies. In fact, in the late 1970s and early 1980s, when Japanese management received tremendous attention from the Western world, Musashi Miyamoto's *A Book of Five Rings* became a best seller in the United States. It is a military text that is reputedly read by most Japanese CEOs. Interestingly, samurai Musashi's book was written around 1645 A.D. and contained many thoughts parallel to Sun Tzu's *Art of War*. Undoubtedly, Musashi must have obtained much of his inspiration from Sun Tzu, whose works had already been translated into Japanese as early as 716 A.D.

It is very important to point out that Sun Tzu's works were known to the top military and political echelons of Japan for more than a thousand years before the rest of the world became aware of it. Throughout this time, it was possible that the Japanese could have perfected the strategies of Sun Tzu – just as they have perfected the works of many other people – so much so that what we witness today has been taken for granted as uniquely Japanese. One thousand years is not a short time and during this period, the Japanese could have institutionalized the thinkings of Sun Tzu into their military and subsequently, corporate strategies and practices. In fact, over such an extended period of time, such influences could have even become intrinsic to Japanese corporate values and behavior.

For years, the Western world has thought that the Japanese economic success would not last. Many have felt and argued that they will probably experience the same fate as the European colonial powers at the turn of the 20th century when their economic power could not be sustained. Indeed, even the once prosperous and powerful United States of post World War II was faced with the same difficulty in sustaining their successes over the last 15 years. Thus, many policymakers and scholars, especially in the US, believe that if market forces were allowed to drive competition, Japan would end up like any other economic power that preceded her and become a US style consumer-driven society.

When the Japanese yen began to appreciate substantially in the mid-1980s against the US dollar, many predicted that the Japanese giant export machine would halt, leading to recession, unemployment, bankruptcies in Japan and a re-alignment of her trade and balance-of-payment surpluses with other nations. While the Japanese did experience some economic discomfort as a result of the appreciating yen – it doubled in value against the US dollar over a three-year period – the results were not what were expected. The Japanese capitalized on the crisis by intensively restructuring their economy, forcing improvements in product designs, marketing techniques and manufacturing. In particular, they made every attempt to cut cost in order to stay profitable and competitive.

Besides addressing the problems within Japan, many companies also began to shift their operations overseas. They used basically a two-pronged strategy in moving overseas. For markets like the United States and Canada where they faced barriers to entry, the strategy was to shift the plants to those markets so as to gain access to the consumers. Japanese automobile manufacturers did exactly this. In 1982 they began to shift their plants to the United States and Canada and by 1989, they had 10 plants located in various regions of North America. In doing so, the Japanese automobile manufacturers not only gained access to the markets, but could also legitimately claim to make contributions to the North American economy. In fact, they have become so successful that they are now threatening the American big three – General Motors, Ford and Chrysler – on their own turf.

The second approach taken by Japanese companies was to shift operations to low cost producing countries in order to lower the costs of production. In some instances, their plants are also sited in countries that give them preferential status. Thus, exports from such countries can still gain access to the developed countries.

Recent statistics have shown how effective those strategies were. Instead of falling apart – as many Western scholars hoped and predicted – Japanese companies came out of the crisis leaner and more combat-fit. They continued with their export offensive and, indeed, the key to Japan's 1988 growth was largely due to the growth in exports – it registered close to 14% and led the economy to an overall growth rate of 4.8%. The trend is almost certain to continue in 1989 and 1990. Prior to the yen crisis, Japanese companies were already dangerous. After the crisis, they became lethal!

9.3 Rethinking of Japan

The seemingly unstoppable successes of the Japanese up to now has begun not only to trouble many Western countries but has also puzzled many scholars as well. The conventional school of thought that the standard rules of the free market would apply and Japan would gradually evolve into an open economy did not seem to work. In fact, a new school of thought – called revisionism – has begun to emerge in the

United States since the mid-1980s. These revisionists include people like former US trade official, Clyde V. Prestowitz, author of *Trading Places* (1988), Dutch journalist and author Karel van Wolferen author of *The Enigma of Japanese Power* (1989), journalist James Fallows, prominent political scientist and academic Chalmers Johnson (who published the well-known 1982 book called *MITI and the Japanese Miracle*) and other prominent US politicians.

These revisionists reject the Western tenet that capitalism and democracy are fundamentally similar everywhere. In particular, they argue that Japan operates on a different set of economic and political imperatives. According to them, Japanese policymakers are mainly interested in making Japan to become a dominant economic power in the world and are less concerned with following market rules. Thus, the Japanese market will only be opened to her trading partners when pushed to the wall – that is, she will not do so voluntarily.

The revisionist view has found many followers in the United States, including policy makers in Washington. Thus, it has generated much anti-Japanese feeling among various groups of people. It even led a vice-president at the US Chamber of Commerce, William T. Archey, to comment that,

> "it doesn't matter how good you are, how hard-working, how
> much you look at the long term, or how much you spend on
> R&D. A Japanese decision to buy your products is not going to
> be based on the market principles we're familiar with"
> (*Business Week*, August 7, 1989).

To turn the tide, the revisionists advocate various measures to break the economic stronghold of Japan, such as seeking guaranteed market shares or measurable results for American products – such as supercomputers, semiconductors and plywood, which are globally competitive – in Japan. Reciprocity in highly protected sectors like banking, construction and insurance should be demanded. In the event that Japan refuses to reciprocate, swift and highly punitive measures should be taken against Japanese products to the US. In addition, the revisionists also demand that Japanese companies should exercise voluntary export restraints in areas that are currently hurting US industries, such as cars and steel. Above all, the revisionists are insisting that Japan must undertake various measures to untangle her various invisible trade obstacles so that American firms can compete effectively in Japan. In a nutshell, these revisionists are actually advocating economic war against the Japanese.

The Japanese, for their part, have not remained oblivious to the noise in America. They have, in fact, carefully tackled the problem on two fronts. First, there is a group of leaders who are urging the Japanese to stand up to the US, and have strummed up nationalistic themes that have struck responsive chords among annoyed Japanese. For example, a Mr Shintaro Ishihara, advocated strongly in his book called *The Japan That Can Say No* that if one does not use Japanese semiconductors, one cannot guarantee precision and that includes American missiles which are using Japanese chips. He suggested that if Japan were to sell the same chips to the Soviet Union, the military balance of power would change immediately. Ishihara has also argued that the problem with the Americans is that their pride is too strong – to the extent of inerasable arrogance, that they ignore the high culture in Japan and elsewhere in Asia.

Besides Ishihara's book, another Japanese publication entitled *Japan as the Enemy, A New Scenario for US Strategy*, written by Kazuhisa Ogawa, a military strategist, also contained a very nationalist appeal. The general theme in Ogawa's book is that American anger at Japan has been increasing on a subliminal level and that Japan is now ranked as the US's third enemy – after the Soviet Union and China. He contended that the only people who don't know this are the Japanese people. The general thesis of books like these, including Morita's well known book which has been translated into English called *Made in Japan* is that Japan is being blamed for an America that has become fat and complacent. Thus, they tend to appeal to an increasing number of Japanese who are getting tired and impatient with complaints by Americans.

The second approach taken by the Japanese is that of influence peddling through soft-side activities. Japanese companies are today spending heavily to shape the way Americans view them. They are donating millions of dollars to US education – from colleges to universities – and various other philanthropic activities. In 1988 alone, Japanese companies donated well over US$310 million to various organizations in America. Besides such soft-side activities to change the average American perception of the Japanese, they have also attempted to shape decision-making in Washington through influence peddling. For example, Japan's new-found clout in Washington surfaced in 1989 when Toshiba Corporation succeeded in defeating efforts to impose harsh sanctions on it because of its involvement in selling restricted technology to the Soviet Union. Japan's lobbyists also succeeded in stalling major trade bills and bills on other issues in Washington.

Beyond the hard and soft approaches taken by the Japanese, they want to reinforce the notion that American problems are not caused by the Japanese, but are largely homegrown. They say the Americans should re-examine themselves and not blame others for their failures. In essence, the Japanese have demonstrated that their economic prowess does not exist in a vacuum. She has now penetrated into the social and political fabric of American society and has begun to shape the agenda for debate in America. The Japanese have made inroads in waging a new war to shape the minds and thinking of the average Americans, their policymakers and their institutions!

9.4 Conclusion

This book started with the contention that a systematic analysis of the analogy between business and war would prove fruitful and illuminating. In some ways it has also proved contentious. Sun Tzu's reflections on the art of winning a military conflict with the enemy, based no doubt on his experiences on the battlefield, have been seen to shed light not only on the nature of the US-Japan trade conflict but also on the different ways in which business life is understood and conducted around the world. Business is a kind of war and the implications for this metaphor vary according to the seriousness with which the analogy is taken. The discussion of bribery in chapter 7 highlights the way in which some individuals, companies or cultures are able to accommodate this practice in a way that would be seen as inexcusable in others. One way of conducting a war may not be seen as acceptable by another side engaged in the actual same war.

The more significant area is, of course, the whole question of the US-Japan trade situation. In an opinion poll published in *Business Week*, 7 August 1989, 68% of the respondents named Japan's economic threat as the greatest danger facing the US; only 22% named the USSR, as a military threat, posing the same degree of danger. Perhaps what is most interesting about this survey is the possibility it suggests about Japan's economic power being *perceived* in terms of a threatening military force. Given the persuasive scope of the basic analogy between war and business perhaps this should not be seen as unduly alarming. What may be alarming is the realization that the US needs to look at the way it has been conducting its trade war with Japan. If the time is opportune for the US to reconsider its business practices it could do worse than begin with a reading of Sun Tzu's timeless classic.

Appendix A: Concepts and principles of war

A.1 Admiral J.C. Wylie (1967)
A.2 Peacock's (1984) functions of war
A.3 Peacock's (1984) principles of war

In order to have a better appreciation of the applications of military strategies to business practices, it is necessary to have some basic understanding of the concepts and principles of war. We will attempt to relate some basics of understanding warfare by discussing the works of US Navy Rear Admiral, J.C. Wylie and US Colonel, William E. Peacock. Their works are chosen rather than say, the works of Karl von Clausewitz (who wrote his influential book *On War* in 1832), primarily because they reflect the contemporary school of thought. In addition, Colonel William E. Peacock of the US Marine Corps saw active duty in Vietnam and Okinawa and worked in the Pentagon. Thus he has had experience in both the planning and implementation stages of war. In discussing the works of these two authors, we will also extract relevant quotations from Sun Tzu's Art of War to show the importance of his philosophies in today's military context and to allow the reader to relate the works of Sun Tzu to modern day military strategy.

A.1 Admiral J.C. Wylie (1967)

The primary aim of the strategist in the conduct of war according to Wylie (1967, p. 91) is to have some selected degree of control over the enemy. This control is exercised through designing a pattern of war such that the center of gravity of war weighs in favor of the strategist and to the disfavor of the enemy.

The "Center of Gravity" referred to by Wylie is the critical point which decides the outcome of the war. The manipulation of this center of gravity depends on four factors. These factors are the *nature, placement, timing* of war and the *weight* of the center of gravity of war.

A.1.1 The nature of war

The nature of war has changed tremendously since the end of the nineteenth century. It was the proliferation of scientific inventions after this period that added new dimensions to the way battles are fought. This has led to two new categories of military conflict, air (this includes nuclear and star-war battles) and guerrilla warfare, being added to the then traditional classifications of sea and continental warfares.

   The basic tenets of the four types of warfares are very similar to each other. In sea warfare, the establishment and exploitation of control of sea routes and sea channels are very often crucial to the establishment of air and land power. It is for this reason that the United States and the USSR maintain large naval fleets in the Atlantic and Pacific oceans. The guarding and control of sea routes are also important for the procurement and movement of supplies and troops both in peace and war times. Thus, the United States, in spite of occasional international protests, still maintains a strong naval presence in the Middle-East.

   Similarly, in aerial warfare the control of airspace is essential to control on land. However, there is no practical way to prevent the enemy from attacking one's forces except to destroy his air power before he has a chance to strike. To have command of the air, therefore, means to be in a position to prevent the enemy from flying while retaining the ability to fly oneself. This scramble for air control has led to many developments in aircraft and related technology such as air surveillance systems (AWACs), sophisticated air-to-air missiles and air refuelling stations. Even the United States' Star Wars concept is premised on dominating air space so as to gain strategic ground advantage.

   In continental warfare, terrain dictates the type of battles that can be fought, the types of weapons to be used, the number and types of troops needed and the nature of deployment. Today, more and more sophisticated weaponry has been developed for ground battles. Some of these help overcome the limitations imposed by the terrain. However, in the final analysis, to capture the objective, it is the enemy that one has to face, no matter who he is.

   Finally, in guerrilla warfare, winning a decisive battle may not be the immediate objective. Rather, small units are allowed to act independently to inflict the heaviest casualties on the enemy's forces, as well as dampen the enemy's morale. Such a strategy is useful when the enemy has a larger force and provided the terrain allows the conduct of such warfare. The Vietnam war is probably the best example of guerrilla warfare at its most effective. Despite superior strengths in numbers and in weaponry, the United States lost the war. The main reason – they were unable to fight the protracted campaign of guerrilla warfare that was waged by the Vietcong.

A.1.2 *The placement of war*

Sun Tzu's *Principle of Choice of Battleground* stated that a key component to winning war is to ensure that the battleground is more advantageous to one's own army than the enemy's. This entails at least two elements – the need to create distinct advantages, such as being the first to occupy key points:

> "Generally, those who reach and occupy the battleground early will have time to rest and wait for the enemy. Those who arrive at the battleground late will have to rush into action when they are already tired and exhausted."

> 凡先处战地而待敌者佚，后处战地而趋战者劳。

> "Therefore, those who are skilled in warfare will always bring the enemy to where they want to fight, and are not brought there by the enemy."

> 故善战者，致人而不致于人。

and the need to choose battlegrounds ignored by the enemy

> "To be certain to succeed in what you attack is to attack a place where the enemy does not defend or where its defense is weak; to be certain to hold what you defend is to defend a place the enemy does not attack or where the defense is invulnerable to attacks."

> 攻而必取者，攻其所守也；
> 守而必固者，守其所不攻也。

In the Vietnam war the Vietcong rarely engaged American troops in the open. Rather, through sabotage and small raids, they forced the

American troops to go after them in the jungles. The result was that American troops were ambushed and booby trapped, and suffered heavy casualties. By luring the US troops into fighting in the jungles, the Vietcong were engaging them on familiar ground and were able to score decisive battles. Those victories were achieved despite the fact that they had inferior weapons.

A.1.3 *The timing of war*

The timing of war refers to the decision of when each engagement is to take place. The importance of timing in war was described in Sun Tzu's words:

> "When the strike of the falcon breaks the body of its prey, it is because of correct timing."

鸷鸟之疾, 至于毁折者, 节也。

The importance of timing cannot be underscored better, especially when it comes to a matter of life and death, like in war situations. The importance and significance of this element is evidenced by the fact that watch synchronization is a "must" excercise in any military briefing before the execution of the battle plan. Every movement, deployment of troops and weapons has to be well-planned and executed. For example, in the capture of an enemy objective such as a hilltop position, the airforce must know when they must begin strafing, the artillery must know when and how long they must bombard and the infantry must know the exact moment to arrive at the objective and to charge up the hill for the final "kill". Any misjudgement of timing may endanger the lives of one's own troops. Imagine the danger if the infantry soldiers arrive way ahead of time at the foot of the hill where the enemy is entrenched – their position can be easily spotted and they have little cover or defense against the enemy's fire. They should arrive just as the airforce has completed strafing and the artillery has begun shelling. At this time, the enemy's troops are heavily pinned down by fire and concentrated on defense. It is thus unlikely that the attacking infantry troops would be threatened.

Note that the elements of placement and timing of war depend heavily on the subjective assessment of the battle situation, the relative strengths of the attacking troops versus the defending troops and many other factors. It becomes evident that such decisions are dependent on the ability and military sense of the strategist.

A.1.4 *Weight of the center of gravity*

As mentioned earlier, the center of gravity as articulated by Wylie refers to the critical point which decides the outcome of the war. In order to tip the weight of the center of gravity of the war to one's favor, Wylie suggested two patterns of strategy, sequential and cumulative. These two patterns stem from varying philosophies of war but they should not be treated as mutually exclusive from one another. In fact, they may have a synergistic effect when used together.

The sequential pattern of strategy treats the war process like a length of chain. Each link is a discrete action which grows naturally out of, and depends on, the one that preceded it. The cumulative pattern, on the other hand, views war as a collection of lesser actions which are not sequentially interdependent. Each individual action is a mere plus or minus in the scoreboard of warfare, summing to a final result that determines victory or defeat.

Interestingly, Sun Tzu had already developed such a similar idea more than 2,300 years ago. According to Sun Tzu:

> "In battle there are only the direct and indirect forces, yet their combinations are limitless and beyond comprehension. For these two forces are mutually reproductive; their interactions are endless like those of interlocking rings. Indeed, who can tell where the variations begin and end?"

> 战势不过奇正，奇正之变，不可胜穷也。
> 奇正相生，如循环之无端，孰能穷之？

A common mistake made by military enthusiasts is to believe that the only way to wage war is to annihilate the enemy. This misunderstanding occurs because they confuse war with a battle. War is the military conflict that two or more countries engage in, while battles are the actual armed struggles that military forces encounter. Thus there are many battles in a war, and winning all the battles does not guarantee victory in the war. Victory in war should be the adequate and appropriate control over the enemy to ensure that the enemy will regain his status as a viable member of the world community. In fact, Sun Tzu advocated such a concept:

> "In the conduct of war, it is better to take the whole state intact than to ruin it; it is better to capture the enemy's army intact than to destroy it; it is better to subdue a division intact than to destroy it; it is better to subdue a company intact than destroy it; and it is better to subdue a squad intact than to destroy it."

凡用兵之法，全国为上，破国次之；
全军为上，破军次之；
全旅为上，破旅次之；
全卒为上，破卒次之；全伍为上，破伍次之。

"For this reason, to win a hundred victories in a hundred battles is not the hallmark of skill. The acme of skill is to subdue the enemy without even fighting."

是故百战百胜，非善之善者也；不战而屈人之兵，善之善者也。

Sun Tzu did not advocate open warfare and confrontation as the first option to be pursued. Rather, it is a measure of the last resort as evidenced by the following comments:

"The highest form of generalship is to attack the enemy's strategy;
The next best policy is to disrupt his alliances;
The next is to attack his army;
The worst policy of all is to besiege walled cities.
Avoid attacking walled cities if possible."

故上兵伐谋，其次伐交，其次伐兵，
其下攻城。攻城之法为不得已。

Sun Tzu also highlighted the importance of defense:

"In the conduct of war, one must not rely on the enemy's failure to come, but on one's readiness to engage him; one must not rely on the enemy's failure to attack, but on one's ability to build an invincible defense."

故用兵之法，无恃其不来，恃吾有以待也；
无恃其不攻，恃吾有所不可攻也。

In sum, we may view the overall concept of war strategies as depicted in Figure A.1. The overall strategy for combat is made up of offensive and defensive strategies. Each of these strategies can again be classified into direct (sequential) and indirect (cumulative) operations or forces, with the possibility of interchange between the direct and indirect operations (forces). It is important to point out that the effects of the interaction between the direct and indirect operations should never be under-estimated. The indirect forces can sometimes be the extraordinary or surprise element in winning the war. This point is put very aptly by Sun Tzu:

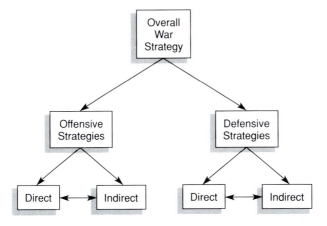

Figure A.1 An Overview of War Strategies

"In warfare, one generally uses the direct force to engage the enemy, but uses the indirect force to win."

凡战者，以正合，以奇胜。

A.2 Peacock's (1984) functions of war

Having discussed the overall concept of war strategy, let us now look at the operational aspects of this concept. According to Peacock (1984), for a military force to fulfill its mission, it is essential that there must be coordination of four functions: military personnel, military intelligence, military operations and planning, and supply and transport. Each of these functions will be briefly discussed, and compared with those advocated by Sun Tzu.

A.2.1 Military personnel

This function refers to the administration of policies that govern the handling of the soldier as an individual. Its areas of responsibility include morale, pay and promotion policies, troop assignments to specific operations, replacing troops if necessary and burial.

Sun Tzu recognized the importance of the military personnel function in his very first chapter on Situation Appraisal. He advocated that there are three aspects to this function – the moral influence of the ruler, the generalship of the commander doctrine.

"The moral influence is that which enables the people to be in perfect accord with their ruler, for which they are willing to accompany him in life and unto death without any fear for danger."

道者，令民与上同意也，故可以与之死，
可以与之生，而不畏危。

"The generalship of the commander refers to the general's qualities of wisdom, sincerity, benevolence, courage, and strictness."

将者，智、信、仁、勇、严也。

"The doctrine refers to the organization, control, signals procedures, designation of military ranks and responsibilities, regulation and management of supply routes, and the provision of items used by the army."

法者，曲制、官道、主用也。

Note that Sun Tzu's treatment of the function of the military was even more comprehensive than those mentioned by Peacock. He highlighted the importance of the human factor (the ruler and the commander) besides the need for systems, organizations and procedures.

A.2.2 *Military intelligence*

This function deals with the collection, evaluation, and final dissemination of intelligence. Here, information regarding the enemy's location, strengths and plans are collected as are data about the weather and the terrain of the battleground. Movements of troops and civilians are traced. Sun Tzu also recognized the importance of intelligence. He called it **foreknowledge** in the planning of strategies.

"The reason why the enlightened ruler and the wise general are able to conquer the enemy whenever they lead the army, and to achieve victories that surpass those of others is because of foreknowledge."

故明君贤将，所以动而胜人，成功出于众者，智知也。

Sun Tzu further advocated the use of people to obtain information and knowledge about the enemy's dispositions and situations.

> "This foreknowledge cannot be elicited from spirits nor from the gods; nor by inductive thinking; nor by deductive calculations. It can only be obtained from men who have knowledge on the enemy's situation."

先知者不可取于鬼神，不可象于事，
不可验于度，必取于人，知敌之情者也。

Thus, it is very important to realize that intelligence must come from humans who are familiar with the enemy. While there has been tremendous advancement in the area of military intelligence technology, such as surveillance equipment, they still have to rely on the human factor for the input or interpretation of data. Sophisticated equipments and systems *per se* cannot win wars without manipulation by the people behind them.

A.2.3 Military operations and planning

The function of military operations and planning includes the preparation of overall strategic plans, tactical plans, types of assault and defense, and alternative plans. As war involves more than one party, and each party may pursue different and varied strategies depending on the conditions prevailing at that time, it is not possible to predict with certainty the pattern of war. Therefore, battle plans cannot be rigid. Rather, various alternative plans must be formulated in anticipation of changing battle and ground situations. In addition, there must also be flexibility in the grouping of forces and units so as to carry out specific assignments and battle plans.

All these factors, interestingly, are covered in Sun Tzu's writings. For example, he developed certain decision rules and guidelines with regard to attack, the use of alternative direct (正) and indirect (奇) forces, the need for concentration of forces, the focus on simplicity of plans. He also wrote about the need to be varied and adaptable in the use of plans in battles:

> "Therefore, do not repeat the tactics that won you a victory, but vary them according to the circumstances."

故其战胜不复，而应形于无穷。

This principle of adaptability has two components, namely, flexibility and the use of initiative. On flexibility, Sun Tzu said:

> "The guiding principle in military tactics may be likened to water. Just as flowing water avoids the heights and hastens to the lowlands, an army should avoid strengths and strike weaknesses."

夫兵形象水，水之形，避高而趋下；兵之形，避实而击虚。

> "Just as water shapes itself according to the ground, an army should manage its victory in accordance with the situation of the enemy. Just as water has no constant shape, so in warfare there are no fixed rules and conditions."

水因地而制流，兵因敌而制胜。
故兵无常势，水无常形；

On the use of initiatives, Sun Tzu commented:

> "If the situation is one of victory, the general must fight even though the ruler may have issued orders not to engage. If the situation is one of defeat, the general must not fight even though the ruler may have issued orders to do so."

故战道必胜，主曰：无战，必战可也；
战道不胜，主曰：必战，无战可也。

It is important to point out here that Sun Tzu did not advocate disloyalty to the emperor or ruler. Rather, his contention was that the general, being close to the battleground, would be the best judge of the outcome of a battle. If he is a capable general, he should be able to make a wise decision and not jeopardize the lives of the troops and the interests of the nation. The bottom line is still to protect the sovereignty of the state. It is interesting to note that the Chinese character for loyalty (忠) literally means the "centering of one's heart" and hence implies, to a large extent, impartiality of decision-making. And loyalty to the Chinese historically refers to loyalty to the state and not necessarily to the emperor.

A.2.4 Supply and transport

The supply and transport function involves moving troops and supplies to the desired location at the planned time. Essential supplies such as food, water, clothing, arms and ammunitions must be transported to the battle front and various support bases using a limited supply of vehicles and other transport means. Such movements must be well co-ordinated and planned as any delay or misallocation can affect the conduct of the war as well as jeopardize the lives of the soldiers. In conventional warfare, the logistical problems become even more critical as an army penetrates deep into enemy territory. The supply routes can often be subjected to ambushes and sabotage. This is one reason why disrupting supplies is one of the main ways to slow down the momentum of an advancing army.

Sun Tzu recognized the significance of this function and advocated that one should be swift in the execution of warfare and not be engaged in a protracted war:

"When the army engages in protracted campaigns the resources of the state will be impoverished."

久暴师则国用不足。

"Those adept in warfare do not require a second levy of conscripts nor more than the required supplies. The necessary military supplies are brought from home and they live by foraging on the enemy. In this way, the army will always be sufficient with food and supplies."

善用兵者，役不再籍，粮不三载；
取用于国，因粮于敌，故军食可足也。

"Therefore, the wise general sees to it that his troops feed on the enemy, for one cartload of the enemy's provisions is equal to twenty of his own; and one picul of the enemy's fodder to twenty piculs of his own."

故智将务食于敌，食敌一钟，当吾二十钟；
萁秆一石，当吾二十石。

The last quotation is especially logical when one takes into consideration the costs and dangers of transporting supplies into enemy territory. In addition, by plundering the resources of the enemy, it also deprives him of the chance to use them to feed and supply his troops. The basic principle is to gain relative strategic advantage over the enemy.

According to Sun Tzu, the impact of supply and transportation cannot be underestimated in times of war. At its worst, it can even impoverish the wealth of a nation:

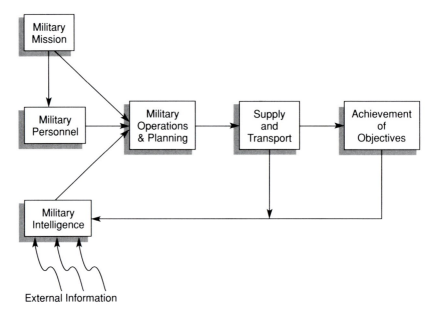

Figure A.2 The Various Functions of War

"The reason why a country can be impoverished by military operations is because of distant transportation; the carriage of supplies over long distances will render the people destitute."

国之贫于师者远输，远输则百姓贫。

In summary, Peacock's (1984) four functions of war in relation to the overall conduct of war can be depicted in Figure A.2. Note that the commander starts the whole process by formulating his mission.

A.3 Peacock's (1984) principles of war

In order to implement the four functions as discussed in the previous section, Peacock (1984) further specified nine principles of war. These nine principles are:

1. The Principle of Maneuver
2. The Principle of the Objective
3. The Principle of the Offensive
4. The Principle of Surprise

5. The Principle of <u>E</u>conomy of force
6. The Principle of <u>M</u>ass
7. The Principle of <u>U</u>nity of command
8. The Principle of <u>S</u>implicity
9. The Principle of <u>S</u>ecurity

The initial letters of these principles form an acronym, **MOOSEMUSS**, which summarizes modern military principles intended to guide the successful execution of war strategies. It would be interesting to compare each of these principles with those advocated by Sun Tzu.

A.3.1 The principle of maneuver

This principle describes the movement one makes in order to place combat power in an advantageous position with respect to the enemy, entailing a careful study and understanding of the grounds and conditions of war. Sun Tzu also articulated this principle very well in his treatise devoting a whole chapter to this subject matter (Chapter VII), and acknowledging the difficulty and intricacy of such a principle:

> "There is nothing more difficult than the art of maneuvering. It is difficult because of the need to make the devious route become the most direct, and to turn misfortunes to advantageous situations."

> 军争之难者，以迂为直，以患为利。

> "Thus, there are both inherent advantages and dangers in maneuvers."

> 故军争为利，军争为危。

The principle of maneuver is illustrated in various places of Sun Tzu's Chapter VII. The following are some examples:

> "War is based on deception. The tactics must react to the changes in situations and forces must concentrate or divide accordingly."

> 故兵以诈立，以利动，
> 以分合为变者也。

"In the early stages of a battle, the spirits of the forces are high; later, they will gradually flag; at the end stage, their spirits are low and thoughts of returning set in. Therefore, those adept in warfare avoid attacking the enemy when their spirits are high, but attack them when their spirits are sluggish and the soldiers homesick. This is control of the emotional factor."

是故朝气锐，昼气惰，暮气归。故善用兵者，
避其锐气，击其惰归，此治气者也。

"Use discipline and orderliness to match the enemy's disorderliness; use calmness to handle a clamorous one. This is control of the mental factor."

以治待乱，以静待哗，此治心者也。

"Use nearness to the battlefield to match the enemy's distance; rest to match enemy's exhaustion; and well-fed troops to match enemy's hungry ones. This is control of the physical factor."

以近待远，以佚待劳，以饱待饥，此治力者也。

"Do not engage an approaching enemy whose banners are well-ordered; do not attack an enemy whose formations are impressive and strong. This is control of the factor of changing circumstances."

无邀正正之旗，勿击堂堂之陈，此治变者也。

The underlying logic of maneuvers, as advocated by Sun Tzu, is to achieve relative superiority of combat power at the point of engaging the enemy, or alternatively, not to be at a relatively inferior position. The main purpose is to gain maximum advantage over the enemy.

A.3.2 The principle of the objective

This principle refers to the need to identify the end to be achieved before the employment of military troops and actions. It requires a careful assessment of the need to resort to military action in order to decide whether such actions are justifiable. Hence, waging war should be based on an objective evaluation of its costs and benefits and the chances of success. The benefits may include factors like economic, political and geographical gains. The costs may include a drain on the national resources and wealth, hardships on troops and citizens or loss of lives. Only when the benefits of war outweigh the costs, and the chances of success are favorable can one wage war, and even so it should be pursued with caution. These warnings have been very well addressed by Sun Tzu in the opening remarks of his writings:

> "War is a matter of vital importance to the State. It concerns the lives and deaths of the people, and affects the survival or demise of the State. It must be thoroughly studied."

> 兵者，国之大事，死生之地，存亡之道，不可不察也。

and the following warnings:

> "Do not move unless there are definite advantages to be gained; do not use troops unless you can succeed; do not fight unless you are in danger."

> 非利不动，非得不用，非危不战。

The seriousness of engaging in war and the need for a cautious approach can best be summed up by the following remarks by Sun Tzu:

> "A ruler must not start a war out of anger; a general must not fight a battle out of resentment. Engage only when it is in the interest of the State; cease when it is to its detriment."

> 主不可以怒而兴师，将不可以愠而致战；
> 合于利而动，不合于利而止。

> "For while anger can be restored to happiness, and resentment can become pleasantness; a State that has perished cannot be restored, and a man who is dead cannot be resurrected."

> 怒可以复喜，愠可以复悦；
> 亡国不可以复存，死者不可以复生。

A.3.3 The principle of the offensive

This principle describes the need for offensive actions to achieve results and to attain success in a military campaign. Sun Tzu also stated similar views in his principle of attack and suggesting that there should be priorities in offensive strategies. These strategies and their underlying

Table A.1 Priorities of offensive strategies

Priority	Rationale
1. The highest form of generalship is to attack the enemy's strategy. 故上兵伐谋，	1. When victory is long delayed, the ardor and morale of the army will be depressed. When the siege of a city is prolonged, the army will be exhausted. When the army engages in protracted campaigns, the resources of the state will be impoverished.
2. The next best policy is to disrupt his alliances. 其次伐交，	
3. The next best is to attack his army. 其次伐兵，	久则钝兵挫锐， 攻城则力屈， 久暴师则国用不足。
4. The worst policy of all is to besiege walled cities. 其下攻城。	

rationale is shown in Table A.1. Note that one should attack the enemy at the earliest stage of the battle. Sun Tzu suggested that the best strategy is to attack the enemy's plan at its inception. Open confrontation, like an all out battle (typical in the ancient ways of be sieging cities) should only be used as a last resort in offensive strategies. However, in the event that one has to fight, there is the need to attack. This need is best summarized by the following comments:

> "Invincibility in defense depends on one's own efforts, while the opportunity for victory depends on the enemy. It follows that those skilled in warfare can make themselves invincible, but cannot cause the enemy to be vulnerable."

不可胜在己，可胜在敌。故善战者，
能为不可胜，不能使敌之可胜。

> "Those who cannot win must defend; those who can win must attack. Defend when one's forces are inadequate; attack when one's forces are abundant."

不可胜者，守也；可胜者，攻也。
守则不足，攻则有余。

Underlying Sun Tzu's remarks is the need to have numerical superiority in force before launching an attack. In addition, the military commander should not assume that the enemy is less prudent in the conduct of war than he is and he should only attack when there are opportunities provided by the enemy, such as when he commits mistakes in defensive tactics.

However, the basic and important point is that the only way to win a battle is to be on the offensive. Invincibility in defense will only guarantee non-defeat, but cannot secure victory. At the same time, a strong defense will not gain territory. The only tenable argument for a strong defense is that it acts as a deterrent to any potential attacking force. This is the reason why many nations in the world choose to build up their defense forces and systems as they act as deterrents to the enemy.

A.3.4 *The principle of surprise*

The principle of surprise recommends that one should act in a way that the enemy cannot react to in an effective manner. When the enemy is surprised and caught off guard, they will not be able to react quickly and effectively. The element of surprise will always cause confusion and disorder in the enemy.

The underlying purpose of deception is to mislead the enemy and to act on the enemy's unpreparedness, thereby increasing the chances of success. In Sun Tzu's words:

> "All warfare is based on deception."

> 兵者，诡道也。

Deception involves the use of illusions, baits and surprises. The following illustrates the concept of illusion:

> "Therefore, when capable, feign incapability; when active, feign inactivity. When near to the objective, feign that you are far away; when far away, make it appear that you are near."

> 故能而示之不能，用而示之不用，
> 近而示之远，远而示之近。

The basic idea is to camouflage your genuine intention so that it keeps the enemy guessing and confused.

The use of baits is the second type of action available under which Sun Tzu saw as constituting the principle of deception:

"Offer the enemy a bait to lure him; when he is in disorder, strike him."

利而诱之，乱而取之

The use of baits may include sacrificing a portion of the force, giving up some previously captured battlegrounds, or yielding a city. These sacrifices are made deliberately to put the enemy in a state of complacency, and are done with the sole purpose of subsequently gaining a more valuable objective. In other words, it is possible to allow the loss of several battles so long as the war is won.

The third dimension to deception is the creation of surprises through unpredictable or multiple courses of actions:

"The enemy must not know where I intend to attack. For if he does not know where I intend to attack, he must defend in many places. The more places he defends, the more scattered are his forces, and the weaker is his force at any one point."

吾所与战之地不可知；不可知，则敌所备者多；
敌所备者多，则吾所与战者，寡矣。

"In the beginning of battle, be as shy as a young maiden to entice the enemy and lower his defenses. When the battle progresses, be as swift as a hare so as to catch the unpreparedness of the enemy."

是故始如处女，敌人开户，
后如脱兔，敌不及拒。

According to Sun Tzu, there are many ways to achieve surprises. One such way is through the use of the direct (*zheng* 正) and indirect (*qi* 奇) forces. The "zheng" force is normally used to engage the enemy, while the "qi" force is used for winning. Another way to achieve surprise is through speed:

"Speed is the essence of war. Capitalize on the unpreparedness of the enemy; travel by the unexpected routes; and attack those places that he does not take precautions."

兵之情主速，乘人之不及，
由不虞之道，攻其所不戒也。

A note of caution, however, should be made about the use of deception in warfare. While the principle seems easy to understand and is very appealing, its application in war is not as simple as one might think. If one wishes to feign disorder to entice the enemy one must first be courageous and well disciplined in order that the deception will appear real and convincing. Otherwise, if the enemy sees through the plot, the consequences can be very disastrous. In the words of Sun Tzu:

> "To feign confusion, one must possess discipline; to feign cowardice, one must possess courage; to feign weakness, one must possess superiority of forces."

乱生于治，怯生于勇，弱生于强。

A.3.5 The principle of economy of force

Economy of force simply means the use of minimum strength applied to a point other than the decisive one in order to pave the way for the application of mass force and power at the point of decision. The idea is to use one's limited available force where it counts most, and is tantamount to shifting the centre of gravity to the advantage of one's main attacking force through graduated efforts, or to create opportunities of relative superiority for the main force. Sun Tzu recognized this principle very well:

> "The strength of an army does not depend on large forces. Do not advance basing on sheer numbers. Rather, one must concentrate the forces and anticipate correctly the enemy's movements in order to capture him."

兵非益多也，惟无武进，
足以并力、料敌、取人而已。

Sun Tzu talked about the roles and possible strengths of small forces when they are used correctly. In simple terms, he saw the advantages and need for nicheing:

> "If I can uncover the enemy's dispositions while concealing mine, then I can concentrate while he must divide. And if my forces are united while his scattered, I can pit my entire strength against a fraction of his at any selected point of attack. There, I will be numerically superior and the enemy will surely be in trouble."

故形人而我无形，则我专而敌分；我专为一，敌分为十，
是以十攻其一也，则我众而敌寡；能以众击寡者，
则吾之所与战者，约矣。

There are many types of military operations that operate on the principle of economy of force. For example, raids on enemy positions are often carried out by small forces, ambushes and sabotages employ the same principle, and much guerrilla fighting operates from this principle. All these activities are designed to disrupt the concentration of the enemy and at the same time to pave the way for major attacks in the future.

To achieve economy of force, one must also rely on other principles such as the principles of deception maneuver and others. At this point, it is important to point out that the application of these principles should not be viewed in isolation. Rather, each principle should be applied with the others to the extent possible. In this way, the interactive effects would be tremendous.

A.3.6 The principle of mass

This principle means that when one engages the enemy at the point of decision, one must have a concentration of superior power with respect to the enemy in order to win the battle. Note that the requisite is a superior power at the point of decision and not in all situations, that is, it is still premised on the notion of relative superiority at the point of engagement. It is also important to point out that this principle does not contradict the principle of economy of force, but rather, it actually complements it. In applying the principle of economy of force, one uses various tactics such as concealing the exact point of attack or using deceptive tactics to disrupt and scatter a larger enemy's force. This makes it possible for a smaller force to take on a much larger (but dispersed) force. However, at the point of engaging the enemy, the attacking force must still maintain military superiority.

Sun Tzu developed certain decision rules with regards to the principle of mass. In understanding these rules, one must also bear in mind that although they were applicable in ancient warfare in China, their relevance has not diminished in today's conventional battles:

"Thus, the art of using troops is as follows:
When outnumbering the enemy ten to one, surround him;
When five to enemy's one, attack him;
When double his strength, divide him;

When evenly matched, you may choose to fight;
When slightly weaker to the enemy, be capable of withdrawing;
When greatly inferior to the enemy, avoid engaging him;
For no matter how obstinate a small force is, it will succumb to a
larger and superior force."

故用兵之法，十则围之，五则攻之，
倍则分之，敌则能战之，
少则能逃之，不若则能避之。
故小敌之坚，大敌之擒也。

Note that modern day usage of forces also follows similar decision
rules. For example, to assault a hill, it is often recommended that the
attacking force must maintain at least a two to three times superiority
over the enemy. This ratio goes up if the assault is conducted at night.
What is interesting, however, is that Sun Tzu also had other ideas in
mind. He recommended that if one is vastly superior, there is no need
for direct confrontation. The best strategy is to surround the enemy and
"choke" him to death. In this way, there is no need to lose lives
unnecessarily. This approach is also consistent with the other principles
elaborated elsewhere in his book. For example, he never advocated
that one should confront the enemy in "death" ground, for example
when he is surrounded. Under such circumstances, the enemy's courage and vigor will be enhanced greatly when attacked as the only way
to escape or live is to fight to death.

Sun Tzu's principle of mass takes into account the situation facing both sides.

A.3.7 *The principle of unity of command*

This principle is very much related to the function of military personnel
as mentioned by Peacock. However, it is important to highlight that the
principle relies heavily on the ability of the commander himself. In his
Chapter III, *Strategic Attacks*, Sun Tzu mentioned 5 ways in which
victories could be predicted:

"He who knows when to fight and when not to fight will win;
He who knows how to deploy large and small forces will win;
He whose whole army is united in purpose will win;
He who is well-prepared to seize opportunities will win;
He whose generals are able and not interfered by the ruler will win."

知可以战与不可以战者胜，识众寡之用者胜，
上下同欲者胜，以虞待不虞者胜，
将能而君不御者胜。

Note that among the 5 ways of predicting victories, the third and fifth aspects are closely related to the "unity of command" principle. In addition, Sun Tzu's principle of unity of command extends beyond that of the field commander alone. It encompasses the role of the ruler and he highlights three ways in which the ruler of a state can cause disunity as well as bring disaster to his army:

> "When ignorant that the army should not advance, to order an advance; or ignorant that it should not retreat, to order a retreat. This is interfering with military command."

不知军之不可以进，而谓之进；
不知军之不可以退，而谓之退；是谓縻军。

> "When ignorant of military affairs, to participate in their administration. This causes the officers to be confused."

不知三军之事，而同三军之政者，则军士惑矣。

> "When ignorant of military command, to interfere in the exercise of such responsibilities. This creates suspicion among officers."

不知三军之权而同三军之任，
则军士疑矣。

The result of such disunity can easily be predicted:

> "If the army is confused and suspicious, the neighboring states will surely create trouble. This is like the saying: 'A confused army provides victory for the enemy.'"

三军既惑且疑，则诸侯之难至矣，
是谓乱军引胜。

A.3.8 The principle of simplicity

In the principle of simplicity, Peacock is concerned that complex plans that appeal to the complex minds of the generals may, in fact, be too difficult for their subordinates to implement and thereby causing the plans to fail. He prefers the direct and simple but well executed plans. Sun Tzu also suggests that successful strategies are often deceptively simple so that their wisdom is seldom noticed:

> "Therefore, the victories won by a master of war never gain him reputation for wisdom or courage."

故善战者之胜也，无智名，无勇功。

It is important to point out that the principle of simplicity does not contradict the need for detailed planning. It refers more to the way in which a plan is carried out and many simple courses of action are often hatched out of very detailed considerations and calculations. In the words of Sun Tzu:

> "... With careful and detailed planning, one can win; with careless and less detailed planning, one cannot win. How much more certain is defeat if one does not plan at all! From the way planning is done beforehand, we can predict victory or defeat."

多算胜，少算不胜，而况于无算乎！
吾以此观之，胜负见矣。

A.3.9 The principle of security

The necessity to maintain a wall of secrecy around war plans is emphasized in this principle. This idea is quite common and we have seen its development into popular phrases like "Top Secret", "For Your Eyes Only", or "On Need To Know Basis". The principle of security is also not ignored by Sun Tzu who advocated secrecy of battle plans in several ways. The first type involves keeping the highest level plans from even the officers and men:

> "He only assigns tasks to his soldiers, but does not explain the purpose; he tells them to gain advantages, but does not divulge the dangers."

犯之以事，勿告以言；犯之以利，勿告以害。

Sun Tzu went a step further in maintaining the wall of secrecy around his plans by suggesting that:

"When war actions are decided upon, block all possible passages of communications and prohibit any dialogue with emissaries."

是故政举之日，夷关折符，无通其使；

Perhaps the ultimate in secrecy could be summed up by the following remarks by Sun Tzu:

"It is the duty of the general to be calm and inscrutable, to be impartial and strict.
He must be capable of keeping his officers and men ignorant of his battle plans.
He must be able to change his methods and schemes so that no one can know his intentions.
He must be able to alter his campsites and marching routes so that no one can predict his movements."

将军之事：静以幽，正以治。
能愚士卒之耳目，使之无知。
易其事，革其谋，使人无识；
易其居，迂其途，使人不得虑。

The above ideas should not come as a surprise to the reader when we consider Sun Tzu's Principle of Deception. It would seem that the ultimate in generalship is the ability to conceal the real intention and objective of the battle plan, yet at the same time, being able to motivate the troops to execute and carry out the plan with the greatest motivation and without fear of death!

Appendix B:
Sun Tzu's Art of War

![gray bar]

It may come as a surprise to many readers to know that Sun Tzu's *Art of War* is, in fact, a very short book. It contains less than 6,200 characters of classical Chinese literary writing. The book has only 13 chapters with each chapter barely a page long. Indeed, the longest chapter (Chapter 11, the Nine Types of Battlegrounds) has about 1,073 characters, while the shortest chapter (Chapter 8, the Nine Variations of Tactics) has only about 248 characters. The average chapter is less than 500 words. It is thus quite a wonder to realize that so much thought and wisdom can be contained in such a short piece of work.

The fact that the original works of Sun Tzu were in literary writing has created some problems in capturing the full meanings and implications of his thoughts. This is largely attributed to the complexity of the Chinese language, writing and culture. In addition, to know the exact meanings and implications of writings, one has to know the circumstances prevailing at the time of the writing. Even today, there are still Chinese scholars (for example, Li Yun of Beijing University, China) conducting research on the historical background surrounding the period around the 4th century B.C. Such research will undoubtedly provide greater understanding of why Sun Tzu advocated certain types of strategies. However, while there is still some contention on the exact meanings of each of the Chinese characters as used by Sun Tzu, there is nonetheless consensus on the basic arguments and propositions of his works. In fact, many modern Chinese translations of Sun Tzu's works have shown little variation.

The bigger problem, however, lies in translating the works into English. As mentioned above, because of the complexity of the Chinese language, culture and writing (especially if it is written in literary Chinese), it is very difficult to capture the full meanings of the Chinese words. For example, the Chinese word, 计 as used in Sun Tzu's opening chapter, can take on several meanings. It could mean one of the following:

1. Plans
2. Planning
3. Estimates
4. Calculations
5. Situation Appraisal

The above meanings are not necessarily exhaustive! In fact, the only way to get a fuller meaning of the Chinese word is to read the complete text in which the word is used. This problem with translation has confounded scholars over the years. To illustrate this problem, Table B.1 shows three varying translations of Sun Tzu's original 13 chapter titles. Note that the problems with translations come about because the original Chinese literary characters contained only one or two characters (the second or third character is common to all the titles, and simply means "chapter").

The problem with translating and interpreting works of ancient history is not unique to Sun Tzu's works. Even the most used book of today – the English Bible – has numerous translations (and amplifications) as a result of the original works being largely in Hebrew and Greek. Nonetheless, all Christians would agree that the meanings and content of the Bible have remained largely similar to the original text. The point is, while there may be some loss of the full richness of meanings as a result of translations and interpretations, the substantive content must be preserved. This principle has not been violated in the case of Sun Tzu's *Art of War.*

As mentioned earlier, the best way to get the closest meaning to the Chinese literary writing is to read it in the context of the full text and the way the word has been used. Accordingly, the writers have boldly translated the 13 chapter titles as shown in Table B.2. In deciding on the use of words, the writers have opted to expand the title where necessary. This has resulted in the use of situation appraisal as a more appropriate description of Chapter I (previous authors have opted for titles like estimates, laying plans, deliberation and planning). The choice of situation appraisal becomes more obvious as one studies the whole of Chapter I of Sun Tzu's works. Similarly, Chapter III has been retitled *Strategic Attacks* and Chapter IV is entitled *Dispositions of the Army* (as this is a clearer description). Chapter V should be more appropriately called *Forces* as the bulk of the chapter written by Sun Tzu deals with the forces (power or energy) that can

Table B.1 Varying translations of Sun Tzu's chapter titles

Sun Tzu		Griffith (1963)	Giles (1910)	Cheng Lin (1969)
I	计 篇	Estimates	Laying Plans	Deliberation
II	作战篇	Waging War	Waging War	Planning
III	谋攻篇	Offensive Strategy	Attack by Strategem	Strategy
IV	形 篇	Dispositions	Tactical Dispositions	Tactics
V	势 篇	Energy	Energy	Formation
VI	虚实篇	Weaknesses and Strengths	Weak Points and Strong	Opportunism
VII	军争篇	Maneuver	Maneuvering	Maneuvers
VIII	九变篇	The Nine Variables	Variation of Tactics	Variations
IX	行军篇	Marches	The Army on the March	Mobilization
X	地形篇	Terrain	Terrain	Terrain
XI	九地篇	The Nine Varieties of Ground	The Nine Situations	Situations
XII	火攻篇	Attack by Fire	The Attack by Fire	Incendiarism
XIII	用间篇	Employment of Secret Agents	The Use of Spies	Espionage

Sources: Samuel B. Griffith, *Sun Tzu: The Art of War*, Oxford University Press, 11th Printing, 1982 (first published in 1963).

Lionel Giles, *Sun Tzu on the Art of War*, Luzac & Co., London, 1910.

Cheng Lin, *The Art of War*, East Asia Pub., Hong Kong, 1969.

be attained as a result of using the right combination of troops, timing and momentum.

The other chapter titles adopted by the authors have remained relatively similar to the previous translations. However, one comment is necessary. Among all the 13 titles, the title of Chapter VI, presents the biggest problem. The direct translation of the words means "fakeness and reality."

However, in reading the chapter, it does not project such a meaning. In fact, in various places of the chapter, Sun Tzu talked about assessing the relative strengths of the enemy. In reality if the adjectives are inserted before the words, they actually mean investigating the real strengths (of the enemy). This has led translators like Griffith and Giles to use similar descriptions like weaknesses and strengths to describe

Table B.2 Translation of the 13 chapter titles

	Sun Tzu	Translation
I	计 篇	Situation Appraisal
II	作战篇	Waging War
III	谋攻篇	Strategic Attacks
IV	形 篇	Dispositions of the Army
V	势 篇	Forces
VI	虚实篇	Opportunism
VII	军争篇	Maneuvers
VIII	九变篇	The Nine Variations
IX	行军篇	Marches
X	地形篇	Terrain
XI	九地篇	The Nine Types of Battlegrounds
XII	火攻篇	Attacking with Fire
XIII	用间篇	Espionage

Chapter VI. However, understanding the strengths of the enemy is also very much related to allowing one to exploit opportunities so as to gain strategic advantages. In fact, a large portion of Sun Tzu's Chapter VI is devoted to assessing the enemy's situation and advice on how to exploit various situations to the attacker's advantage. Hence, the more appropriate description of this Chapter VI is provided by Cheng Lin's title of *Opportunism*.

Throughout this book, the authors have attempted to provide the closest meanings in terms of translating from Sun Tzu's original writings. To enable those readers who are knowledgeable in literary Chinese, the relevant direct quotations from Sun Tzu's works are reproduced so as to allow comparisons.

Bibliography

Abell D.F. (1980). *Defining the Business: The Starting Point of Strategic Planning*. Prentice-Hall, Inc.: Englewood Cliffs, New Jersey.

Abernathy W.J., Clark K.B. and Kantrow A.M. (1981). The New Industrial Competition. *Harvard Business Review,* (Sept/Oct 1985), pp. 68-81

Ansoff H.I. (1965). *Corporate Strategy.* McGraw-Hill: New York.

Ansoff H.I. (1969). *Business Strategy.* Penguin: Harmondsworth

Ansoff H.I. (1979). The changing shape of the strategic problem. *Strategic Management: A New View of Business Policy and Planning* (Schendel D.E. and Hofer C.W., eds.), pp. 30-44. Little Brown: Boston

Bracker J. (1980). The historical development of the strategic management concept. In *Academy of Management Review,* **5**, 219-24

Buzzell D.R., Bradley T., Gale and Ralph G. M. Sultan (1975). Market Share: A Key to Profitability. *Harvard Business Review,* Vol. 53, No. 1, (Jan/Feb 1975), pp. 97-106

Carter V.B. (1965). *Winston Churchill: An Intimate Portrait.* Harcourt Brace: New York

Clark J.B. (1987). *Marketing Today: Successes, Failures, and Turnarounds.* Prentice-Hall, Inc.: Englewood Cliffs, New Jersey

Clifford D.K. Jr. and Cavanagh R.E. (1985). *The Winning Performance: How America's High-Growth Midsize Companies Succeed.* Bantam Books, Inc.: New York

Corey E.R. and Steven H.S. (1971). *Organizational Strategy: A Marketing Approach.* Division of Research, Harvard Business School.

de Bono E. (1971). *Lateral Thinking for Management.* Penguin: Harmondsworth

de Bono E. (1978). *Opportunities.* Penguin: Harmondsworth

Drucker P.F. (1971). What we can learn from Japanese Management. *Harvard Business Review,* (Mar/Apr 1971)

Drucker, P.F. (1974). *Management: Tasks, Responsibilities, Practices.* Harper & Row: New York

Drucker P.F., Dupuy R.E. and Dupy T.N., eds. (1970). *The Encyclopedia of Military History from 3500 B.C. to the Present.* Harper & Row: New York

Glueck W.F. and Jauch L.R. (1984). *Business Policy and Strategic Management* 4th edn. McGraw-Hill: New York

Griffith S.B. (1971). *Sun Tzu: The Art of War*. Oxford University Press: Oxford

Hertz D.B. (1969). *New Power for Management*. McGraw-Hill: New York

Hofer C.W. and Schendel D.E. (1978). *Strategy Formulation: Analytical Concepts,* West Publishing: St. Paul

Hobbs J.M. and Heany D.F. (1983). Coupling strategy to operating plans. In *Strategic Management* (Hamermesh R.G., ed.), pp. 335-45. John Wiley & Sons: Chichester

Kotler P. (1984). *Marketing Management* 5th edn. Prentice-Hall: New Jersey, Englewood Cliffs

Kotler P., Fahey L. and S. Jatusripitak (1985). *The New Competition*. Prentice-Hall: New Jersey, Englewood Cliffs

Lamb R.B. (1984). *Competitive Strategic Management*. Prentice-Hall: New Jersey, Englewood Cliffs

Levitt T. (1960). Marketing Myopia. *Harvard Business Review,* Vol. 38, No. 4, (Jul-Aug 1960), pp. 45-56

Lorange P. (1980). *Corporate Planning: An Executive Viewpoint*. Prentice-Hall: New Jersey, Englewood Cliffs

Naylor T.H. (1970). *Corporate Planning Models*. Addison-Wesley: Reading MA

Ohmae K. (1983). *The Mind of the Strategist: Business Planning for Competitive Advantage*. Penguin: Harmondsworth

Peacock W.E. (1984). *Corporate Combat*. Maple-Vail: London

Porter M.E. (1980). *Competitive Strategy*. Free Press, Macmillan: New York

Porter M.E. (1985). *Competitive Advantage*. Free Press, Macmillan: New York

Schendel D.E. and Hofer C.W., eds. (1979). *Strategic Management: A New View of Business Policy and Planning*. Little Brown: Boston

Schoeffler S.R., Buzzell R.D. and Donald F.H. (1974). Impact of Strategic Planning on Profit Performance. *Harvard Business Review,* Vol. 52, No. 2, (Mar-Apr 1974), pp. 137-45

Steiner G.A. (1979). *Strategic Planning: What Every Manager Must Know*. The Free Press, Macmillan: New York

Steiner G.A., Miner J.B. and Gray E.R. (1982). *Management Policy and Strategy* 2nd edn. Free Press, Macmillan: New York

Steiner G.A. (1979). Contigency Theories of Strategy and Strategic Management. In *Strategic Management: A New View of Business Policy and Planning,* (Schendel D.E. and Hofer C.W. eds.) pp. 405-16. Little Brown: Boston

Stripp W.G. (1985). Sun-Tzu, Mushashi and Mahan: The Integration of Chinese, Japanese and American Strategic Thought in the International Business. In *Proc. Inaugural Meeting of the Southeast Asia Region Academy of International Business,* Chinese University of Hong Kong, 1985, pp. 109-18

Tilles S. (1963). How to Evaluate Corporate Strategy. *Harvard Business Review,* Vol. 41, No. 4

Tilles S.(1963). Making Strategy Explicit. Business Strategy (Ansoff H.I., ed.), Penguin: Harmondsworth

The Falklands Campaign: The Lessons, presented to the Parliament by the Secretary of State for Defence by Command of Her Majesty, December 1982. London: Her Majesty's Stationery Office

Unkovic D. (1985). *The Trade Secrets Handbook: Strategies and Techniques for Safeguarding Corporate Information.* Prentice-Hall: New Jersey, Englewood Cliffs

Webster's New Collegiate Dictionary. (1981). G&C Meriam

Wee C.H. (1985). The Experience Curve: Concept, Implications and Limitations. *Singapore Management Review,* Vol. 7, No. 2, (Jul 1985), pp. 33-44

Wee C.H. (1985). Managing in a Recession. *Singapore Business,* Vol. 9, No. 9 (Sept 1985), pp. 45-7

Wee C.H. (1986a). An Outline of Sun Tzu's Art of Strategic Warfare: Applications to Marketing. In *Singapore Marketing Review,* (Mar 1986), pp. 63-7

Wee C.H. (1986b). Sun Tzu's Art of War: Prerequisites for Strategic Planning. In *Proc. Academy of Int.Bus.* S. E. Asia Regional Conference, Vol. 1, National Chiao Tung University, Taiwan, 30-44

Wylle J.C. (1967). *Military Strategy: A General Theory of Power Control.* Rutgers University Press: USA

Index